PROS AND [COMIC] CONS™

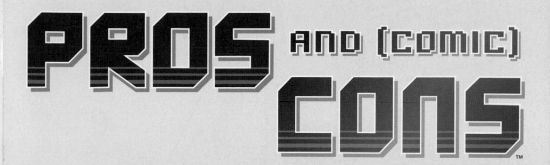

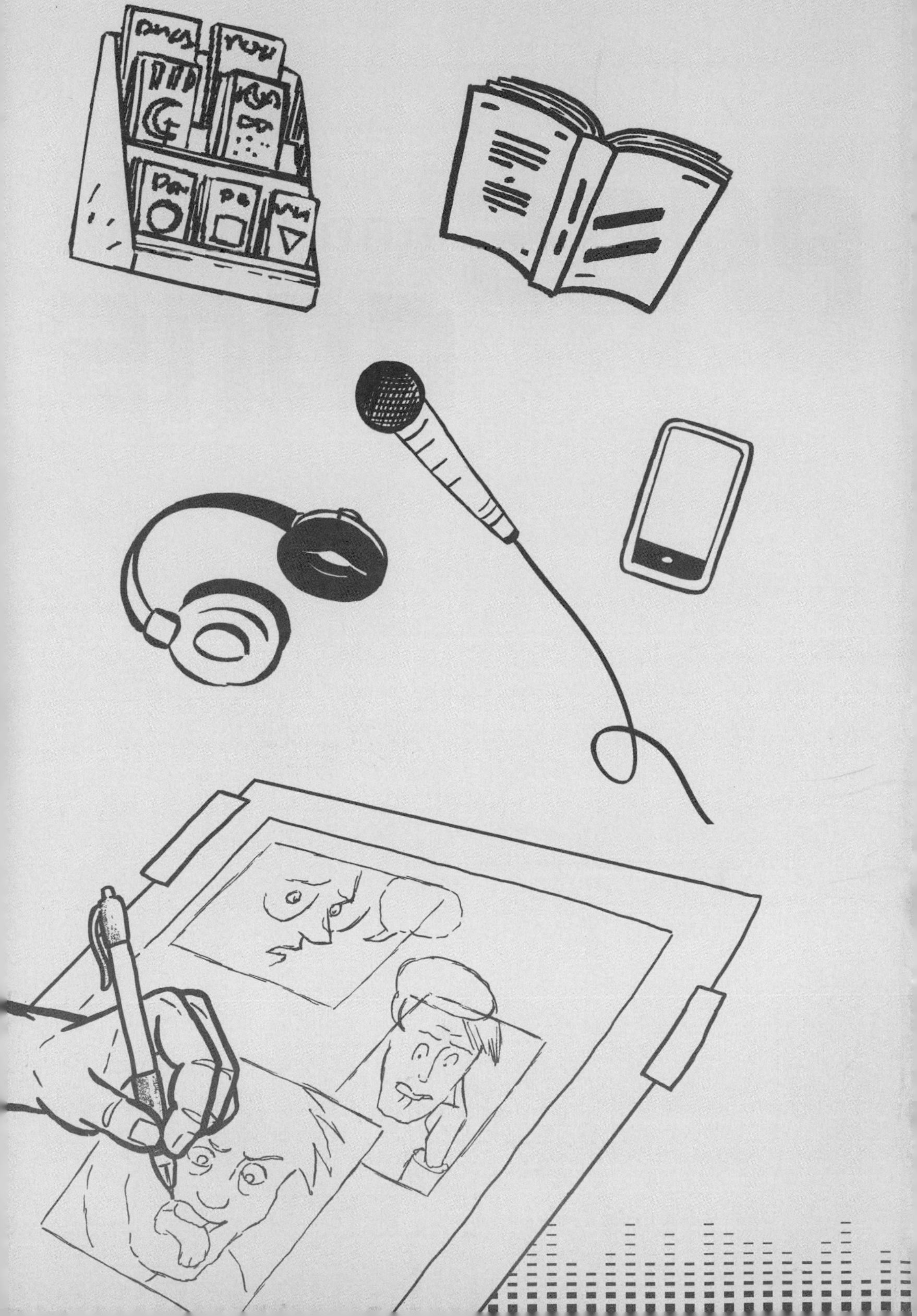

PROS AND (COMIC) CONS™

EDITED BY
HOPE NICHOLSON

with edits from NYALA ALI

Cover Art by COLLEEN COOVER

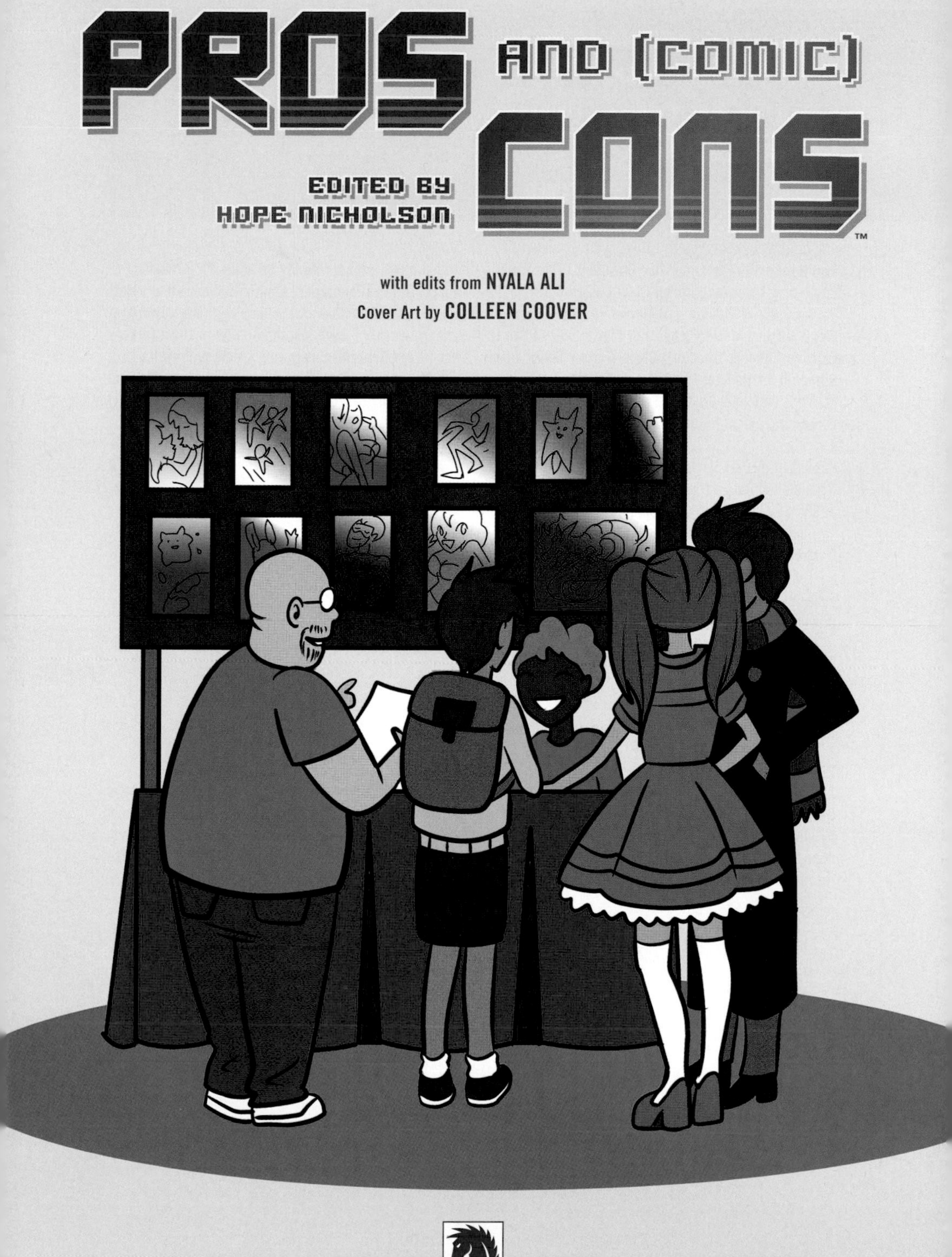

DARK HORSE BOOKS

President and Publisher **MIKE RICHARDSON**

Collection Editor **DANIEL CHABON**

Assistant Editors **BRETT ISRAEL** and **CHUCK HOWITT**

Designer **ANITA MAGAÑA**

Digital Art Technician **SAMANTHA HUMMER**

Neil Hankerson Executive Vice President I **Tom Weddle** Chief Financial Officer I **Randy Stradley** Vice President of Publishing I **Nick McWhorter** Chief Business Development Officer I **Dale LaFountain** Chief Information Officer I **Matt Parkinson** Vice President of Marketing I **Cara Niece** Vice President of Production and Scheduling I **Mark Bernardi** Vice President of Book Trade and Digital Sales I **Ken Lizzi** General Counsel I **Dave Marshall** Editor in Chief I **Davey Estrada** Editorial Director I **Chris Warner** Senior Books Editor I **Cary Grazzini** Director of Specialty Projects I **Lia Ribacchi** Art Director I **Vanessa Todd-Holmes** Director of Print Purchasing I **Matt Dryer** Director of Digital Art and Prepress I **Michael Gombos** Senior Director of Licensed Publications I **Kari Yadro** Director of Custom Programs I **Kari Torson** Director of International Licensing I **Sean Brice** Director of Trade Sales

Published by Dark Horse Books
A division of Dark Horse Comics LLC
10956 SE Main Street I Milwaukie, OR 97222

DarkHorse.com

First edition: May 2019
ISBN 978-1-50671-167-6

10 9 8 7 6 5 4 3 2 1
Printed in China

To find a comics shop in your area, visit comicshoplocator.com

PROS AND (COMIC) CONS

TABLE OF CONTENTS

INTRODUCTION

By HOPE NICHOLSON

My favorite part of conventions are the goodbyes.

"It was so good to see you!"

"I look forward to your next book!"

"What's next? ECCC? TCAF? Heroes? SDCC?"

These stock statements are such a common end of convention moment that it's become a comforting ritual, a closure to moments of companionship with friends but a promise that we will meet again. I joke that comic conventions often feel like summer camp, in that intense friendships are formed, only to lapse into occasional online interactions, until the time of the next con when they are renewed again with hugs, banter and meals shared. Some friendships will fade away entirely after the convention, while others will grow stronger after time.

Personally, I don't have one group I hang out with cons, though I admit I'm occasionally envious of groups, of both the bros packed five to a room, doing shots of whiskey before coming down to the bar to hang out in an impenetrable wall of testosterone, and the far-too-cool-and-so-young artist types of all various genders, in outfits that I would have believed could only exist in comics, similarly tightly knit and speaking a language that consists of mostly gestures and unknown internet lingo. There's a relationship between comic creators that grows over time at cons, and for some people, these bonds help create essential confidantes and collaborators.

At the larger cons, I rotate between gatherings of casual friends, sharing a quick bit of information or laughing at a few jokes, praising them for their past success or encouraging them for future pitches, before moving on to the next, spending only a few minutes with any one group or person at a time. Part of this is less being a social butterfly and more a sense of neuroticism that in order to prevent anyone from finding out how deeply uncool I am, I should just get in-and-out at lightning speed. But comic conventions are a good place for neurotic people, as an admission of anxiety or nervousness is often matched by the person you're talking to (a friend this year asked me in a SDCC bar, "Is it possible you're as neurotic as me?" I replied, "Oh no, much more.").

It isn't unusual, not by far, that comics take up our every waking thought. How to make more, who to work with next, will fans like the next book, will sales be strong, will your publisher honour your book with their limited and precious marketing budget, are all little things that occupy our minds as we rush from one project to the next to keep our heads above water (PS this is all very unhealthy and we are all very tired). It certainly isn't the money that drives me to attend cons, though I do have friends who have made tens of thousands in a single weekend, I've been lucky to break even when I table. It's the feeling of "Yes. All this work is now acknowledged. I have done well." It's a true and earnest validation from your peers and readers that for some reason all the likes, RTs, Goodreads reviews, and royalty cheques can't come close to matching.

At SDCC 2018, I met contributor Sina Grace for the first time and he earnestly looked me in the eyes and apologized profusely for not turning in any artwork yet for this book (never mind that he was already two months early). His apology was rooted in that he needed to see SDCC again, to walk the halls, to drive the same highways, in order to keep the memories fresh in his head for the story. I can relate, and writing this introduction two days after that same con has helped me keep the feelings fresh as well.

My memories of this weekend are scattered, whirling from meetings, to panels, to signings, grabbing sandwiches, canned champagne, granola bars, and energy drinks from various booths as I rushed along to keep me going. These memories exist in small moments, my roommate Megan Kearney asking everyone in our Dark Horse signing line to hold up their *The Secret Loves of Geeks* books (which made me cry), a fan asking where she can see herself as an ace Desi woman in pop culture and my fellow panellists giving her earnest and useful advice and comfort, strolling down the waterfront past midnight with an artist I admire, jumping into the Marriott pool to hang out with a friend because we were both too lazy to walk around. I still exist right now in all the good moments before my anxiety will inevitably make me start to question things like "Wait, do my new friends secretly think I'm boring?" "Did I talk about my love life too much?"

"Am I ever going to hear back about that movie deal?"

In this book, you will read Trina Robbins's story of her experience at SDCC in 1977, and I see striking similarities to the SDCC I know in 2018. Both of us have been serenaded by artists and spent most of our time sunning by the pool (actually, for the past three years, me and Trina always make a point of going to the pool together and sharing margaritas in the sun). Going back ten years before her story to 1967, we get the premiere fanboy experience of a young teenage Bud Plant growing his comics empire while taking a road trip across the USA to meet his comic idols.

I know that I've had bad convention experiences, the ones where no one knows me, where I receive no dinner invites, where sales are low and I feel that all my work is useless, where fights are had with partners and crying in my hotel room ruins the week. So I can relate, too, to the feelings of frustration and longing for recognition on Erik Radvon's story, and the weird impulse that keeps us going back anyway.

In fact, the last few events I've attended have been remarkably the opposite of SDCC. My last intern, Shaneela, teases me because at my BIG GLOBAL BOOK LAUNCH in 2018, where we thought a line-up in the store was for me, in fact it was for a *Yu-gi-oh!* tournament, and we sold no books at all. That same book had a packed panel and signing at SDCC three months later. Comics sometimes make no sense! And when you've had a string of bad conventions or events, it can weigh so heavy on your heart. And it can be hard to listen to others tell you to persevere and keep trying when every rejection drives you further away from the thing that you love the most, and sometimes you do need to take a break, to rest up and fight again.

I hope this book helps you. Because I know that it's not easy. And I know that it can hurt. And I also know that the time will come when everything, for at least one weekend, will be wonderful again and you will feel fresh and fed and renewed with energy. Keep in mind that so many of these stories are from creators who've made it, looking back at the path they've taken, and sharing how many years it took them to make it to where they are today. And these paths are all different, but our stories of struggle are the same! From publishers and editors, to authors, comic artists, writers, historians, retailers, bloggers, and journalists, each one of us is an equal in our passion for this industry and our drive to work together to make it a better place for all newcomers.

And if you've never been to a convention before, or can't travel as often as you'd like, I hope that this book feels like the biggest, most glamorous, exciting, and fulfilling event you've ever been to! Like our previous anthology collaborations, *The Secret Loves of Geek Girls* and *The Secret Loves of Geeks*, these accounts are all true stories of vulnerability and openness, so you get the real truth of why we keep performing these bizarre rituals of tables, panels, fans, and friends. Come sit behind our table and have a chat. And see you next con.

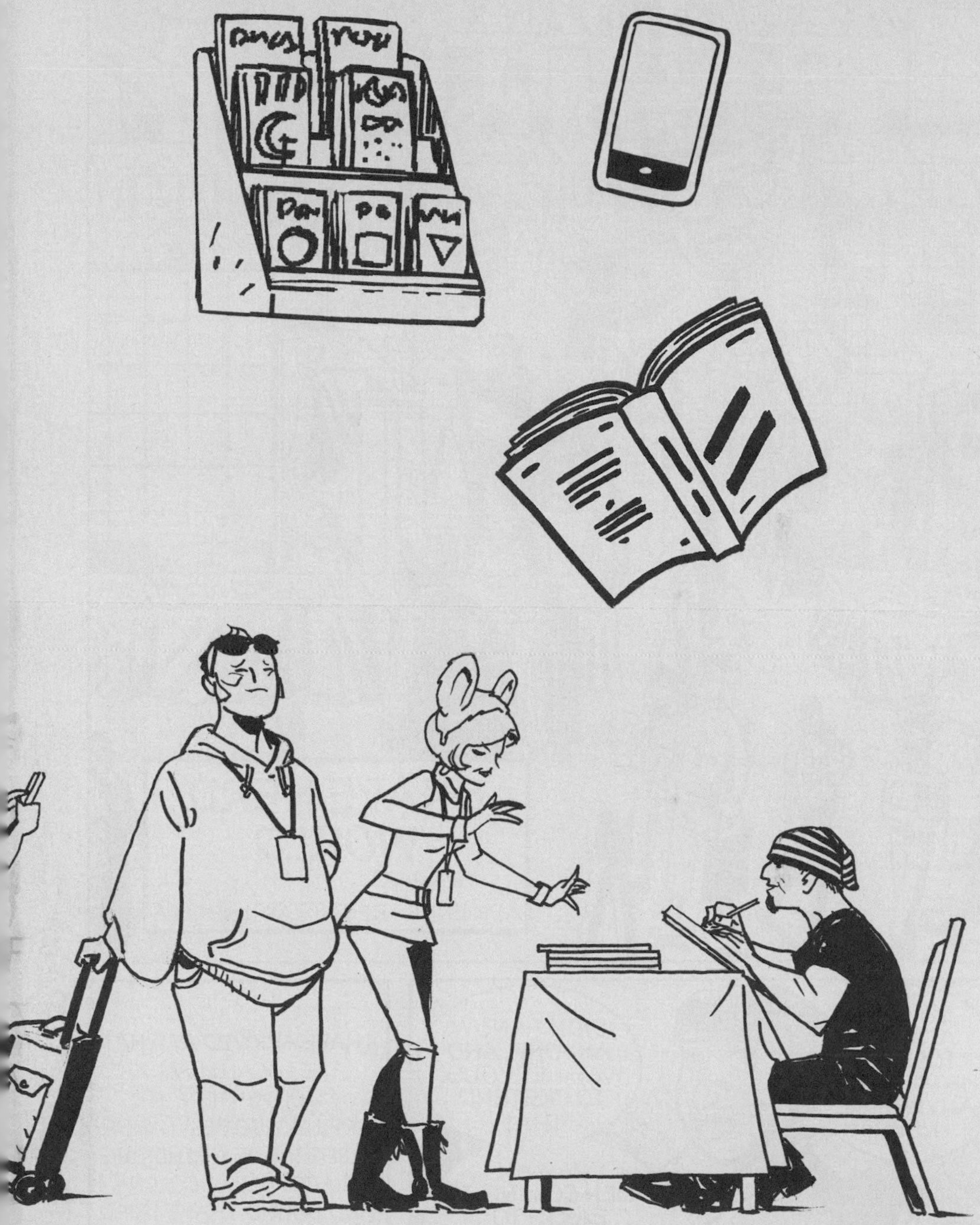

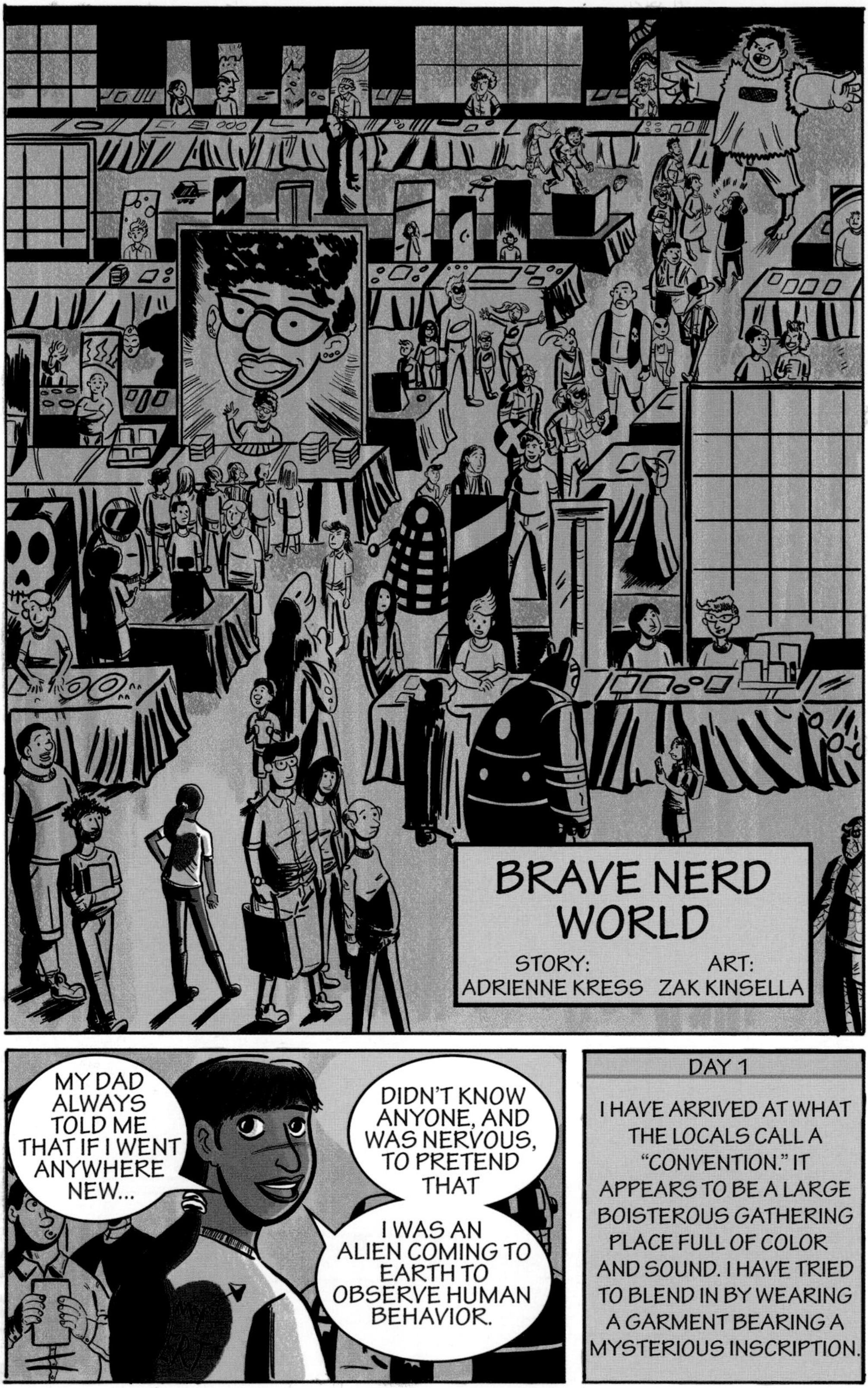
BRAVE NERD WORLD
STORY: ADRIENNE KRESS
ART: ZAK KINSELLA
MY DAD ALWAYS TOLD ME THAT IF I WENT ANYWHERE NEW...
DIDN'T KNOW ANYONE, AND WAS NERVOUS, TO PRETEND THAT
I WAS AN ALIEN COMING TO EARTH TO OBSERVE HUMAN BEHAVIOR.
DAY 1
I HAVE ARRIVED AT WHAT THE LOCALS CALL A "CONVENTION." IT APPEARS TO BE A LARGE BOISTEROUS GATHERING PLACE FULL OF COLOR AND SOUND. I HAVE TRIED TO BLEND IN BY WEARING A GARMENT BEARING A MYSTERIOUS INSCRIPTION.

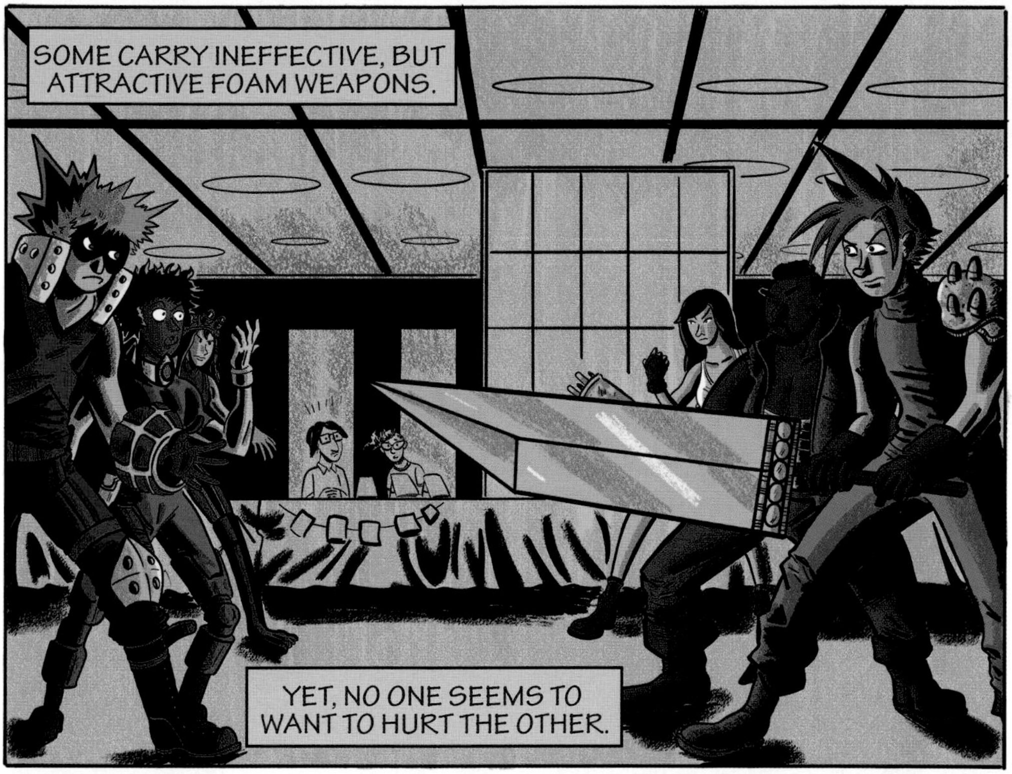
SOME CARRY INEFFECTIVE, BUT ATTRACTIVE FOAM WEAPONS.
YET, NO ONE SEEMS TO WANT TO HURT THE OTHER.

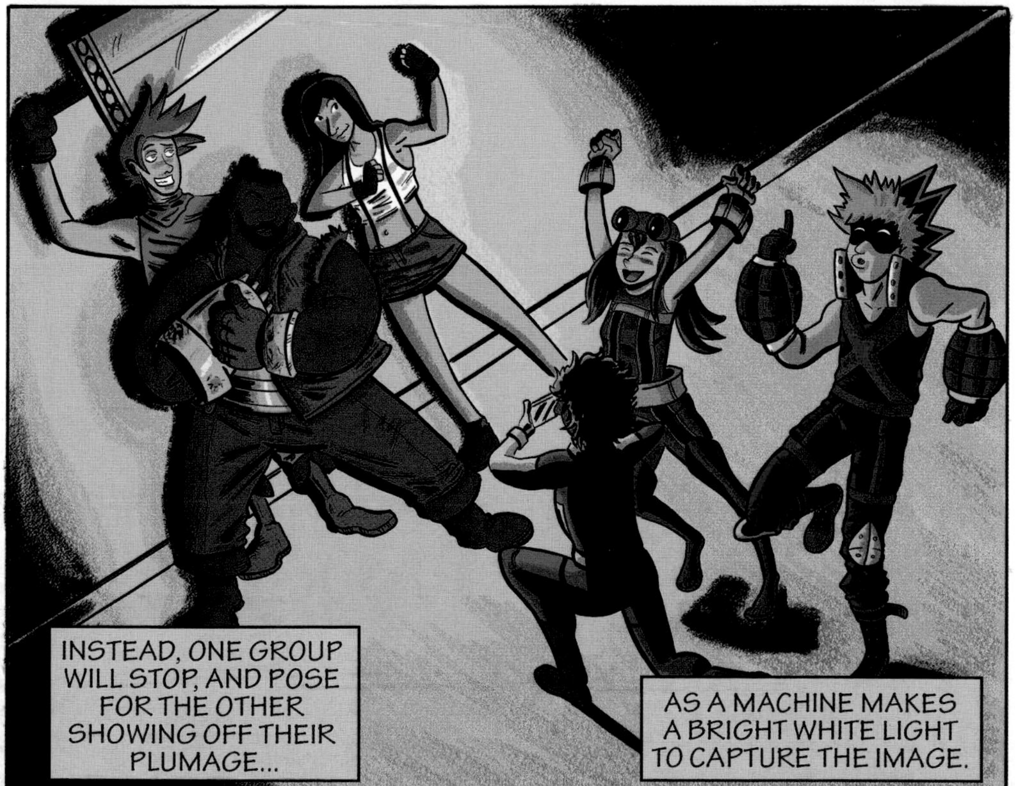
INSTEAD, ONE GROUP WILL STOP, AND POSE FOR THE OTHER SHOWING OFF THEIR PLUMAGE...
AS A MACHINE MAKES A BRIGHT WHITE LIGHT TO CAPTURE THE IMAGE.

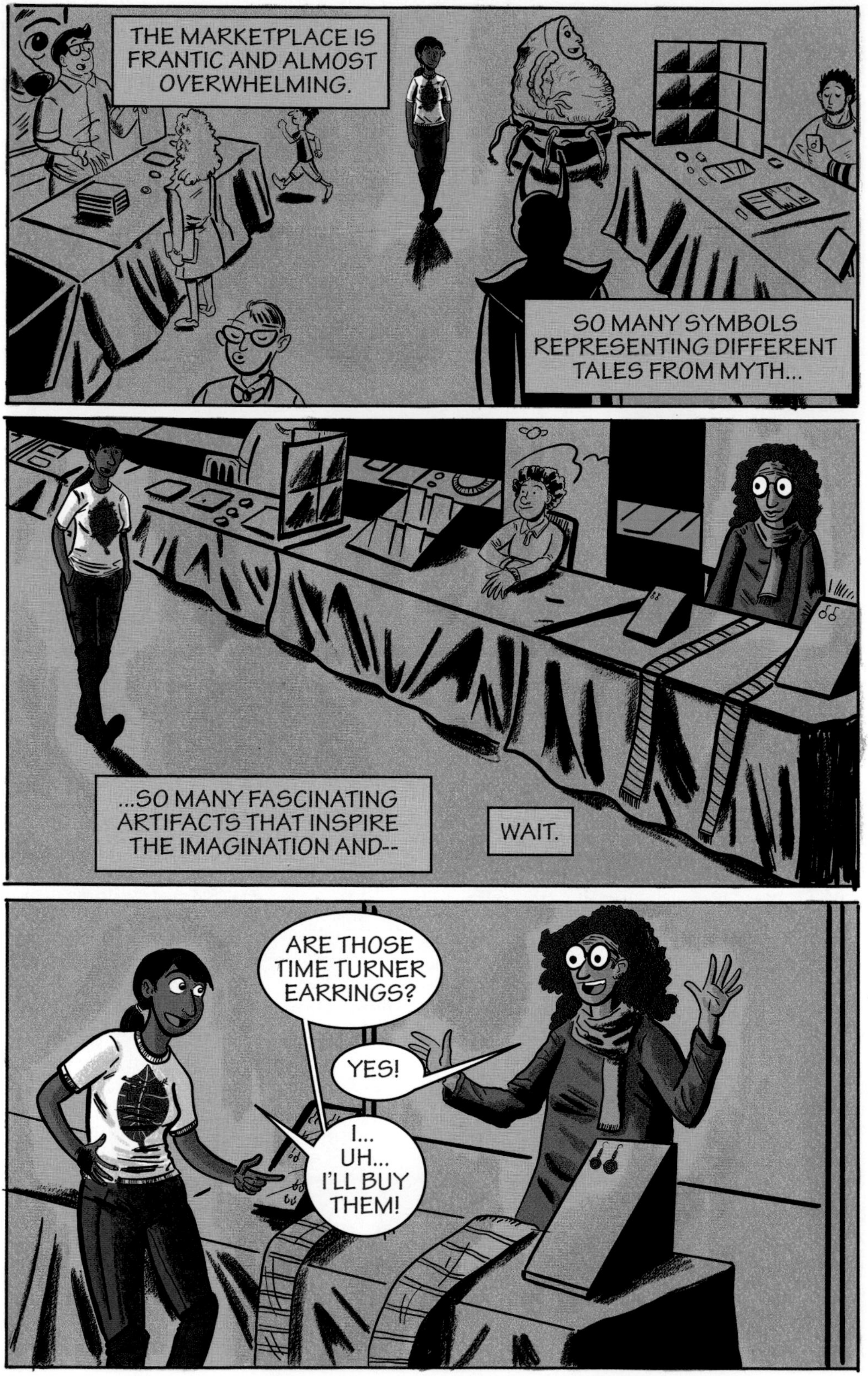
THE MARKETPLACE IS FRANTIC AND ALMOST OVERWHELMING.
SO MANY SYMBOLS REPRESENTING DIFFERENT TALES FROM MYTH...
...SO MANY FASCINATING ARTIFACTS THAT INSPIRE THE IMAGINATION AND--
WAIT.
ARE THOSE TIME TURNER EARRINGS?
YES!
I... UH... I'LL BUY THEM!

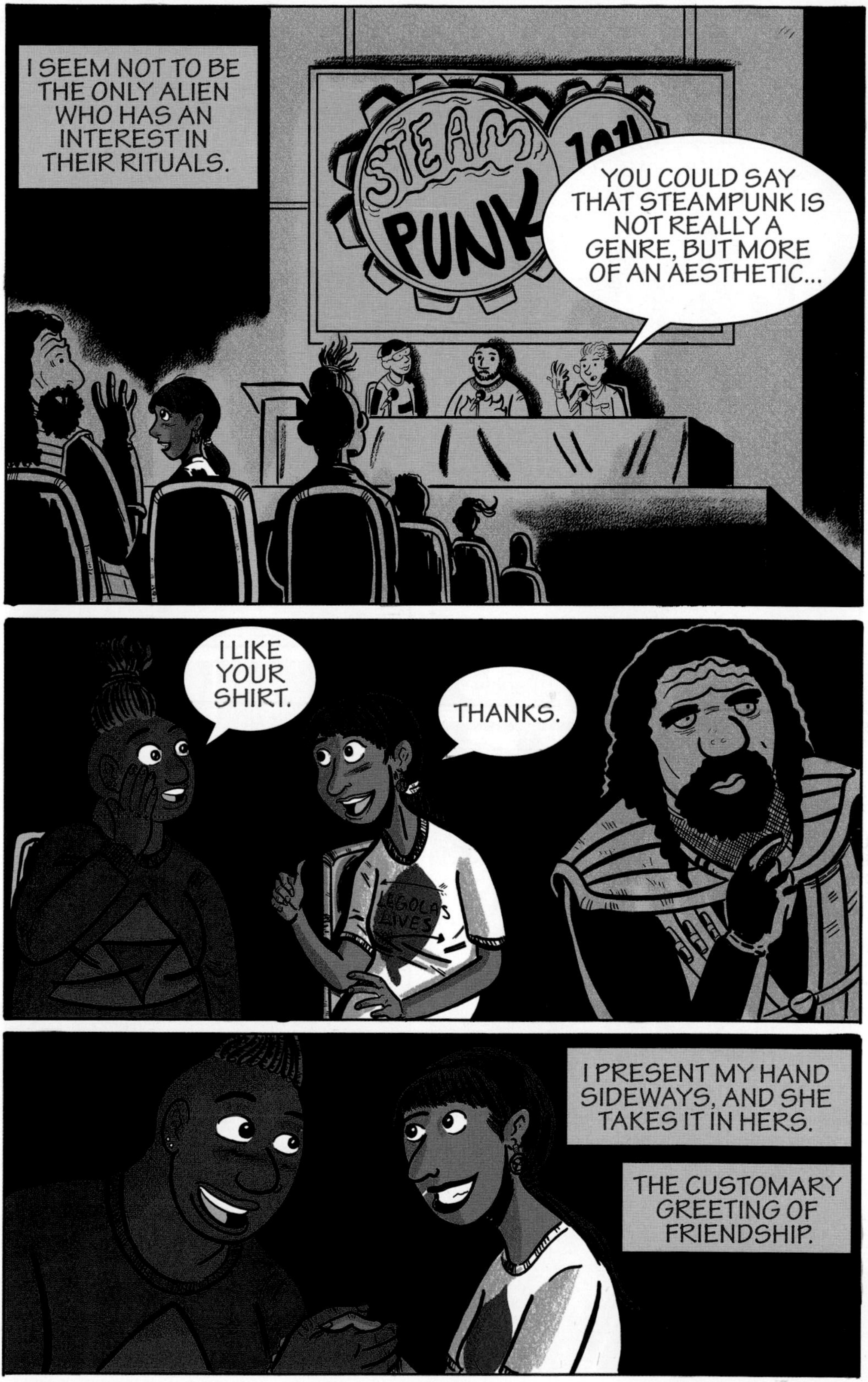
I SEEM NOT TO BE THE ONLY ALIEN WHO HAS AN INTEREST IN THEIR RITUALS.
STEAM PUNK
YOU COULD SAY THAT STEAMPUNK IS NOT REALLY A GENRE, BUT MORE OF AN AESTHETIC...
I LIKE YOUR SHIRT.
THANKS.
LEGOLAS LIVES
I PRESENT MY HAND SIDEWAYS, AND SHE TAKES IT IN HERS.
THE CUSTOMARY GREETING OF FRIENDSHIP.

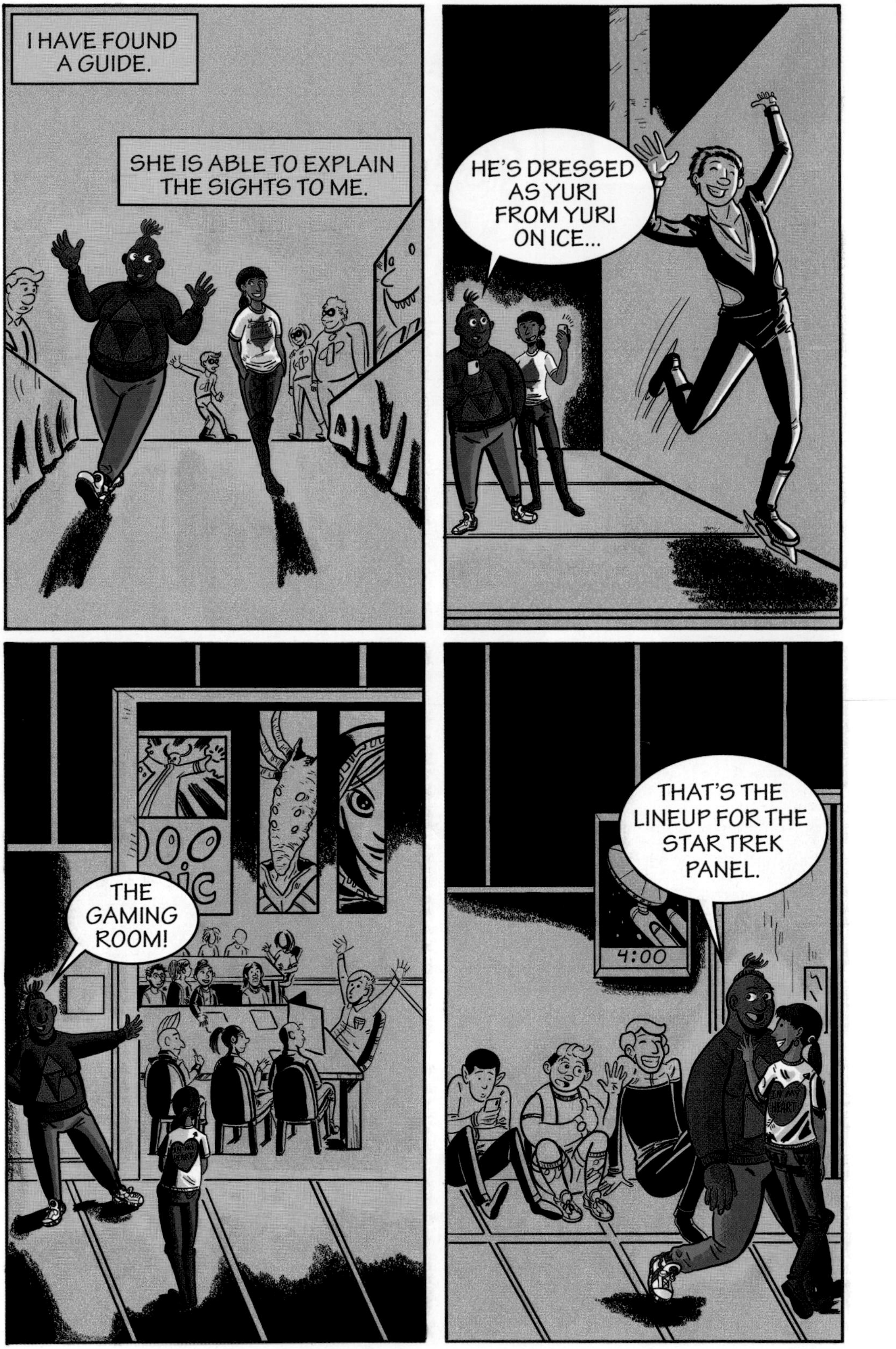
I HAVE FOUND A GUIDE.
SHE IS ABLE TO EXPLAIN THE SIGHTS TO ME.
HE'S DRESSED AS YURI FROM YURI ON ICE...
THE GAMING ROOM!
THAT'S THE LINEUP FOR THE STAR TREK PANEL.
4:00

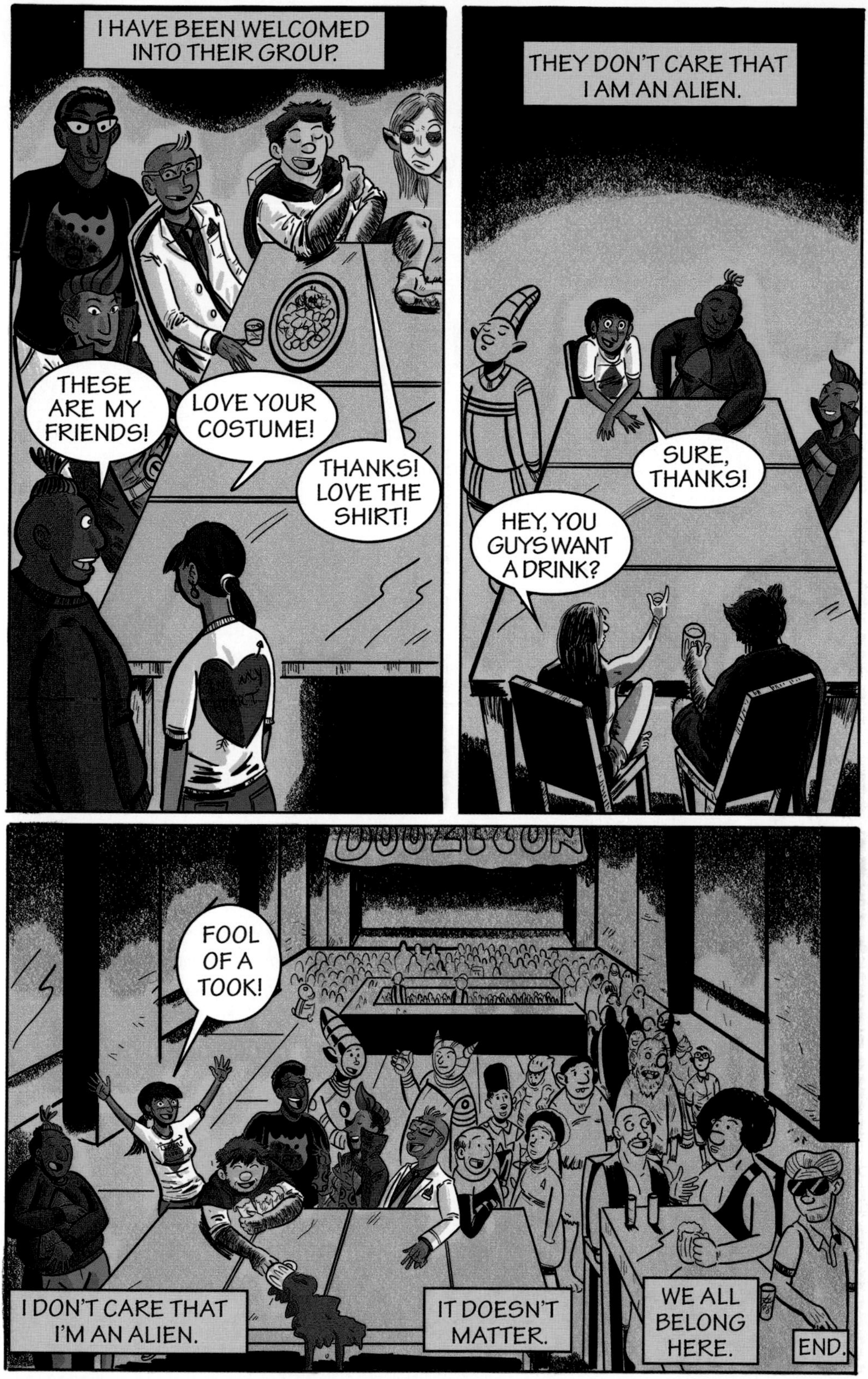
I HAVE BEEN WELCOMED INTO THEIR GROUP.
THESE ARE MY FRIENDS!
LOVE YOUR COSTUME!
THANKS! LOVE THE SHIRT!
THEY DON'T CARE THAT I AM AN ALIEN.
SURE, THANKS!
HEY, YOU GUYS WANT A DRINK?
FOOL OF A TOOK!
I DON'T CARE THAT I'M AN ALIEN.
IT DOESN'T MATTER.
WE ALL BELONG HERE.
END.

This story was originally written in 1992 on the occasion of Richard Finn's Portland Comic Book Show, and reflects the industry as it was then. That year, the American Continental Circus was preparing its performance just outside the convention doors.

ONLY LONELY MADMEN

Diana Schutz

It's unmistakable. That rich, loamy, sweet stench of animal shit, I mean. And it assails my senses on an already hot July morning, like Sandburg's fog, coming on little cat feet, silent and curious at first, then sinewy and suffocating all at once. It's an uncommon fragrance for the urban outdoors, miles away from those yawning fields of country cowpies, but this Rose City parking lot is shriveling my nose just as if I'd been napalmed. Twenty years and a continent away from Vietnam, I'm dodging still cars moored outside the Memorial Coliseum, seeking sanctuary in the Assembly Hall, headquarters of the Portland Comic Book Show. There's no cause for alarm. Or is there?

My name is Diana Schutz, and I'm . . . a comic book fan.

Four elephants, naked but for the weighted chain binding their stump-like ankles, sway in the stifled air, lifting first one foot, then the other, in unison, a four-part harmony, tapping a massive toe on scorched pavement to keep the beat, trunks curling up and around like the dance of a conductor's baton, in slow motion. They have no tusks, have long forgotten the eleven-foot upper incisors forcibly removed by the safari dentist—neither a degreed surgeon nor painless, for that matter. They no longer need their ivory weapons. Elephants have no enemies—besides man. And they lost that war a long time ago.

I'm standing in line with Tom and Wes, 13-year-old twins who flank me as we shuffle, lifting first one foot, then the other, to lighten the hour-long wait for an autograph from the star of today's comics convention, Sergio Aragonés. The twins are only dimly aware of Sergio's *Groo the*

Wanderer, one of the moribund breed of comical comics, a *funny*book—at one time a label applied to the entire medium. Nor are Tom and Wes really aware of Sergio's considerable, thirty-year contribution to *Mad*, his innumerable, tiny, rapid-fire but no less painstaking silent caricatures—pantomimes—that limn the pages of that venerable magazine whose gap-toothed mascot is perhaps the most familiar face in America. These Portland twins, each named by a different parent, have paid their two-dollar admission, netting them two free autographs by the *Mad* marginals master himself, and by god they're going to get their money's worth!

Their friend approaches, wielding a limited edition Spider-Man print—number 9 of 50—signed by local artist Randy Emberlin, an inker for Marvel. The kid wears that preadolescent scorn for women in comics, a look that flies up, up and away once he learns I'm a comic book editor. Eyes agape but teenage pride yet intact, he lets Wes—or is it Tom?—exhale the sigh of envy. "Luhh-*cky*!" pronounces the twin, whichever one it is. "That's a fun job. Get to read comics all day."

I've heard this before, and smile, ceding them their four-color fantasy. There's time enough for life's empty truths. Read comics all day? Not a chance.

I read 'em at night, just like I used to as a little girl, in the much maligned Weisinger era of '60s Superman titles—the proverbial flashlight cocked under the cloak of bedcovers, haloing the heroes of my young years: Supergirl, Super-Horse, Streaky the Super-Cat, and Superman's girlfriend Lois Lane. I don't remember any super-elephants in those comics of the Silver Age, but with DC's Mort Weisinger in the editorial ring, there might well have been!

"Head up! Head up!" barks the assistant trainer, a short, sour man dressed in showtime black-and-white. Wanda grudgingly lifts her cumbrous chin, her 45-year-old trunk looping up and over to form an arch framing the slim man's passage. He's gone to confer with Robert, poor Robert of the sweaty blue work suit and broken teeth, heaving some dusty carriage-type thing onto the elephant's hulking back. Robert works for the American Continental Circus, and he's wise in the ways of elephants. He's dressing them right now, in black leather bondage outfits with mirrored anklets, primping them here, in this $4 parking lot, for their Portland performance. Really, he'd rather be in the conditioned air of nearby Assembly Hall, trading his minimum wage for the latest issue of The Jaguar. *Robert, too, is a comic book fan.*

The line has hobbled ahead, and I can see Sergio from where I stand, his thick handlebar mustache sparkling with more silver than I recall. That Mexican mustache was black as India ink when first we met, some ten years ago, as I hosted him from store to store in my pumpkin-colored Volkswagen, a guest of the Comics & Comix chain in northern California. I don't need to wait in this line, straining to see Sergio who even now is telling stories to my friend Steve in those incredible, rolling Latin rhythms and cadences.

Maybe he's talking about his first job for DC Comics, an issue of *Young Romance* written as a favor to editor Joe Orlando, who was scrambling to beat the "dreaded deadline doom," as Marvel's Stan Lee used to call it. Sergio sent Joe out to lunch, then finished the story before the editor even had time to digest. Maybe Sergio is describing the legendary Bill Gaines, the long-haired, long-bearded father of *Mad*, whose EC line of horror comics so inflamed a *Better Homes and Gardens* psychiatrist named Freddy Wertham that the good doctor publicly branded the entire industry, in the now infamous *Seduction of the Innocent*, as the wellspring of juvenile delinquency in 1950s McCarthyite America.

By now I've grown bored with the twins, their creepy movie monsters, and steroid saviors. I should march right up to the front of the line, drop a quick kiss on Sergio's bronzed cheek, murmur something true about how charmed I am, as ever, just to see him—and then get the hell out of there, perhaps for a quick search of the dealers' room, which, on a lucky day, might be inclined to yield an affordable copy of *Shock SuspenStories* #6, with its classic bondage cover, or even better, *Action Comics #252*, featuring the first appearance of Supergirl, the Maid of Steel, one of those 10¢ comics my mother threw out like so much trash, now listing on the collector's market for upwards of $540 in mint condition and for which I would gladly starve through a thousand lunches just to possess once more. Yes, I am a comic book fan, just as much as Wes and Tom and their girl-shy companion with the $10 Spider-Man print. And so, I wait.

Asian elephants are smaller than their African counterparts, though their tonnage is every bit as stupefying. Their faces, particularly, are somewhat less immense—and their ears flap with a wingspan considerably stunted next to Walt Disney's Dumbo. "Dumbo's African," Robert nods. These elephants—sad, lumbering creatures whose dignity might still be found stalking the grasslands of India like some out-of-work ghost—continue to rehearse their act, swinging to and fro in the summer swelter for an audience of genetically engineered

equines—a miniature horse and donkey—and Omar, the half-blind camel.
Dressed in an Arabian-style black tasseled cape, through which his blond hump
protrudes, Omar seems unperturbed by both the elephants and his one jellied
eye; he's working some tuft of bracken around his lower jaw, an astonishing,
lopsided lower jaw that wobbles and bobs at impossible angles over large, rotted
teeth. Omar too is preparing for the show, his left foreleg poised six inches above
the pavement. (Is the camel really practicing his dance? Or is there something
more sinister to the crook of his hoof? Is he in pain? Is he in pain?)

At 9 a.m., 200-plus early birds threading the parking lot, positions staked
at dawn, bob past lumbering convention doors, now swinging wide to
reveal a dot-matrix signboard that shouts in black-and-white:
GET YOUR FAVORITE
SUPER HERO DRAWN
FOR ONLY $5.00!!
OR *BECOME* A
SUPER HERO FOR
THE SAME PRICE!!!!
Underneath, hand-printed in red marker, as if an afterthought: WHAT
A BARGAIN!!

I shuffle slowly past, spellbound—I mean, *become* a superhero? That's
the ultimate fantasy, of course. It's what stirred our imaginations as children,
unheard and powerless in an adult world. It's what continues to bind us,
as if shackled to nostalgia by a persistent yet purposive sensation that exis-
tence should offer something . . . well, *more* than these little lives we inherit.
I'd always wanted to be Linda Lee Danvers, the Girl of Steel, Superman's
orphan cousin from the doomed planetoid Argo. This was my chance!

As it turns out, this was my chance to be *drawn* as Supergirl by 16-year-
old Willie, who, with his 14-year-old production manager, has hit upon
the convention's best scam, from their table directly opposite the entryway.
In addition to those $5 sketches, they are hawking—with the finesse of
the most accomplished carnival barker—*Flip Side* #1, an ambitious if ama-
teurish "fanzine" of superhero illustrations and strips. "Ya need money,"
Willie informs me, his eyes never leaving the Bristol on which an impossibly
muscled demigod slowly takes shape. "That's what ya need."

At 16, this young entrepreneur is already wise in the ways of business.
This business of comic books, at one time dependent on the sweatshop
labor of otherwise failed "fine" artists, has emerged from the darkest of

its four-color ages to provide better than a living wage for the talented freelancers who write and draw the commercial monthlies. After years of watching their paneled pages fed through the shredders, comic book artists have successfully regained the right to their own original art, which they can resell to collectors for hundreds—sometimes thousands, or even tens of thousands—of dollars. Writers and artists now have the option, also, of owning the *characters* they create—unheard of in the days of Siegel and Shuster's Superman or Joe Simon and Jack Kirby's Captain America. A royalty system, initiated by Eclipse Comics in 1978 and now *de rigueur* at all the companies, finally cuts creative teams in on the not-insubstantial profits of this multimillion-dollar industry, wherein royalties on a three-issue *Legends of the Dark Knight* can be exchanged for the down payment on a brand-new hillside home in the suburbs: "the house that Batman built."

Robert introduces the elephants to the stranger who has escaped the comic book convention. He is perhaps a little wary of her interest, but takes advantage of this, his only moment in the spotlight. "That's Wanda, Pattie, Tika," he points in succession, "and that's Queenie making love to the camel." Indeed, the youngest of the four elephants has wrapped her trunk around Omar's prodigious lower jaw in a brazen display of interspecies French-kissing! Robert laughs affectionately. He takes care of these sorry animals whose eyes no longer flash with ferocious freedom. He watches them "to make sure they don't go nowhere" (as if they had anywhere left to go) . . . and he shovels their shit, he admits finally, apologizing for the term: "Manure. Whatever you wanna call it." He will never buy a hillside home with his circus salary.

My friend Steve Duin is a comic book fan. In his secret identity, he writes an often-controversial column for the daily newspaper. Not too long ago he interviewed Stephen Fishler, owner of the New York-based Metropolis Comics, a mail-order collectibles service specializing in Golden Age titles from the 1940s. Fishler had this to say about his consumer base:

"If you go to a convention, you'll see a lot of strange people. I've always wondered: Are these normal people who have been turned strange by comic books? Or were they strange already and comic books just attracted them?

"A lot of people who buy books from me are very secure and have a well-rounded life. But there are others . . . comic books are their life. If you were to break into their house and steal their collection, they wouldn't have any reason to live. They'd be hanging from a rope in no time."

They're all here today, the members of this *unique* culture: Tom and Wes, the 13-year-old twins, and Willie the comic book wannabe, who dismisses an even younger artistic hopeful, refusing to critique his portfolio of pencil tracings, because 16-year-old Willie, who's paid $57 for his table, after all, needs to "sit here and do business." There's the couple dressed in all-black—a nod to Neil Gaiman—with Oregon-blanched faces. And the young man who goose-steps by in tall leather boots, chains at his side, *DEATH* inscribed in ornate letters on the back of his torn leather jacket, which hangs heavy from his shoulders despite, or perhaps because of, the sweltering outside sun. There's a bonneted baby, wheeled around by her underage mom, who boasts that this is baby's *tenth* convention, though she's not yet a year old. Yes, they're all here, the *Sandman* fans; the Archies, Bettys, and even Veronicas; from the Baby Hueys to the triple-XL super-hero T-shirts—worn by The Legion of Mikes, as Cat Yronwode once called them, for obscure reasons, back before she became Eclipse's Editor in Chief, when she was still a struggling writer working out of her Missouri homestead. They're here today, at the Portland Comic Book Show, this collection of ragtag humans, and they're on the prowl: for the $14.95 limited edition collector's mug whose handle is the Batman scaling a Gotham City building with glow-in-the-dark windows. For *Star Trek* movie stills, original *and* next generation. For Michael Benson's *Better Dead Than Red*, his $6 paean to the glory years of "Commie madness." For 1953's one-and-only *Thrilling Adventures in Stamps*, with the enormous Nazi airship exploding on its cover. For the near-pristine copy of *Jumbo Comics*, starring Sheena, Queen of the Jungle, in her leopard-skin camisole (that my friend Steve has already triumphantly scored). For the $16 *Flaming Love* #2, promising Torrid Tales of Turbulent Passion, which I will pass up, not without some regret, in favor of the less steamy *Real Love* #27, with its overwrought stories and L. B. Cole artwork. For the two-volume set of Human Freaks and Oddities trading cards, perhaps (paraphrasing Huxley) to reassure them by day and even while they are asleep, that in spite of all the terror, all the bewilderment and confusion, they are unshak-ably, inarguably, or at least comparatively . . . *normal!* And I am one of them, a comic book fan, clutching my hardcover Artist's Proof copy of *The Groo Chronicles*, "the expensive edition," as the title page wryly notes, staving off reality in this never-ending line, tapping my toe, shifting my weight from foot to foot in anticipation of Sergio's characteristic signature, which is always more than a simple scribble, sometimes a self-caricature or a quick penning of Alfred E. Neuman or the not-quite-redoubtable Groo—Sergio, whose artist's fingers have drawn nonstop since the early morning hours with two free autographs a person, extras at 25¢ per, all proceeds going to the local Make-A-Wish Foundation.

In Tim Burton's *Batman Returns*, Bruce Wayne's butler, the indomitable Alfred, asks our hero, with some reproach: "Must you be the only lonely madman in town?" Indeed not. And today, at Richard Finn's Portland Comic Book Show, all 1,500 of us have come together.

She's crying now, this odd woman, this stranger with her peculiar penchant for elephants, unbidden tears blossoming from the corners of her eyes like some wild, exotic flowers as she vainly tries to poke them back in. "Liberate the elephants!" she wants to scream. "Liberate the elephants!" Robert shakes his head, uncomprehending. He doesn't understand the complex emotions of elephants and women. Turning away, he slaps Wanda's rump and adjusts her halter for what must be the fifteenth time that day, as the noble beast lifts her large eyes upward in mute recognition of the open, untamed sky. She sways, lifting first one foot, then the other, shuffling to the whistle of long-forsaken breezes—not a dance step at all, Robert corrects the stranger, but merely a move to keep her magnificent bulk from settling in one spot. Wanda waves her body to and fro for comfort only in this unusual Portland sun, and the warm Indian grasslands remain just a detail, on a folded map tucked away in someone's collection, forever out of sight.

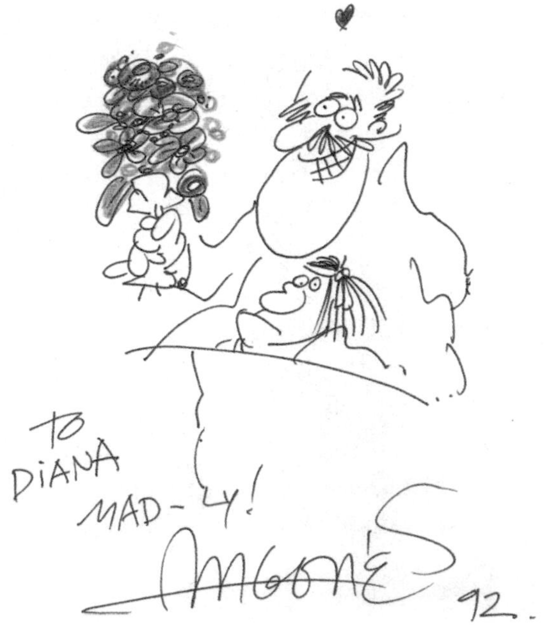
TO DIANA
MAD-LY!
ARAGONÉS
92.

Groo™ © 2019 Sergio Aragonés. Used with permission.

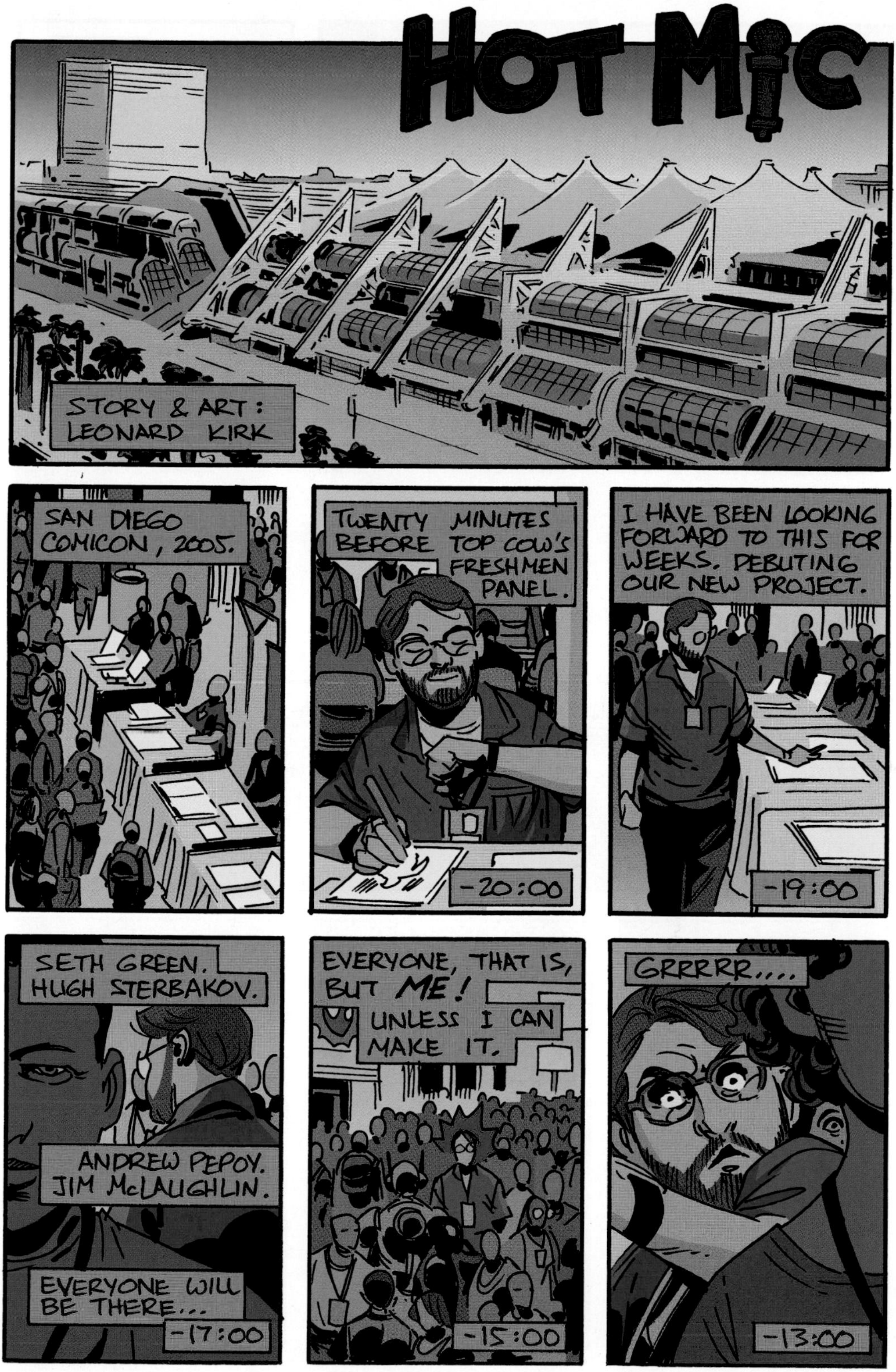
HOT MIC
STORY & ART: LEONARD KIRK
SAN DIEGO COMICON, 2005.
TWENTY MINUTES BEFORE TOP COW'S FRESHMEN PANEL.
-20:00
I HAVE BEEN LOOKING FORWARD TO THIS FOR WEEKS. DEBUTING OUR NEW PROJECT.
-19:00
SETH GREEN. HUGH STERBAKOV.
ANDREW PEPOY. JIM McLAUGHLIN.
EVERYONE WILL BE THERE...
-17:00
EVERYONE, THAT IS, BUT *ME*!
UNLESS I CAN MAKE IT.
-15:00
GRRRRR....
-13:00

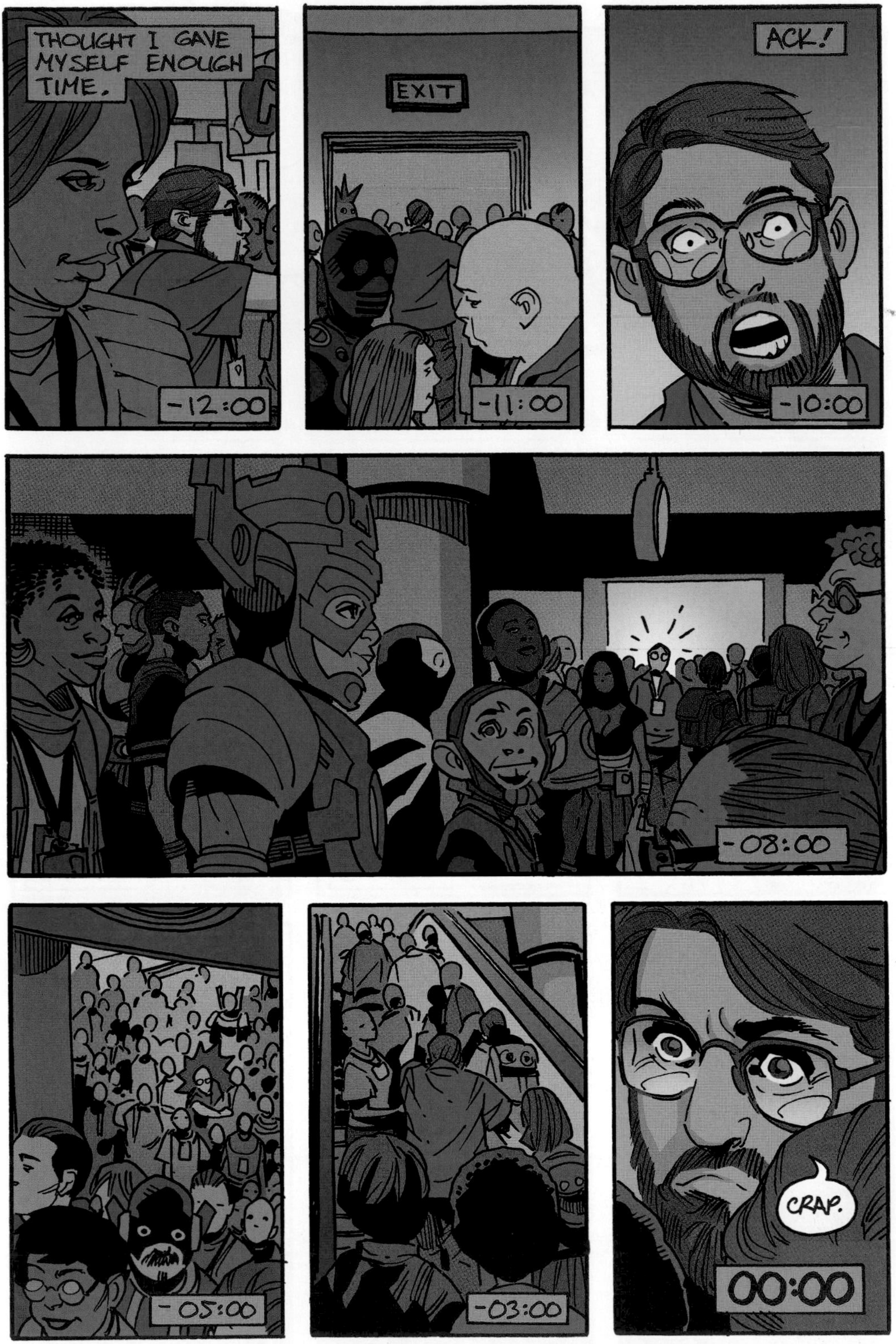
THOUGHT I GAVE MYSELF ENOUGH TIME.
-12:00
EXIT
-11:00
ACK!
-10:00
-08:00
-05:00
-03:00
CRAP.
00:00

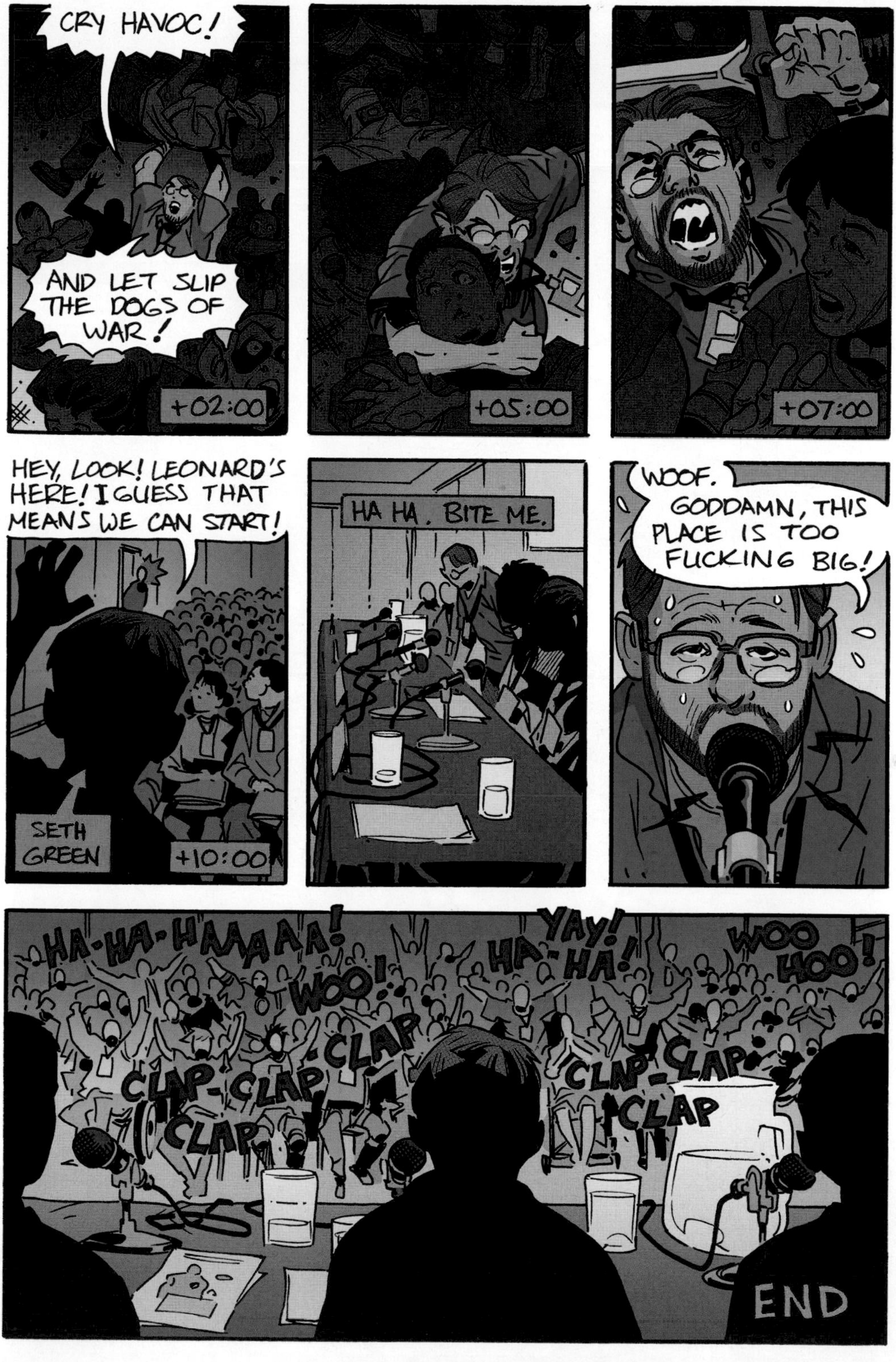
CRY HAVOC!
AND LET SLIP THE DOGS OF WAR!
+02:00
+05:00
+07:00
HEY, LOOK! LEONARD'S HERE! I GUESS THAT MEANS WE CAN START!
SETH GREEN
+10:00
HA HA. BITE ME.
WOOF. GODDAMN, THIS PLACE IS TOO FUCKING BIG!
HA-HA-HAAAAAA!
YAY!
HA-HA!
WOO HOO!
WOO!
CLAP-CLAP-CLAP
CLAP
CLAP-CLAP
CLAP
END

ONLY IN...

Ah, San Diego Comic-Con. There's nothing like it, anywhere. Ever.

If there is a god, it is hard to imagine that *he* would have been able to imagine such a gathering.

It is such a spectacular vomitorium of all that pop culture has become--that, in any given moment of any given moment, you are bound to see, or hear, or smell something that you could find only at San Diego con.

This is one of those stories.

And even if you haven't been to the con, you've seen their crazy antics on E! Entertainment television, running around Cannes film festival...

Now, one of the Troma cast of characters-- in particular, Sgt. Kabukiman NYPD-- was hovering around our booth quite a lot.

I think he is a fan of mine-- it's hard to tell. Because, as the show progressed, his dialogue, though enthusiastic, became increasingly slurred...

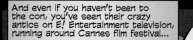

Well, they are always at San Diego, and always, proudly, gleefully, making a shitload of noise.

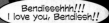

Bendissshhh!!! I love you, Bendissh!!

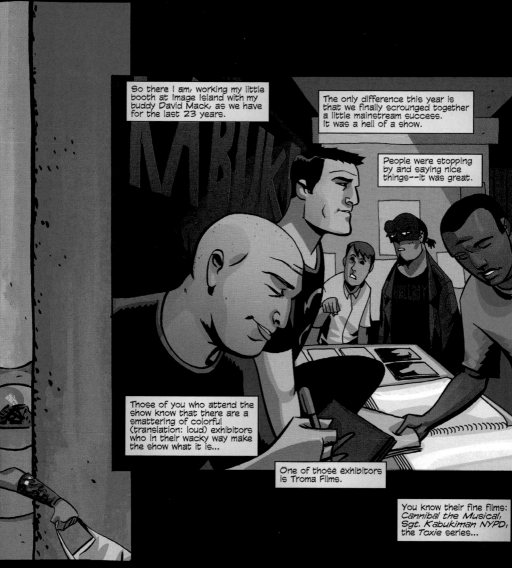

So there I am, working my little booth at Image Island with my buddy David Mack, as we have for the last 23 years.

The only difference this year is that we finally scrounged together a little mainstream success. It was a hell of a show.

People were stopping by and saying nice things--it was great.

Those of you who attend the show know that there are a smattering of colorful (translation: loud) exhibitors who in their wacky way make the show what it is...

One of those exhibitors is Troma Films.

You know their fine films: *Cannibal the Musical*, *Sgt. Kabukiman NYPD*, the *Toxie* series...

Now, though he was certainly embarrassing the shit out of me, the person whose nerves he was *really* getting on was David Mack.

Particularly a drunk-as-fuck Sgt. Kabukiman.

But we are polite young men, and we let Sgt. Kabukiman be himself.

BENDISSSHHH!!

You have to understand... David's book *Kabuki* is a very serious and personal artistic statement, and he didn't even want this Sgt. Kabukiman hanging around, confusing potential readers into thinking that the two of them might have any connection.

Sgt. Kabukiman has *nothing* to do with *Kabuki*.

I LOOOVE YOU!!!

Cut to later in the show...

Marvel had set up a couple of interviews for me to do.

Which was nice--because if there is anything this little story will tell you, it's that I love to talk endlessly about myself...

I don't remember who the interview was with...

(I'm not that big an airhead. It's just that the con is total chaos, and I can't remember who it was.)

But I *do* remember it was for Spider-Man, it was some Canadian thing, and it was a live broadcast.

And I am doing my interview face-- the happy comics creator face-- which, for those scoring at home, is in direct contrast to the face I make when I am actually *making* the comics.

Oh, I always loved Spider-Man, so you can imagine how exciting--

And while I was yammering on, I noticed this girl out of the corner of my eye...

...and I immediately recognized her as Julie from *The Real World: New Orleans.*

(Or, as most of you will remember her, the very cute, and very horny, Mormon girl.)

And there she was, smiling at me.

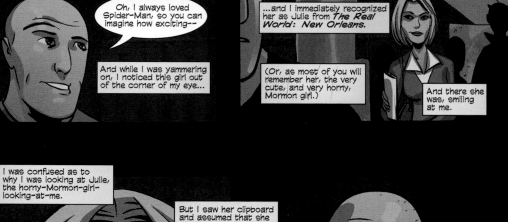

I was confused as to why I was looking at Julie, the horny-Mormon-girl-looking-at-me.

But I saw her clipboard and assumed that she must be associated with the show, and continued on...

I think the appeal of Spider-Man is that he has real, everyday problems...

And as the interview went on, I noticed out of the other corner of my other eye a figure coming towards me.

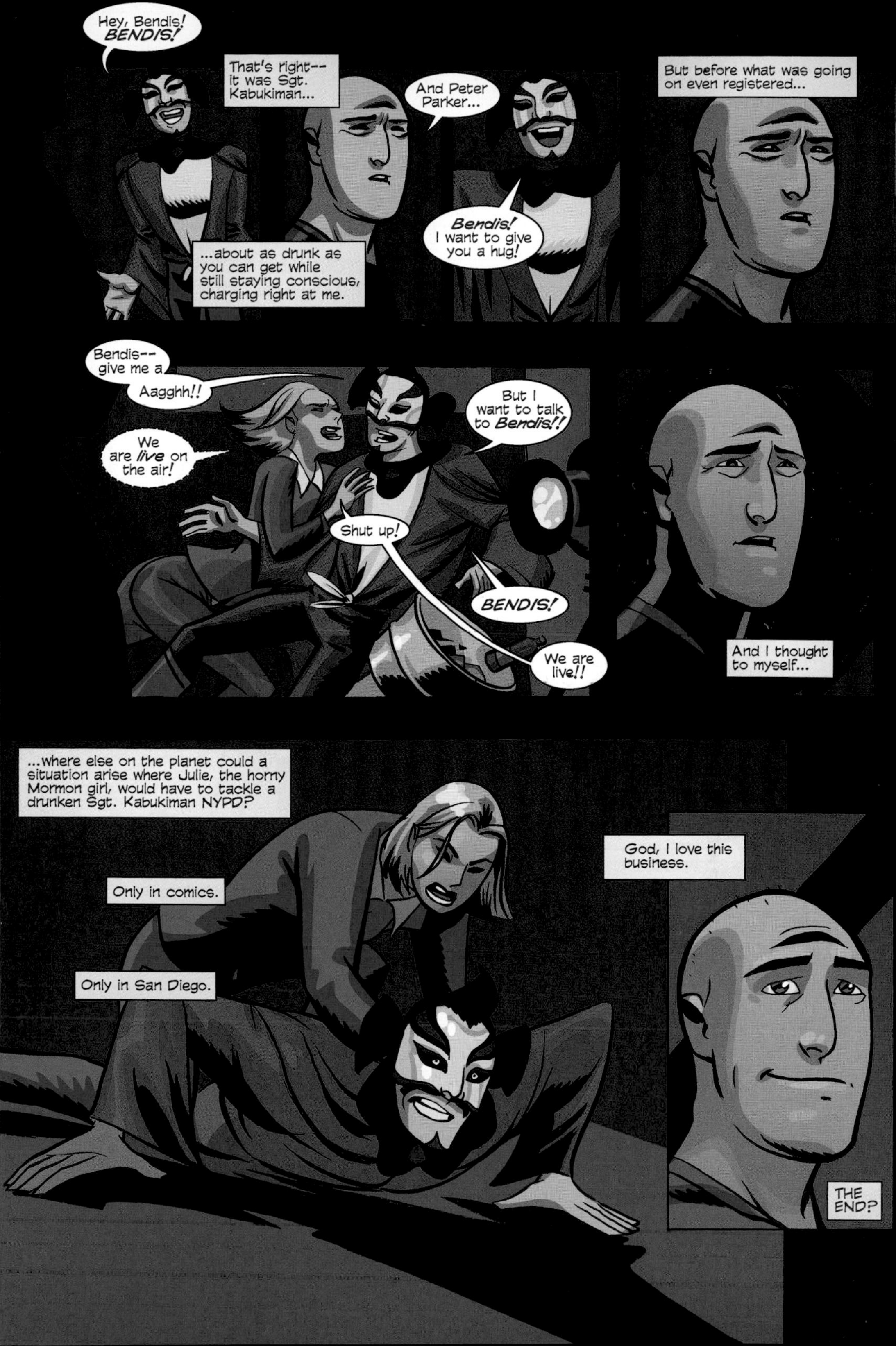

Hey, Bendis! BENDIS!
That's right-- it was Sgt. Kabukiman...
...about as drunk as you can get while still staying conscious, charging right at me.
And Peter Parker...
Bendis! I want to give you a hug!
But before what was going on even registered...
Bendis-- give me a
Aagghh!!
We are live on the air!
But I want to talk to Bendis!!
Shut up!
BENDIS!
We are live!!
And I thought to myself...
...where else on the planet could a situation arise where Julie, the horny Mormon girl, would have to tackle a drunken Sgt. Kabukiman NYPD?
Only in comics.
Only in San Diego.
God, I love this business.
THE END?

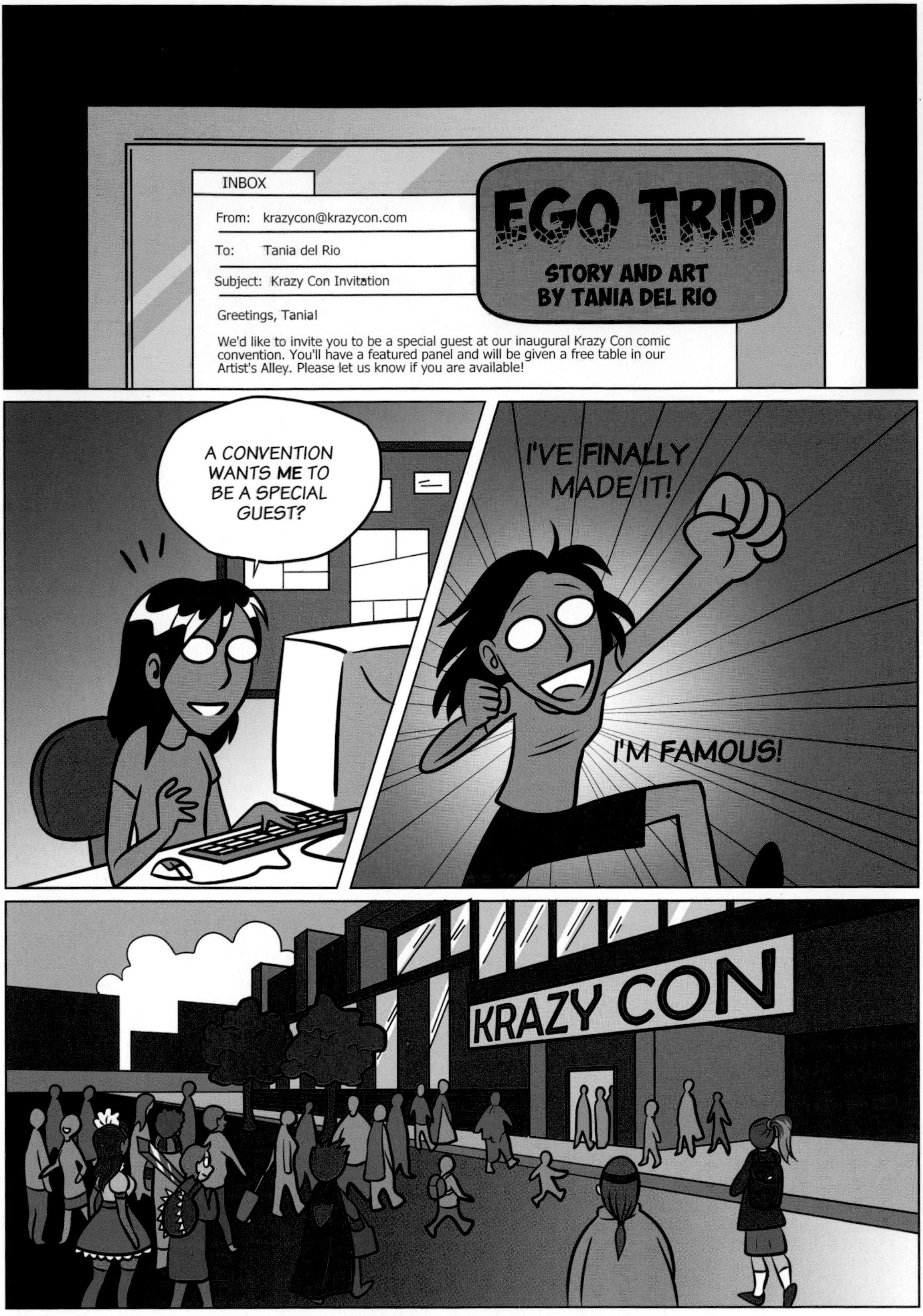
INBOX
From: krazycon@krazycon.com
To: Tania del Rio
Subject: Krazy Con Invitation
Greetings, Tania!
We'd like to invite you to be a special guest at our inaugural Krazy Con comic convention. You'll have a featured panel and will be given a free table in our Artist's Alley. Please let us know if you are available!
EGO TRIP
STORY AND ART BY TANIA DEL RIO
A CONVENTION WANTS ME TO BE A SPECIAL GUEST?
I'VE FINALLY MADE IT!
I'M FAMOUS!
KRAZY CON

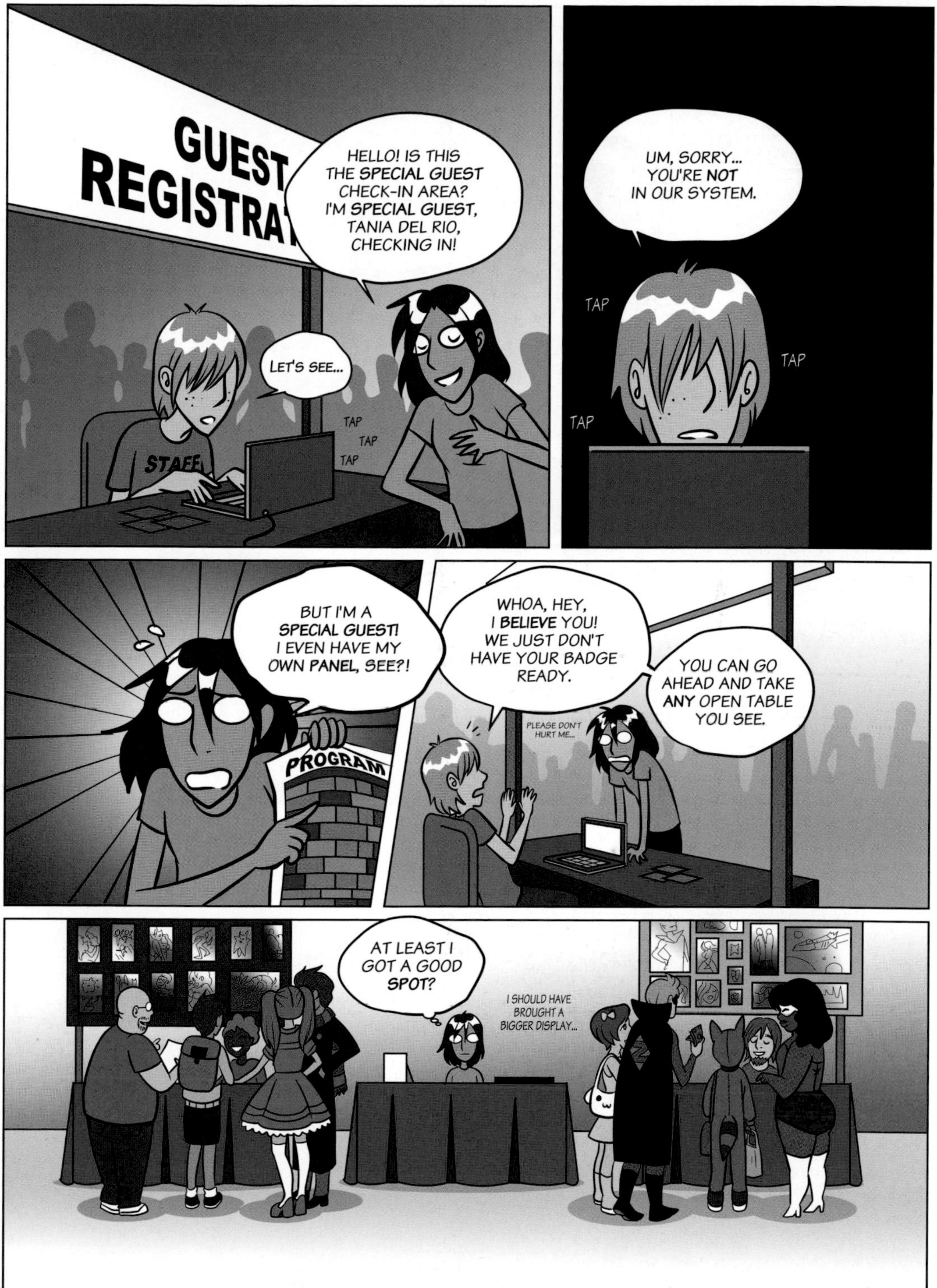
GUEST REGISTRAT
HELLO! IS THIS THE SPECIAL GUEST CHECK-IN AREA? I'M SPECIAL GUEST, TANIA DEL RIO, CHECKING IN!
LET'S SEE...
STAFF
TAP TAP TAP
UM, SORRY... YOU'RE NOT IN OUR SYSTEM.
TAP TAP TAP
BUT I'M A SPECIAL GUEST! I EVEN HAVE MY OWN PANEL, SEE?!
PROGRAM
WHOA, HEY, I BELIEVE YOU! WE JUST DON'T HAVE YOUR BADGE READY.
PLEASE DON'T HURT ME...
YOU CAN GO AHEAD AND TAKE ANY OPEN TABLE YOU SEE.
AT LEAST I GOT A GOOD SPOT?
I SHOULD HAVE BROUGHT A BIGGER DISPLAY...

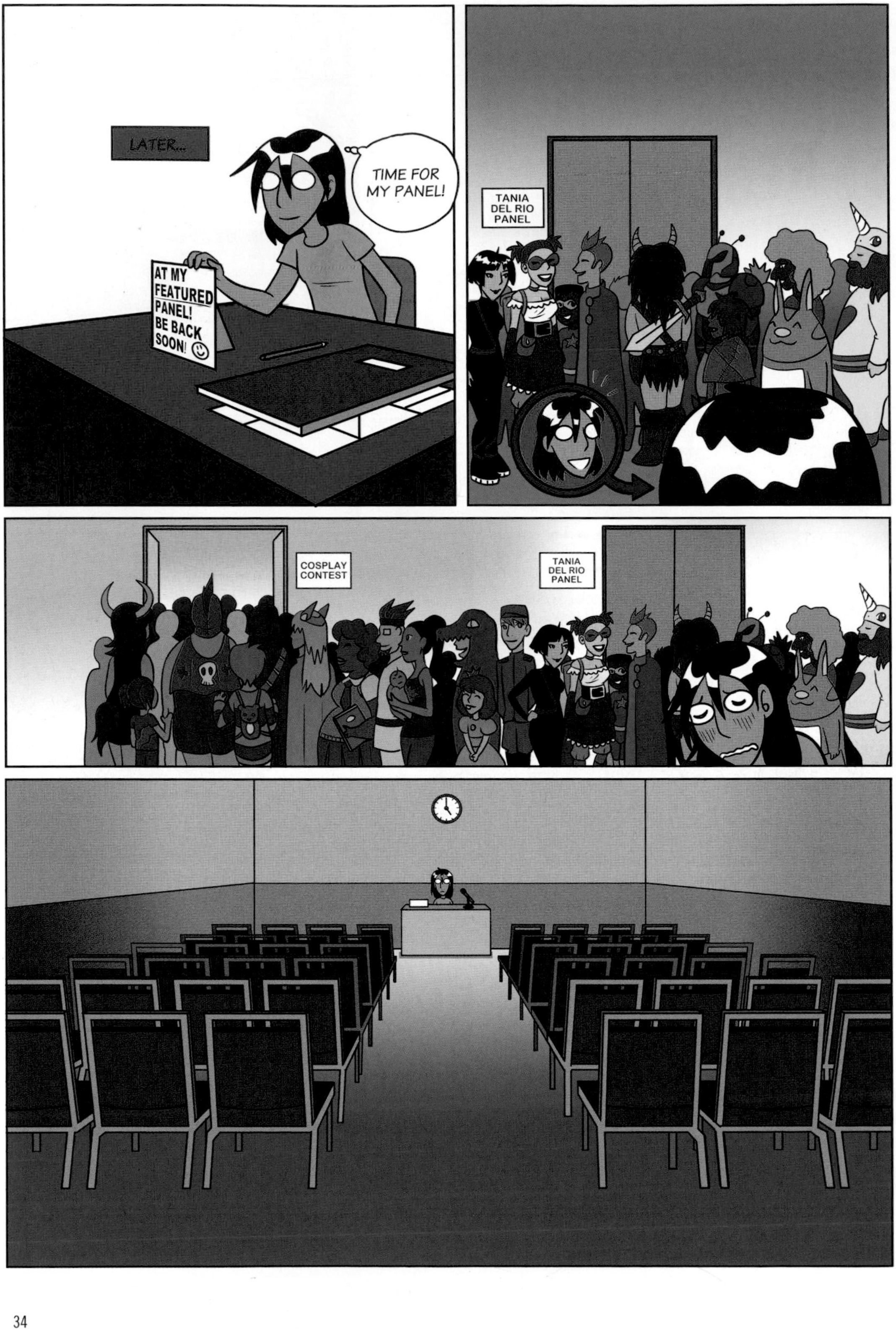
LATER...
TIME FOR MY PANEL!
AT MY FEATURED PANEL! BE BACK SOON! ☺
TANIA DEL RIO PANEL
COSPLAY CONTEST
TANIA DEL RIO PANEL

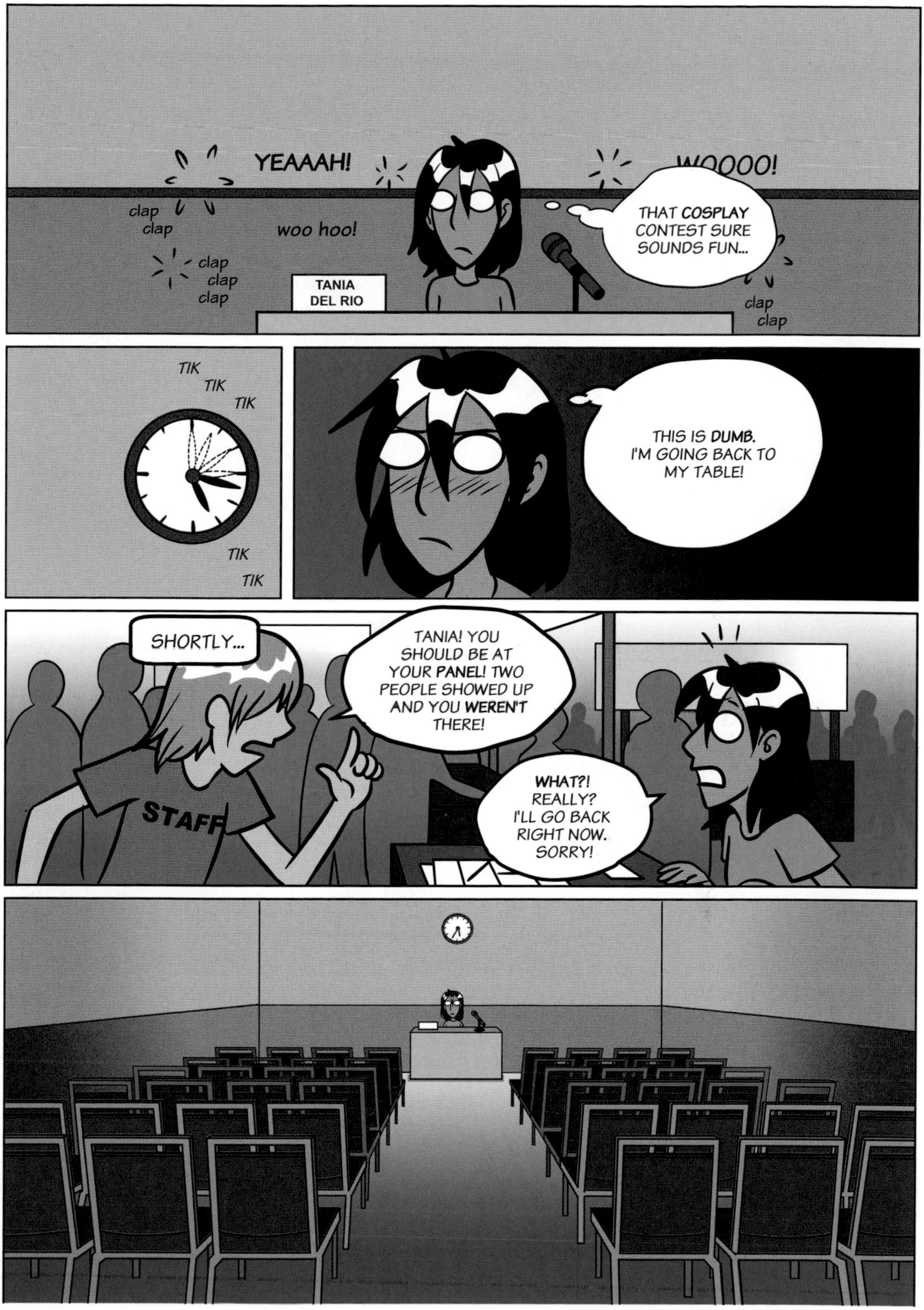
YEAAAH!
WOOOO!
clap clap
woo hoo!
clap clap clap
TANIA DEL RIO
THAT COSPLAY CONTEST SURE SOUNDS FUN...
clap clap
TIK TIK TIK
TIK TIK
THIS IS DUMB. I'M GOING BACK TO MY TABLE!
SHORTLY...
TANIA! YOU SHOULD BE AT YOUR PANEL! TWO PEOPLE SHOWED UP AND YOU WEREN'T THERE!
STAFF
WHAT?! REALLY? I'LL GO BACK RIGHT NOW. SORRY!

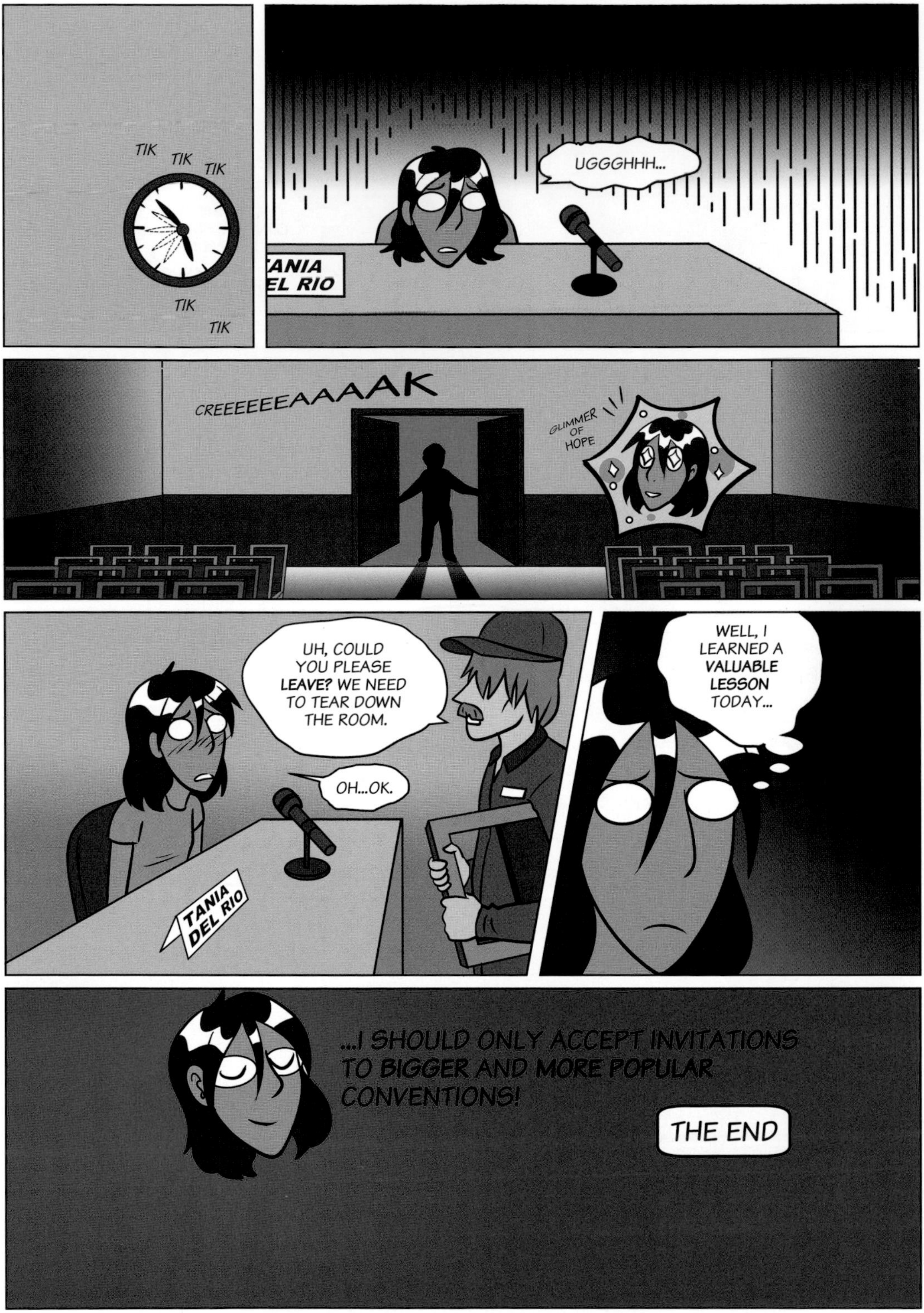
TIK
TIK
TIK
TIK
TIK
UGGGHHH...
TANIA DEL RIO
CREEEEEEAAAAK
GLIMMER OF HOPE
UH, COULD YOU PLEASE LEAVE? WE NEED TO TEAR DOWN THE ROOM.
OH...OK.
TANIA DEL RIO
WELL, I LEARNED A VALUABLE LESSON TODAY...
...I SHOULD ONLY ACCEPT INVITATIONS TO BIGGER AND MORE POPULAR CONVENTIONS!
THE END

A QUEER GUIDE TO COMIC CON

Anthony Oliveira

A good functional definition of queerness (if I can get a little nineties for a second) is the eruption of the unusual into the ordinary. Personally, my annual calendar is punctuated by four such mega-queer events: in Fall, we have Halloween (in which straight people descend on The Village despite our most frightening attempts to scare them off), in Winter, we have Christmas (in which we commemorate the halcyon occasion when three old queens showed up with accessories and perfumes and tried to give a baby a makeover), in Spring, there is of course Pride (when we throw a party as an excuse to close the roads to infuriate the heterosexuals), and, in the late summer, the queerest event of all: Comic Con.

What follows, then, is my guide to getting the queerest time out of your convention. You don't have to be queer to use it, but as with most things in life, queer people will get more out of it.

Prep

I highly recommend going with friends if you can, and getting to know their interests, even if you don't share them, so you can be a good partner in the hunt. Many years ago I was lucky enough to make a nerdy best friend (Hi John!) and have had the lifelong pleasure of getting to go with him to most cons ever since. John is straight, which goes to show they are not all terrible, with a little rummaging, you might also find a decent one!

Dating at cons is also possible—whether bringing your own or attending one of the new dating events some conventions host.

That being said, going alone (which I have *also* done plenty of times) is its own pleasure. Being a good date to yourself is an important life skill to have. One great way to do this is to make your social media into a kind of living diary of the experience. Tweet your search for that back issue, Instagram your Artist Alley finds or celebrity run-ins, curate a Facebook album, etc. I basically owe my whole twitter account (and subsequent career!) to nothing other than live-tweeting nerdy queer joy; you can certainly do the same! Digital spaces are the number one way queer people find each other now; access the hive-mind!

Spend some time looking at and thinking about the con schedule—is there an app? A program? If going with friends, sit down in advance and make a loose plan. What is important to everyone? What panels or signings do you need to attend? When are the cosplay meet-ups you want to photograph?

Have a loose budget. A rough amount for daily buys, and a rough floating amount for Big Gets (this year: my new, light-up Infinity Gauntlet that I have no room in my apartment for!), will help you colour inside the lines a little.

Also, look outside the program—are any of the gay bars or facilities planning any events? Comic conventions aren't always great about inclusivity, and if you're coming in from out of town, the area around convention halls is often a cis-heterosexual wasteland. Do a google to find where the city's queer neighbourhood is (if they have one—or several), and see if anything cool is happening there. Drag shows are a perfect post-con party because they're fun, bright, and social, but surprisingly passive—you don't have to dance or socialize if you're tuckered out! Just relax and enjoy the show. And tip your performers!

Cosplay – Wearing It

Cosplay is my absolute favourite thing about comic conventions. It is also in many respects the queerest. It is the nerdier cousin of drag—drawing on many of the same skills, and engaged in the same interplays of performativity, burlesque, and showpersonship that inform the drag tradition. The dude in that Mister Freeze costume might be as straight as it gets, but as he sparkles in glittery silver makeup and cascades dry ice onto the convention hall carpet, whether he knows it or not, he stands on the shoulders of drag.

Cosplay is also frequently the site of genderplay: femme bodies dressing up as their favourite anime princes, or masc bodies enjoying the carnivalesque of dressing up as Pokemon trainer Misty or the Princess of Power, She-Ra. Cosplay, like Halloween, is (as Buffy Summers once said), a chance to come as you *aren't*.

This also means that queers basically have the cheat codes for cosplay! So use them. Many is the time I've seen a great costume ruined by makeup mistakes that my drag performer friends wouldn't be caught dead making. Avail yourself of online tutorials—there's one for every look and every kind of armor or cape!

I think cosplay basically breaks down into three tiers.

TIER ONE is cosplay that amounts to a specific but basically "civilian" outfit with a prop or element of make-up or two—Steven Universe in his star shirt and sandals with a shield, or Marceline the Vampire Queen in her flannels and maybe some fangs. This is my personal favourite tier to wear to a convention, because it's a) fun, b) invites conversation and/or photos (with you or that you take with other cosplayers), but c) doesn't in any way hamper moving comfortably through a crowd or require maintenance or care of the costume. It basically makes the costume a part of your day, but not its focus—some pictures, but also some browsing, some panels, some lunch, etc.

TIER TWO is the more advanced level—basically a faithful reproduction of a character or look that nevertheless stays within the bounds of the basic human frame: the paladins of Voltron, or Spider-Man, Princess Peach, Magneto, etc. These are obviously a lot of fun, but they come with a higher level of custodianship and demand—people will want pictures everywhere you go, an unfortunate jostle might damage your jetpack, and your pizza slice might get grease on your elven cloak.

TIER THREE is the costume that gets crowds of photo-takers and kids. It's festooned in lights; it's shooting out fog; it takes you a second to figure out where the person even is inside its animatronics. These are the Daleks, the Juggernauts, the Alien Queens. This person's con experience is basically to stand in the larger hallways and be bombarded by attention—a lot of fun, but weirdly also a form of community service (which many conventions recognize, and issue them special badges for their efforts).

All of these are great ways to experience cons, and great things to see at cons! Just recognize they will inform the kind of experience you have, and you should decide in advance which is right for you. Also consider mixing and matching your days—maybe Saturday you wear your nine-foot Onslaught costume while Sunday it's just you in your cute Dark Phoenix tee rummaging through Artists Alley!

And remember, your costume exists in a shared space with others. That means basic safety concerns (no realistic weaponry, no sharp or unyielding edges) but also exhibiting sensitivity and thoughtfulness. Don't put a Nazi armband on your Red Skull or Hellboy costumes. Don't appropriate or mock real human cultures not your own (or fictional ones that closely approximate real ones), and for the love of God, if you find yourself applying make-up to your skin that is a REAL HUMAN SKIN TONE NOT YOUR OWN, stop right the heck there.

Pack for repairs (most comic conventions now have a cosplay triage area; check your maps!) and find out if there's a scheduled meet-up for other cosplayers in your fandom so you can take maximum photos!

Cosplay – Enjoying It

When taking pics of cosplay: ask first, show them the results, and then ask if they're on twitter/Instagram so you can tag them. Asking for photos produces a better picture, and indeed if they don't like it they'll almost always pose again. Also, it's a great way to strike up conversation! If I'm not tagging them immediately (some photos need edits!) then I keep an open note file on my phone of their @ for later.

Tier Three costumes sometimes do not need this step, nor do Group Meet-Up events; everybody knows the deal in these situations! Similarly, occasionally a person in costume will be doing something that merits a candid photo (recently I got a great shot of a Maleficent archly texting someone on a bench). In these situations, I will simply introduce myself afterward, and show them the photo so they can see how cool it was. If I don't feel brave enough to do that or think the photo is too embarrassing to show them, then I probably shouldn't have it, and will delete it anyway.

Cosplay is never consent. This means that someone's outfit being revealing does not mean you get to leer or touch them or cat-call. Never mock a costume either aloud or online, and if you take a photo of a costume only to realize it's compromising or embarrassing in a way you didn't intend or the person wouldn't appreciate, simply consider it a loss and don't post it.

The Outfit

If you're dressed as a civilian (also a perfectly valid choice!) you're still gonna want to give your look some thought. In all human interactions, but especially in spaces like a convention, for better or worse our bodies are a text people read—the primary site from which assessments are made, conversations will spring, and opinions formed. So express yourself!

First of all be clean—cons are close quarters, and no one wants to smell a shirt taking a second lap. When I was a kid comic cons were stinkier, but blessedly the hygiene of the nerd community is trending towards improvement. Conversely, and for the same reason, don't overdo any scents, as some people are sensitive or allergic. I am a perfumed dandy, so this is hard for me, but I long ago discovered the advanced but highly rewarding world of having a signature milder daytime and a signature nighttime scent (honestly scent-buying is the best because you get all the joy of shopping with none of the bummer of clothes not fitting; I highly recommend it).

Non-cosplay dress for cons is a broad spectrum, but you'll be fine with fun casual. Most comic cons run warm, as they're frequently in summer and almost always pushing venues to capacity. Temperatures fluctuate wildly—warm, crowded sunlit atriums or paths giving way to cavernously over-air-conditioned lecture halls. Assume you'll be down at various points to a t-shirt/single layer, but I always pack a cardigan in my bag.

If you are not a mobility device user, you will be on your feet ALL DAY—so wear a sensible and comfortable shoe, preferably closed-toed as you will get tread on occasionally in the crowd.

My default con outfit is: a fandom or graphic tee (one for each day of the con), jeans, a statement sneaker, and a cardigan with some pins on it.

Shirts And Pins

The fandom tee is not just a fashion choice; it is a conversation piece. "I like your shirt!" is a way a stranger can indicate "I am available for a conversation, and we have this thing in common!"

My choices are almost always queer-adjacent—my Captain America shield in rainbow colours, or my "ALT MASC" rainbow pink unicorn shirt. This helps me find my fellow queers in a crowd. My "Magneto Is Right" tee invites conversation about minority politics; my Steven Universe star locates other soft boi sweethearts, etc. The graphic tee is the equivalent of a Care Bear Stare; it beams itself into public spaces like a beacon: "Here is what I love! Do you love this too?"

Similarly, the enamel pin or button have long been a staple (and even a stereotype) of queer flagging. Gay dudes used to use hankies to say what we were into; now a button can function to signal your own community participation! I like to wear a rainbow pin because especially for folks visiting from out of town who may not get to pass through as many queer spaces as I am lucky enough to, this can be a way to signal their inclusion and that they have a place here, even if we never talk. Similarly, pronoun pins (indicating your pronouns are "He/Him," "They/Them," or others) are also a great item to wear—even if you're cis and conventionally gender-presenting, they signal you are interested in fostering spaces and conversations that are inclusive and affirming.

Also a heads-up: make sure you're comfortable with what you're wearing because as I said, anything and everything WILL become a conversation piece with fellow fans, vendors, and talent! A pin is more modular than a shirt—if you decide your newfound identity is not something you want to talk about all day, you can just pop it off.

"Nice shirt" or "I love [fandom you're wearing]!" can always be met with a "thanks!" This can be the beginning of a conversation or the whole of it, depending on the social cues—be respectful of people's boundaries, and firm with your own. A reminder that some fans are neuro-divergent, and may have trouble reading social cues you think are polite.

You'll also probably need a bag. I like a messenger bag rather than a backpack because I am short and they hit other people less in crowds and I can more easily access their contents, but go with what you're comfortable with.

Supplies

So, you're all dressed and you've got some kind of bag. You'll also need: a cardboard tube for your posters and prints, and a firm sleeve/book to tuck things in. You will think you do not need these things *right up until* you see that glorious map of Hyrule or something, and now your newest and most precious possession is also your flimsiest, moving through a crowd of careless paper-bending bulldozers.

You're going to be taking pictures, consulting an app, texting your friends, tweeting all day—have a charger and ideally a battery pack!

It's also not a terrible idea to pack a sharpie with you for signatures!

Have some cash, because you'll want coins for small purchases, and want to avoid sketchier debit/credit machines. The only times I've ever had my credit card cloned was at an unscrupulous point-of-sale device at a con booth.

Take a second and think about it: your body is a weird machine whose job is to pilot you happily to fun things. What might it need to do this? Have whatever medicine you'll need. Con crud (the tendency for people to get sick after conventions) is real, and it is *not* spectacular. I am very allergic to dust, and books and old toys are basically just inert dust-collecting objects, so I need my allergy medication. Breath mints keep you fresh, especially in stale air. Also, I like to have a packet of those little facecloths, because they are like taking a three-second spa day in the middle of an oily, junk food-ridden afternoon. Your mileage may vary if you're the makeup wearing type (blue face paint or otherwise).

Speaking of: pack a healthy snack, and some water. Both are in short supply or ludicrously expensive on-site. You can get (better) pizza later!

Where's your lanyard? DO YOU HAVE YOUR LANYARD? One time my boyfriend left his lanyard on the kitchen island and we didn't notice until we got there and it took half the day to go back and get it. LEARN FROM OUR SUFFERING. HAVE YOUR LANYARD.

Booth

There's basically two kinds of booths—the corporate booth, and the artist/indie booth (a great many of which are in Artist Alley). The corporate booth is staffed by people of varying interest in their wares and varying levels of acting ability in feigning said interest; you owe them your good manners, and you should feel very free to take the free things they may offer, but this is pretty low stakes; they're mostly here to rep a brand.

Artist Alley is my favourite place at comic conventions, and it is often where the queerest content lives. This is where you'll find your Stucky and

Klance art, your kinkier sculptural pieces and your cute coin-purses. But it can also be more emotionally fraught, as the interactions that occur here are much more personal! When talking to an artist, feel free to be genuinely complimentary and enthused. If a card is offered, give it a polite moment of inspection (mentally connecting card to face), and take it. If you're unsure about pricing, ask. Do not haggle. However, vendors absolutely do not want to lug things home, so the last day is a good chance to price-check. Artists do not owe you a discount because you like their work. Do not lie if you're not interested; "thanks for letting me look!" is a perfectly valid way to end an interaction. Don't let yourself be pressured into sales you'd like to think about—"I'm going to do a lap and probably think about this print the whole time" is a very common thing for me to say, and about half the time I do decide to come back for it.

If you're a creator, whether touring or tabling, have a card and a little pitch ready for other creators you meet, and make sure the card directs them to your work! The model dressed as Iron Man or Black Widow might not help you get your portfolio to Marvel, but you may meet the perfect artist or writer for your next project! A brief intro and digital follow-up is the way to go; respect the fact that some people might just be polite and are trapped at their booth.

I am a voracious comic reader but I actually buy very few comics at cons; mostly I'm coming home with a Tanuki Mario mug or a homemade Phantom of the Paradise helmet—and original queer content the big publishers are too scared to actually represent. Save money for Artist Alley, and give it your queer love and time.

If you buy something, posting a photo of it on social media is never amiss, and a great use of that business card that artist just gave you! Lift up your fellow queers!

Panel

Panels are a great way to vary your day, to give yourself a rest, and to see some of the biggest and most important creators, artists, and actors talk about their craft. They can also by far be the most hit-and-miss con experience in terms of diverse content and queer inclusiveness. Sometimes I will look around the room for a classic creator's panel or an older property and it is a sea of the same straight white dude. This is a red flag; there will be jokes and comments that will gross me out. On the flipside, a recent *Steven Universe* cast panel I attended was one of the most wholesome, affirming events I've ever seen, as fans sang songs in costume accompanied by a ukulele.

It isn't snobby to know who the writers or creators of your favourite properties are, and following their careers is a shortcut to finding quality you enjoy. Attend their panels! They'll direct you to other great stuff!

At panels, don't be afraid to ask a question—but it better be a *question*. Do not give a long preamble. You may thank the creator for something that particularly touched you or influenced you. Being abstruse or con-frontational isn't going to get you the kind of attention you want—even if you're right, the vibe will be so toxic and your effort so uphill that it is almost never worth it. If you love a person's stuff, it's also perfectly fine to introduce yourself after.

Social / Last Thoughts

The main thing to remember is something that Shredder once told his mutant children in *TMNT 2* (a cinematic masterpiece burned into my brain): *go; play; have fun!*

That being said, comic cons are, like any major event, also kind of stressful—they can be over-stimulating, or uncomfortable, or occasionally upsetting. If you're not having fun, take a second to recalibrate, de-stim-ulate, or change your body chemistry with a snack before diving back in.

Nerd communities are havens for the socially awkward. That is no excuse to be rude. Always remember that being a fan is never a competition. Never interrogate or quiz. I would also just generally encourage you to cultivate a spirit of generosity, curiosity, and care (in cosplay and in life); you won't always understand what you're looking at and some things may raise your eyebrows (whether costumes or wares or art), but Pride Parade rules apply: don't yuck other people's yum. Many things have a context, and sometimes that context escapes us.

Be wise, learn to trust your instinct for who is a bad person trying to ruin someone's day (whose goal you can frustrate simply by ignoring them), who lacks your critical sensitivity and has just made an unfortunate call, and who may have reasons or an audience whose contours you cannot foresee.

Do not police other people's bodies—there is not a "right" size or right racial or gender presentation for cosplay, and not all these dimensions are immediately or wholly legible. Keep in mind that BIPOC (Black, Indigenous, and People of Colour) may be white-passing, and that drag rules generally apply for cosplay, which means addressing cosplayers by the name and pronouns of the character they are performing is generally good practice, as they are in a "performance" mode, but be willing to be corrected. When meeting someone new, try not to presume their pronouns; the current thinking is generally to ask if you must, but only if you must; "they" will suffice until a social cue presents itself. This policy may age or change.

It is worth pointing out that kids will be around; it is also worth pointing out you should care about that pretty much exactly as much as you decide to. Your queerness is not inherently offensive or sexually overt, and indeed in a milieu full of pin-ups and print-screened body pillows, your sexual overtness may not necessarily be out of place either.

Honestly, it is very possible you will be the queerest thing those kids see all year, so be the hero you wish *you* had seen as a kid. In any case, you owe no deference to cis heterosexual hegemony. Kiss your partners, ship your ships, ask your queer panel questions loudly and insistently, wear your flag capes, take up space.

As in all things, let nothing stand which offends your dignity. Live in defiance, and be brave enough to be kind.

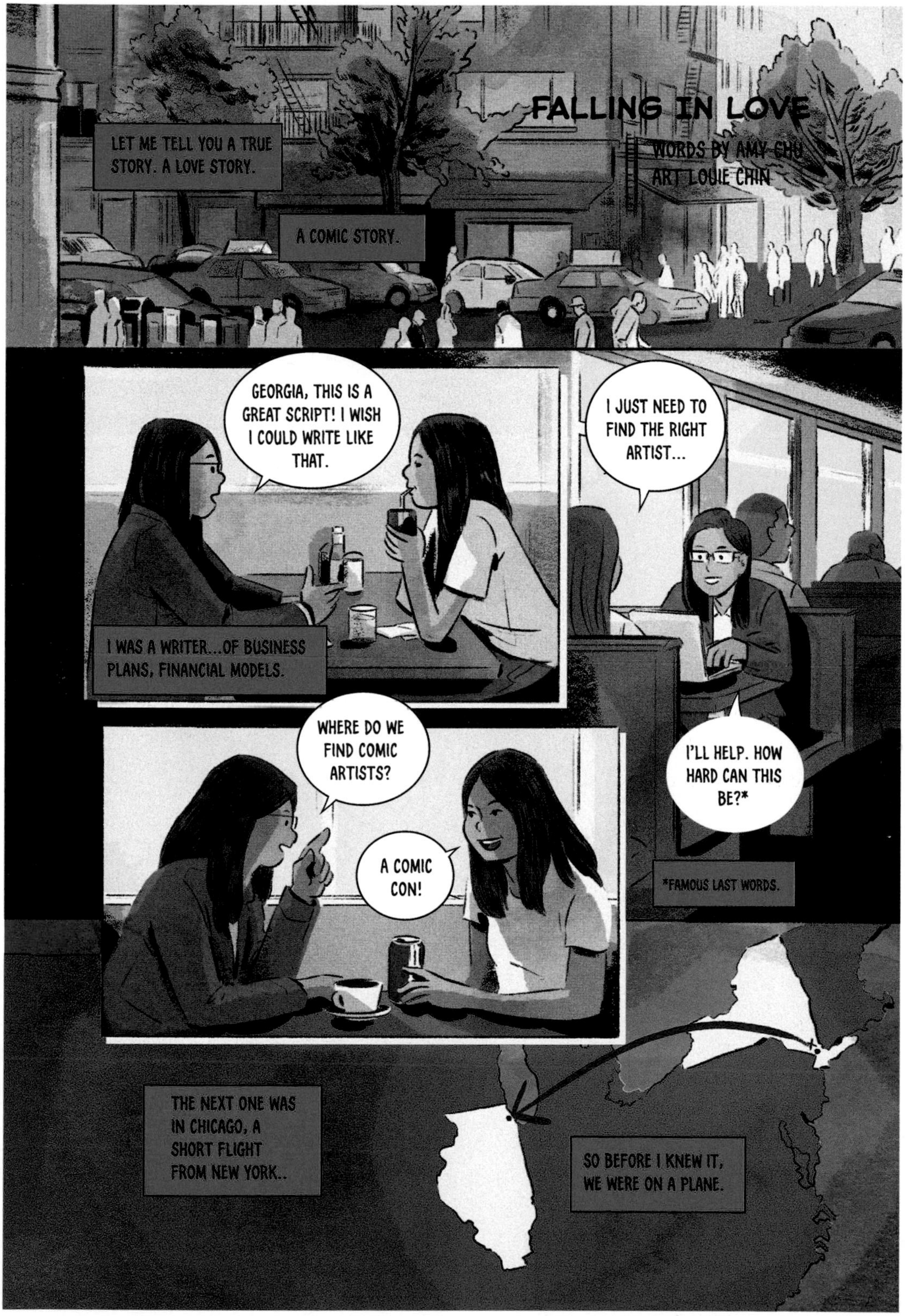
FALLING IN LOVE
WORDS BY AMY CHU
ART LOUIE CHIN
LET ME TELL YOU A TRUE STORY. A LOVE STORY.
A COMIC STORY.
GEORGIA, THIS IS A GREAT SCRIPT! I WISH I COULD WRITE LIKE THAT.
I WAS A WRITER...OF BUSINESS PLANS, FINANCIAL MODELS.
I JUST NEED TO FIND THE RIGHT ARTIST...
I'LL HELP. HOW HARD CAN THIS BE?*
*FAMOUS LAST WORDS.
WHERE DO WE FIND COMIC ARTISTS?
A COMIC CON!
THE NEXT ONE WAS IN CHICAGO, A SHORT FLIGHT FROM NEW YORK..
SO BEFORE I KNEW IT, WE WERE ON A PLANE.

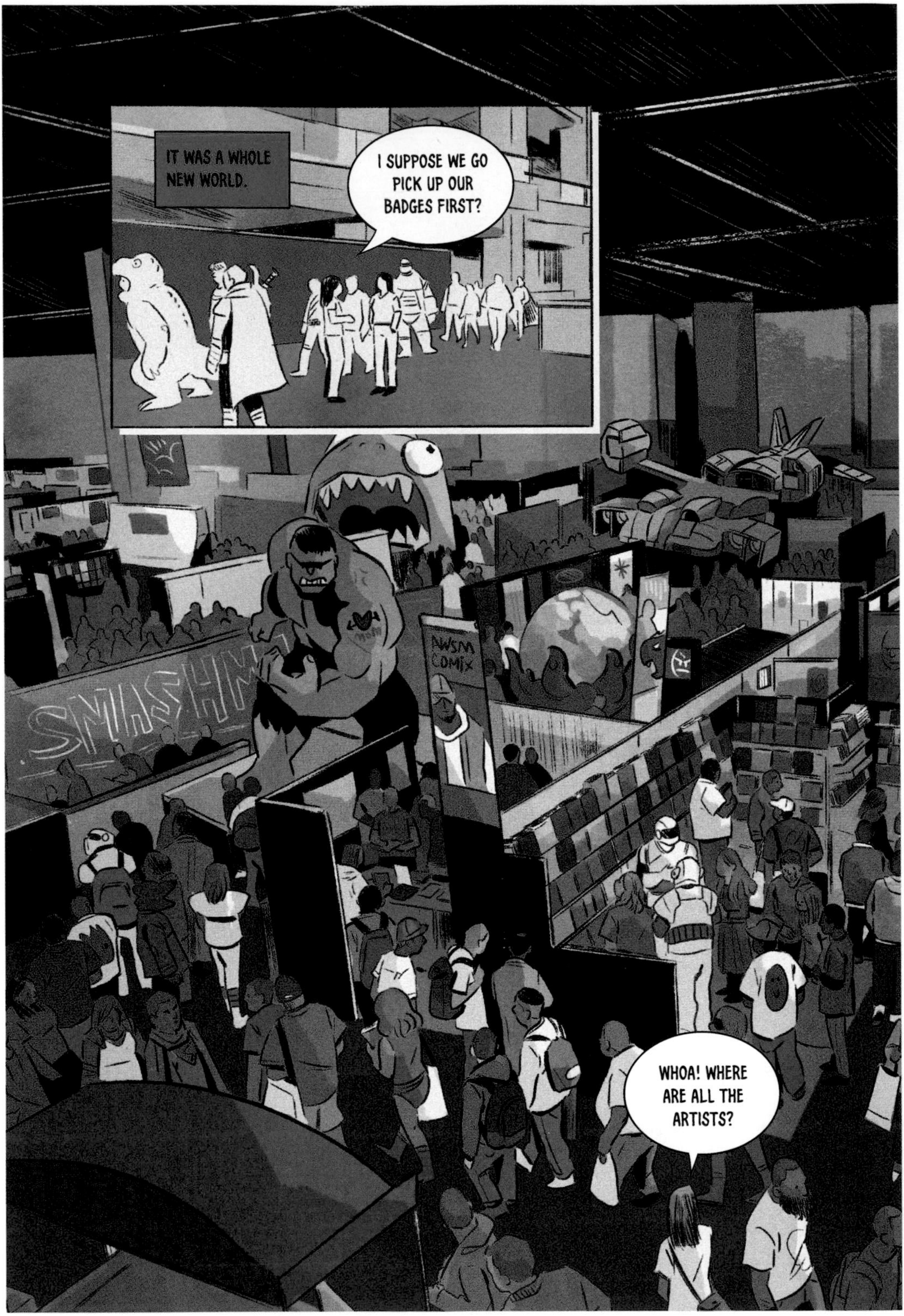
IT WAS A WHOLE NEW WORLD.
I SUPPOSE WE GO PICK UP OUR BADGES FIRST?
SMASH
AWSM COMIX
WHOA! WHERE ARE ALL THE ARTISTS?

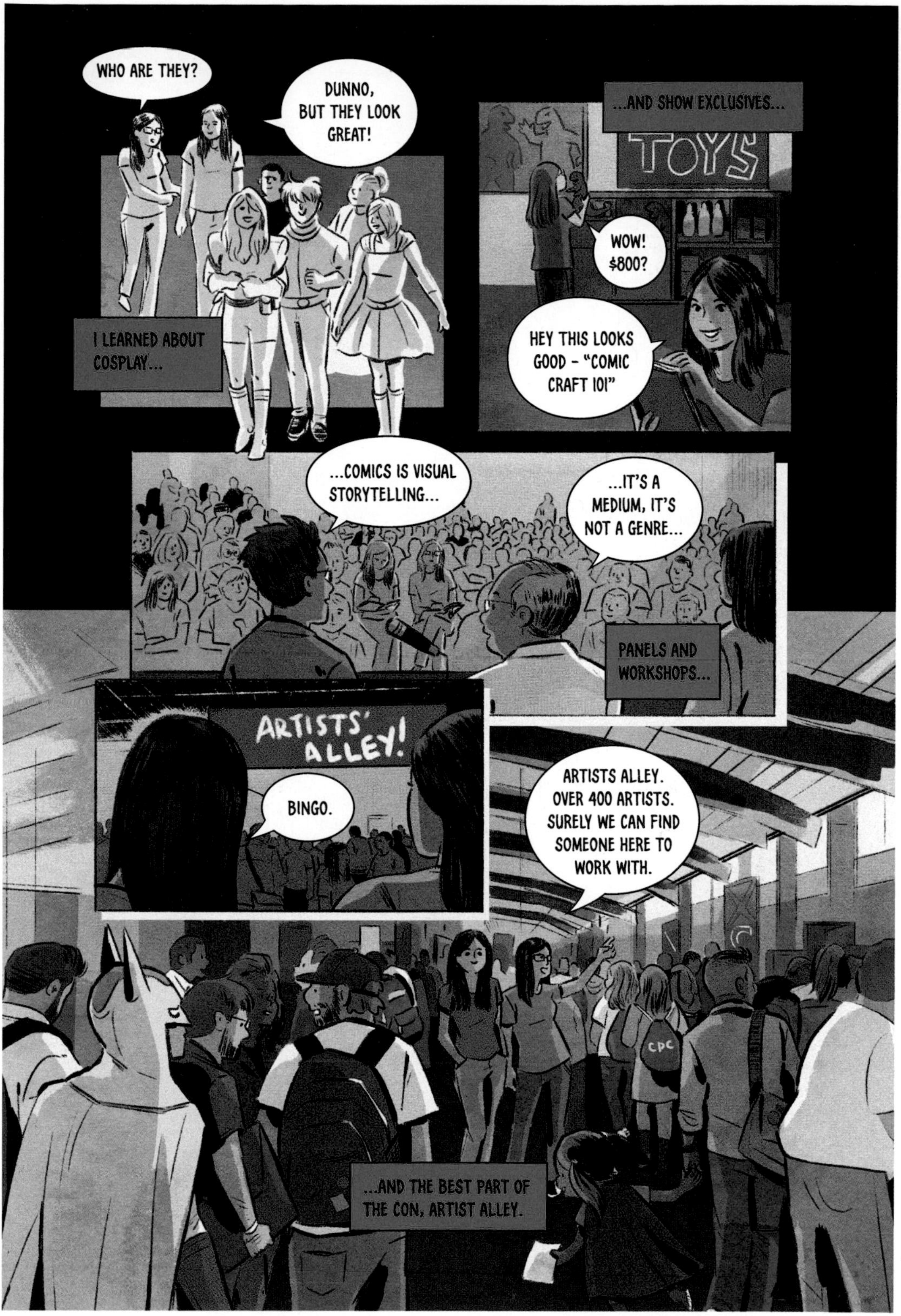

WHO ARE THEY?
DUNNO, BUT THEY LOOK GREAT!
I LEARNED ABOUT COSPLAY...
...AND SHOW EXCLUSIVES...
TOYS
WOW! $800?
HEY THIS LOOKS GOOD - "COMIC CRAFT 101"
...COMICS IS VISUAL STORYTELLING...
...IT'S A MEDIUM, IT'S NOT A GENRE...
PANELS AND WORKSHOPS...
ARTISTS' ALLEY!
BINGO.
ARTISTS ALLEY. OVER 400 ARTISTS. SURELY WE CAN FIND SOMEONE HERE TO WORK WITH.
CPC
...AND THE BEST PART OF THE CON, ARTIST ALLEY.

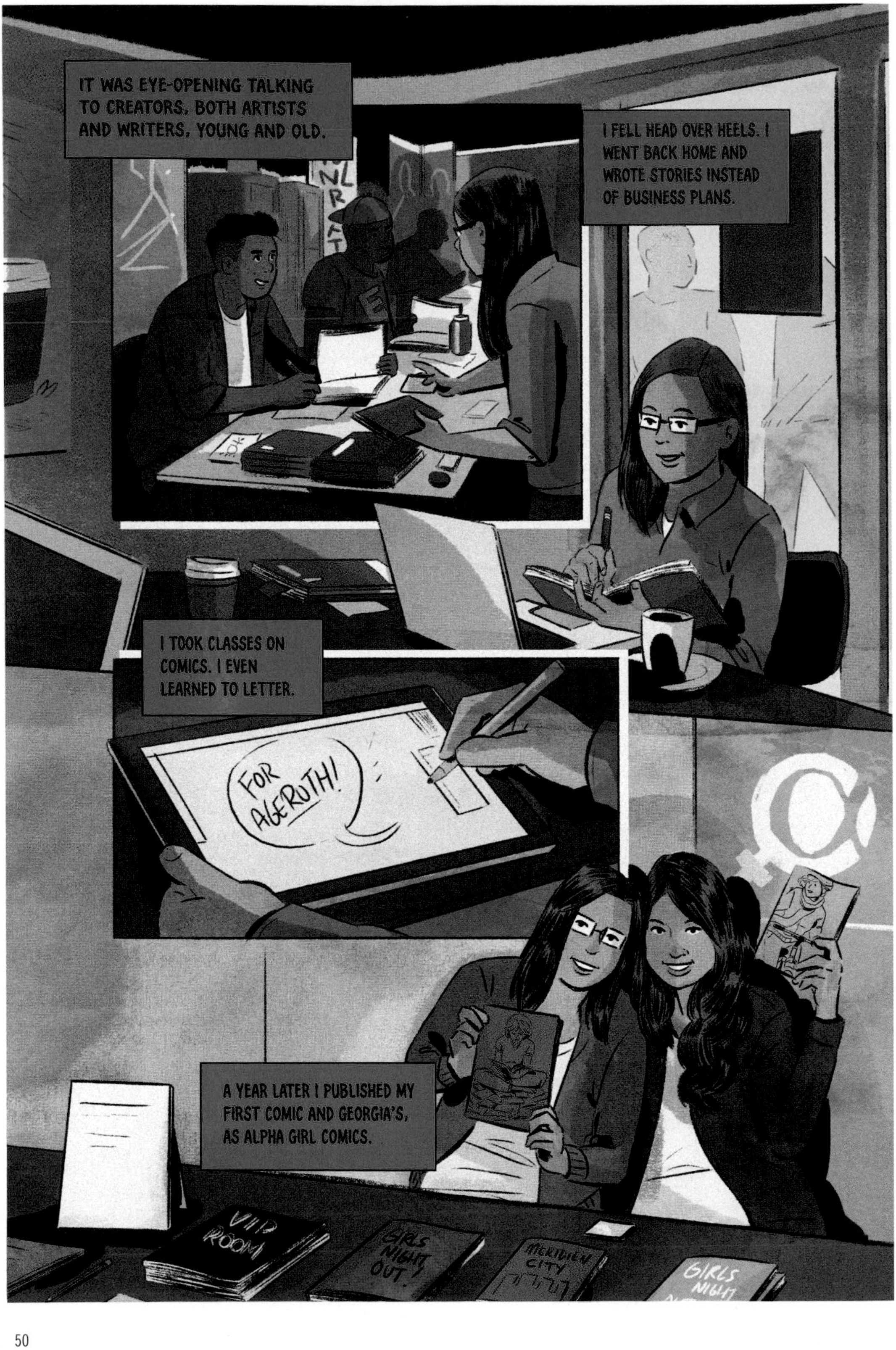
IT WAS EYE-OPENING TALKING TO CREATORS, BOTH ARTISTS AND WRITERS, YOUNG AND OLD.
I FELL HEAD OVER HEELS. I WENT BACK HOME AND WROTE STORIES INSTEAD OF BUSINESS PLANS.
I TOOK CLASSES ON COMICS. I EVEN LEARNED TO LETTER.
FOR AGEROTH!
A YEAR LATER I PUBLISHED MY FIRST COMIC AND GEORGIA'S, AS ALPHA GIRL COMICS.
VIP ROOM
GIRLS NIGHT OUT!
MERIDIEN CITY

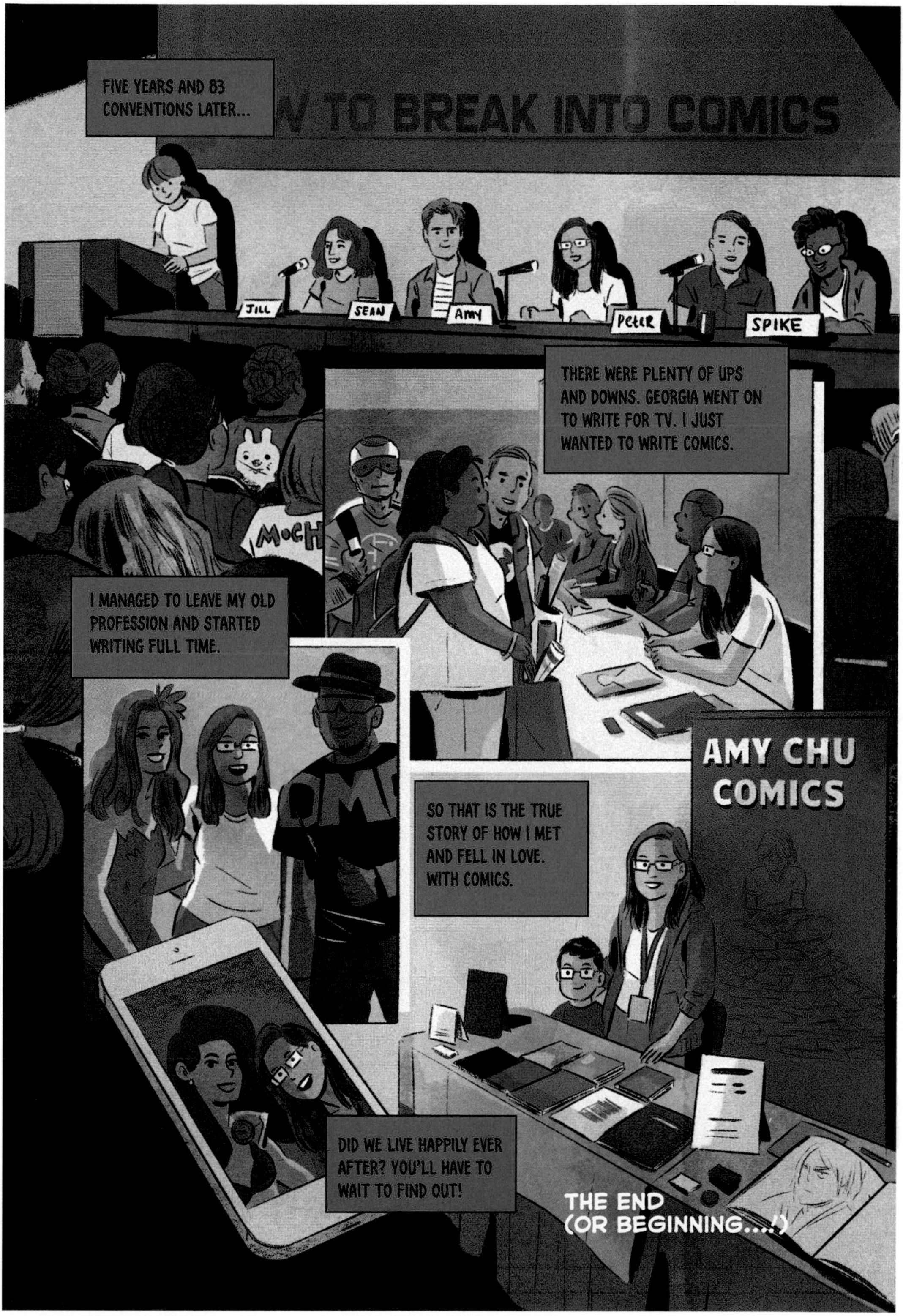
FIVE YEARS AND 83 CONVENTIONS LATER...
W TO BREAK INTO COMICS
JILL
SEAN
AMY
Peter
SPIKE
THERE WERE PLENTY OF UPS AND DOWNS. GEORGIA WENT ON TO WRITE FOR TV. I JUST WANTED TO WRITE COMICS.
MOCH
I MANAGED TO LEAVE MY OLD PROFESSION AND STARTED WRITING FULL TIME.
AMY CHU COMICS
SO THAT IS THE TRUE STORY OF HOW I MET AND FELL IN LOVE. WITH COMICS.
DID WE LIVE HAPPILY EVER AFTER? YOU'LL HAVE TO WAIT TO FIND OUT!
THE END
(OR BEGINNING...!)

NEVER WEAR COMFORTABLE SHOES TO A CON

Tia Vasiliou

Just about any con survival guide starts with this piece of advice: wear comfortable shoes.

I never trust anyone who tells me to wear comfortable shoes. It implies a situation will almost certainly be uncomfortable. It implies I will have very little choice in the matter. Look, if I'm going to be uncomfortable, it will be in a situation of my own making, thank you very much. I mostly wear heels at cons, because I am never more uncomfortable than when I feel underdressed. I will smile and shine as blisters form and my shoes pool with blood (true story) as long as they're an impressive pair of shoes. Blisters heal after all, and you can always make new blood, but the glory of impressive shoes is forever.

My most impressive pair of shoes is probably the black pony hair Mary Janes that once belonged to Kim Gordon of Sonic Youth (she was selling some of her wardrobe to raise money for charity. I didn't like, knock her down and steal them off her or anything). I call them my magic shoes because I can always seem to conjure my favorite things or people anywhere I wear them. I'll mention a song I want to hear and suddenly the DJ will play it. A friend who couldn't join the party somehow arrives. One time, I reached into my purse after a night of post-con karaoke and discovered a bag of peanut butter M&M's. To this day I have no idea how it got there, but I'm going to say it was the magic shoes. Yes, I'm a little superstitious. And I firmly believe that putting some blood into the universe can get me back a little something worthwhile. Let's just say these shoes are not built for comfort, and are totally worth it.

I mainly just wear those candy-conjuring magic shoes to convention after-parties, my gold distressed ankle boots are usually my favorite for the con floor. I spray painted these ankle boots gold and distressed them myself, in an attempt to pass them off as something I might have fished out of a glamorous Milano haute couture dumpster. "International High-Fashion Trash Witch" is very much my aesthetic. Boots like these are an excellent go-to for any occasion where you want to be just a teensy bit smug about wearing shiny high heels to walk around a con all day, but still want to look like you didn't try too hard (spoiler alert, however it may appear, I am always trying very hard.) Don't let the wedge heels fool you into thinking they're more comfortable. That's a rookie mistake. They're still five inches tall. But get yourself shoes with a sturdy platform, and no matter how high the heels, you'll at least be able to brave the convention center Starbucks line . . . and then run full tilt to the panel for which you're about to be late because you were standing in the convention center Starbucks line. Ask me how I know.

Even my lone pair of flat shoes that you miiiiight catch me wearing at a con (Doc Martens) are shiny pewter, rather than the standard-issue goth black. And side-note? If you ever do catch me wearing these at a con, it's a pretty good indication that I have entirely given up on life. Please be a dear and prepare the funeral pyre, and/or bring me an iced coffee.

Wearing heels at a convention is mostly me trying to trick myself into feeling a little more secure in the sea of chaos that inevitably is every convention floor. It says to my exhausted body, "I am probably going to be able to find a comfortable place to sit at any given moment." It reassures my frayed nerves, "I am in control of my experience here." Reverse psychology, I guess. That's a thing, right? *I am impervious to pain and could do this all day! I'm invincible!*

Are any of those things actually true? Ha. Not really. Okay, maybe the last one is a little bit true. I do have a weirdly high pain tolerance and very strong ankles capable of withstanding hours of walking in heels. But I have learned that when you need to be *on*—for work or for social situations— sometimes it's all about appearances. It just needs to *seem* true. And the most important person you have to convince is yourself. You've got this. You are Super-You.

"Are we our true selves at cons?" a friend mused, as we discussed our elaborate wardrobe and grooming preparations ahead of SDCC.

"No," I replied, "But I think we are our best selves."

Listen. I know how it sounds. But the part of me that gets whiny and anxious and overwhelmed is not my best self, especially not when I'm trying to work. If putting myself in a pair of heels can bring out another part of me—the charming, focused, confident part—I can take a few blisters for the cause.

I always manage to pack in my carry-on luggage no fewer than three, but usually more like five, sparkly party dresses and several pairs of shoes (high-heeled, obviously). I don't know how I can get what is essentially a Sephora pop-up past airport security, but I start collecting sample sizes of all my beauty essentials months in advance, and my quart-sized, TSA-approved baggies seem to have some Mary Poppins magic. All my bags do, really. I bring like four outfit changes per day. *In a carry-on.* I don't usually end up wearing most of what I bring, but I couldn't *possibly* be expected to anticipate what my "best self" will feel best wearing at any given moment, so it's good to be prepared.

Over-preparing has always played a big role in my convention-going.

Before I worked in comics, I was pretty terrified by the idea of conventions. I am a *very* anxious person. I'm not great with crowds. Or germs. I get claustrophobic when I'm not in control of how I move through a space. I don't mean that I just don't like these things. No one likes these things. But for me, when the anxiety goes unchecked, it's more of a "take me to the hospital, I think I'm dying" sort of thing. It's usually under control, but it takes a lot of work. And even when I focus on keeping myself calm, every time a stranger bumps into me I die a little inside.

So, yeah, conventions seemed scary. But I also really wanted to get more involved in comics, to make some friends, to be connected. Maybe even get a job. I worked up a little nerve and attended a few cons in cosplay, to do a little incognito reconnaissance and get the lay of the land. Preparing the costumes helped to channel some of my pre-con nervous energy, and then I was able to walk the con floor as a badass comic book character, rather than as a real person who might actually start crying from the stress of having thousands of germy strangers surrounding me. And you know what? It worked. It was awesome.

Things changed a lot when I started attending cons for my job with a large digital comics retailer. I was going to moderate panels, conduct creator interviews, and appear in podcasts and videos for social media, so I couldn't exactly cosplay away my con anxieties. As if my terror of the crush of germy strangers wasn't enough of a challenge, I'm also very much an introvert. Even though I somehow do love attending them, the entire nature of cons—an intense long weekend of socializing—is spectacularly psychologically draining. And, needless to say, these are not great traits for a professional trying to do their job. You have to be around a million people, and literally no one who is trying to focus on work in the midst of a con has time to console a neurotic, exhausted bundle of anxiety. I had to figure out a way to alleviate some of these issues so I could focus in order to do my job.

When I thought about how to handle my first convention as a pro—SDCC so, you know, no pressure—I saw no reason I couldn't apply the same anxiety management principles I'd developed when I cosplayed. So, just like I did before, I poured all of my anxiety into preparation. I would essentially cosplay the best, most confident version of myself. I would cultivate an aura of being so *on* that even if I felt a little off underneath, no one would notice because surely a person who wears red lipstick and high heels all day at a con couldn't be too much of a mess, right? *Right?!*

I will never forget my ballet teacher who (jokingly, I *think*) advised us to stomp on our own toes before going onstage to perform a piece with a lot of bourrées—fast, miniscule steps accomplished by fluttering on the tips of your toes so it looks as though you're floating. I don't think I need to point out that ballerinas are not actually weightless. Bourrées hurt like hell. You certainly forget to be nervous when you're concentrating on transcending physical pain to appear beautiful and lighter than air.

Whether or not my ballet teacher meant for me to take this lesson literally, it's served me well. I simply don't have time to be nervous at a convention, and the small, persistent bite of pain from high heels is perhaps a familiar reminder that I need to transcend all the anxiety and put on my best performance. I essentially give the anxious part of myself some mental busywork to keep her out of the way so my "best self" can get the job done.

I know it seems superficial, that I just spend a ridiculous amount of energy suffering for the sake of my appearance and call it my "best self," but there's a lot more to it than that. Here's the thing about people with anxiety:

most of us know we have it, and that when it's bad, it becomes a problem for other people. On the whole, a lot of the ways people cope with their anxiety simply mitigates it being too much of a problem for other people. For us, the anxiety is often still very much there, just under the surface, the worst of it kept out of sight by unwarranted apologizing, or excessive fidgeting, or any number of quirks. What I'm saying is, if you notice someone doing something that seems a little ridiculous, like insisting on wearing high heels all day at cons, just consider that they might have a really good reason for what they're doing. We're all doing our best.

Whether it's for anxiety, vanity, or some other equally valid reason, I'm certainly not the only person who goes extra hard for their convention wardrobe. I'm not saying that I'm doing anything particularly revelatory or special. In fact, it occurred to me recently that if you only see me at conventions, you might not realize that it's all an elaborate performance of magical thinking. You might think this is just how I dress all the time. But the truth is, I could not keep up my convention level of glam on the regular. It isn't who I am, it's just a thing I have to do sometimes.

So, things have been going great with me and my high heels. It's only been a handful of years since I've been going to conventions, but I think I've accomplished a lot. I got a job. I made some friends. And even though cons are stressful, I love spending time with my con-friends. They are extraordinarily talented, creative, smart, funny, insightful, kind people. They are photographers and cosplayers and critics. They're publishers and PR mavens and editors. Artists and writers. A lot of them make comics. And then there's me. I don't really make anything. What exactly am I contributing to this space? Sometimes I look around and I'm like, why on earth do these wonderful people let me hang out with them?

I think people with anxiety tend to have thoughts like this all the time. *Oh my God, does everyone secretly hate me?* I know I think this approximately seventeen times per hour. Especially in a place with as much concentrated talent as a convention. And the social armor that is lipstick and high heels and a fabulous dress starts to morph into a more harmful purpose. Because in a somewhat destructive, completely arbitrary and not at all advisable way, I often feel that if I can't contribute talent, I ought to at least contribute to the aesthetic. I can be the décor.

This is a terrible way to think of yourself, by the way. Because it traps you in this place where *appearing* as your "best self" actually starts to preclude your ability to contribute anything meaningful to a social gathering or relationship. Rather than acting as a buffer that gives you room to relax and be yourself, it becomes a barrier and prevents you from *actually being* your "best self." It's supposed to be mental busywork, not your entire personality.

Of course I can't speak for my con-friends but, being the wonderful people they are, I suspect they would still like me even if I wasn't wearing high heels. It's only my own compulsive anxiety that insists on high heels for my performance. Not only is this staggeringly unhealthy, if I am being reasonable even I would admit that it is patently false. I wouldn't be surprised if most people didn't even notice what I'm wearing. The performance is entirely for an audience of one: me. And it's important that I not lose sight of it as exactly what it is—a performance.

I no longer go to conventions to do a million panels and interviews and social media videos for my job, but attending them still feels like a thing I need to do every few months. I mean, don't get me wrong, it's also very much a thing that I want to do. Like, for fun . . . This is supposed to be fun, right? And it is fun. But I'm starting to wonder if it would it be possible to perform as my "best self" without the flash of sequins and the bleeding toes and obsessively put-together outfit. Would the world end if I turned up in jeans and Docs?

Turns out, no. The world keeps spinning. I tried it and I actually . . . just had a really nice time with my friends. I bought some art and went to panels. I talked to people and had some drinks and *it was fun*. Wait, that's a thing? You can just . . . do that? Oh. Okay. There's probably a life lesson I could learn from that experience, if I were the sort of person who learned life lessons.

Is it possible that I have intrinsic value as a person? Am I *already* my "best self?" No, that can't be right. It's got to be the high heels.

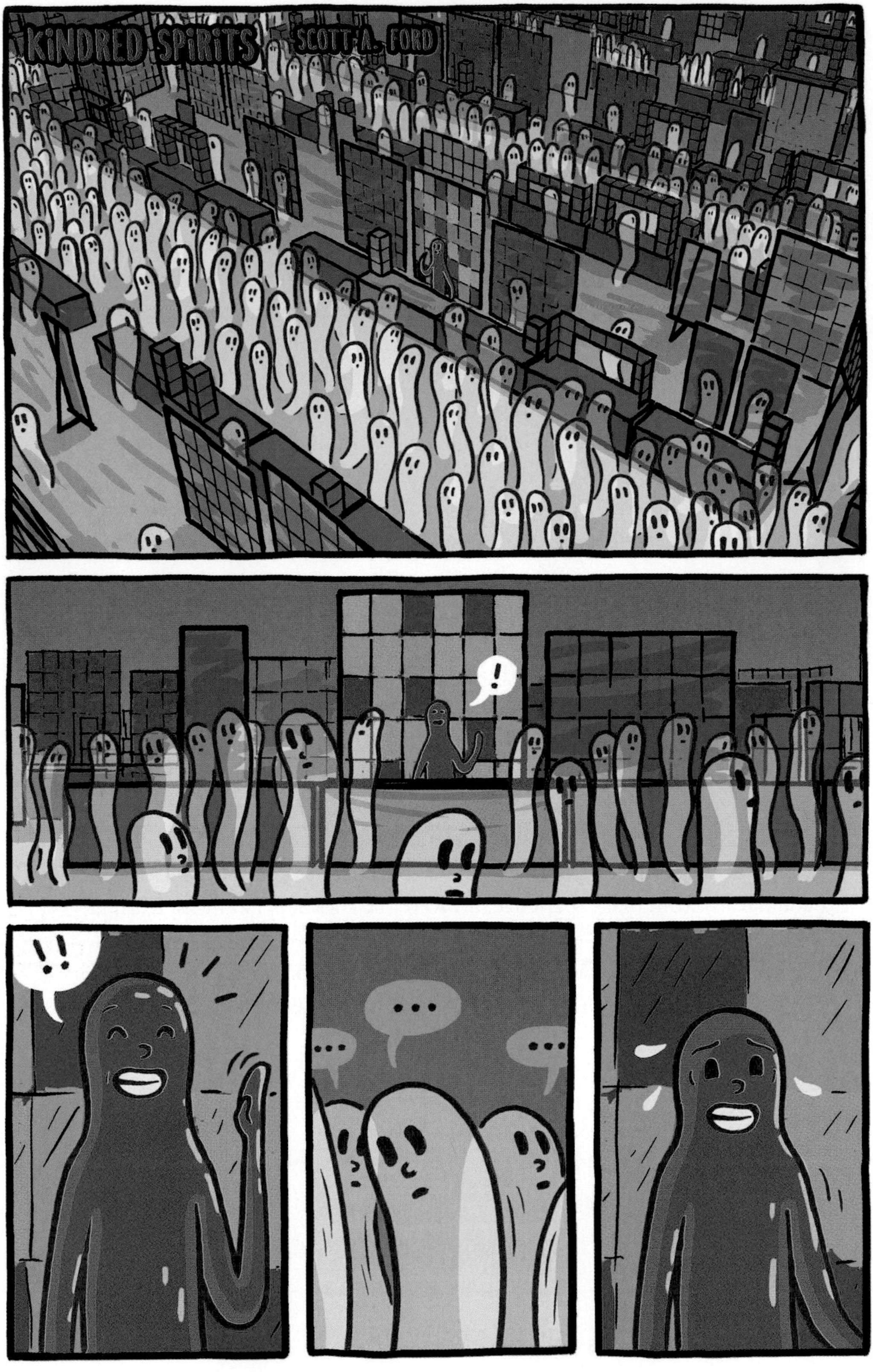
KINDRED SPIRITS
SCOTT A. FORD
!
!!
...
...
...

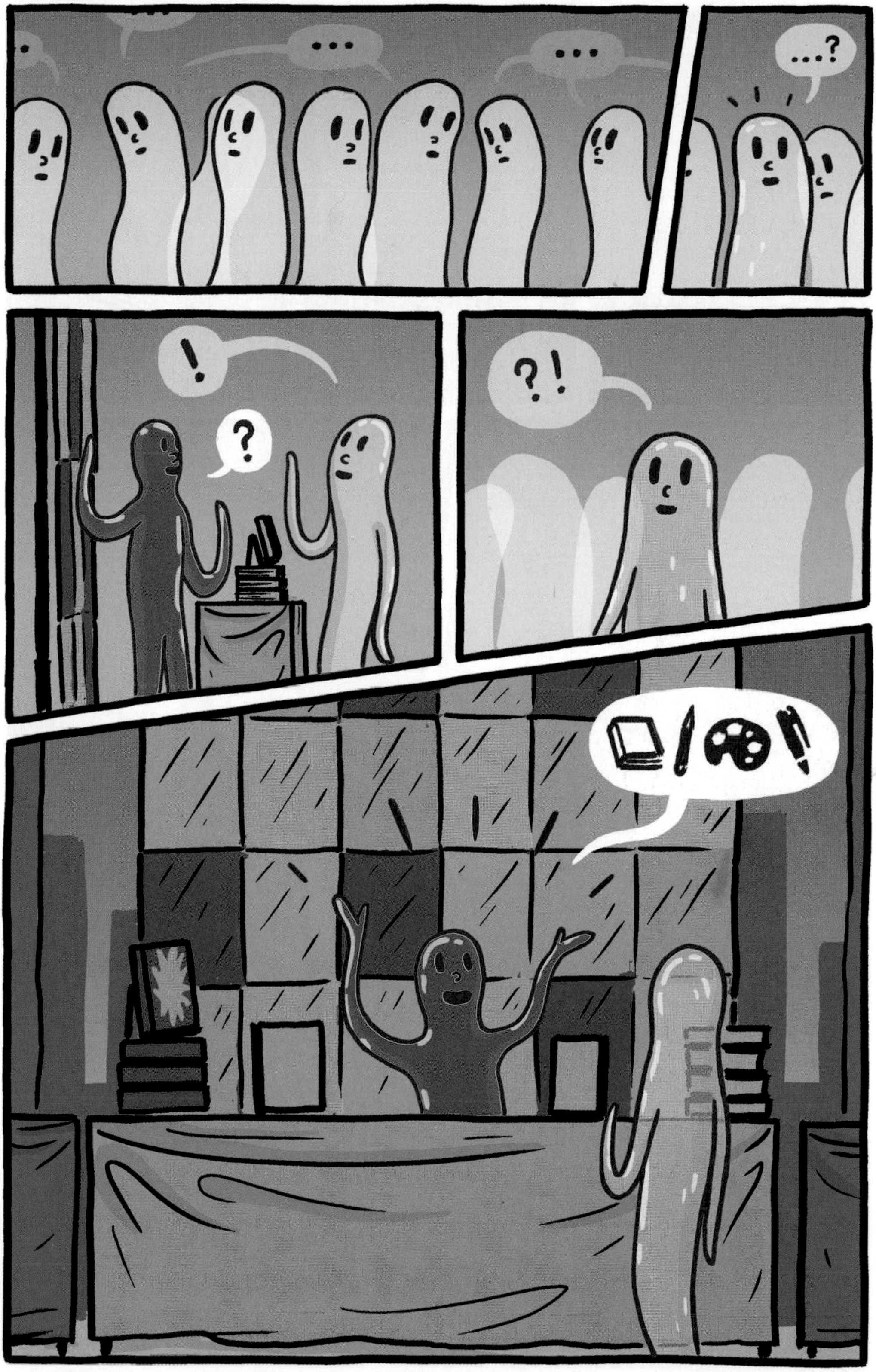
...
...
...
...?
!
?
?!

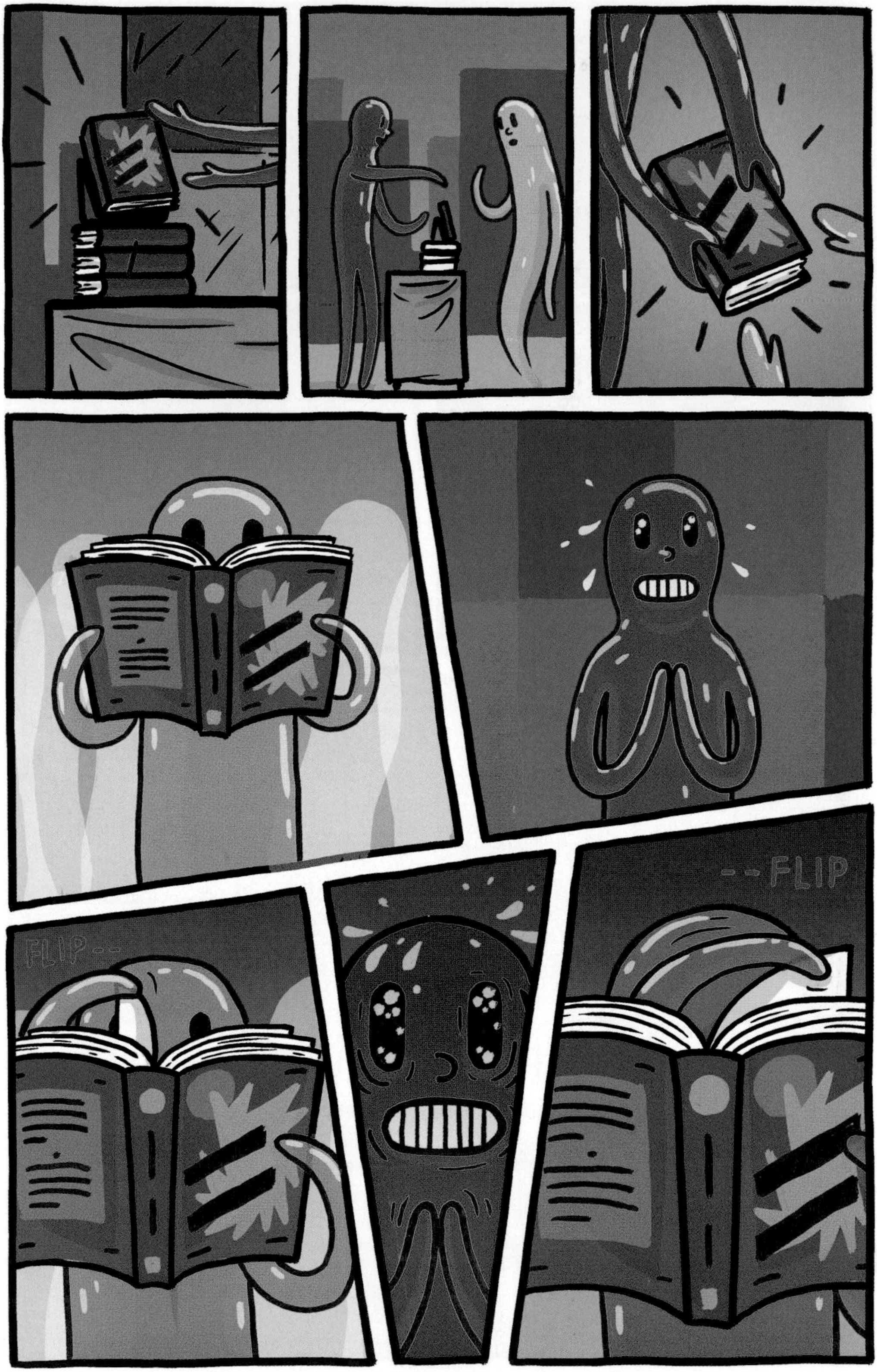
FLIP--
--FLIP

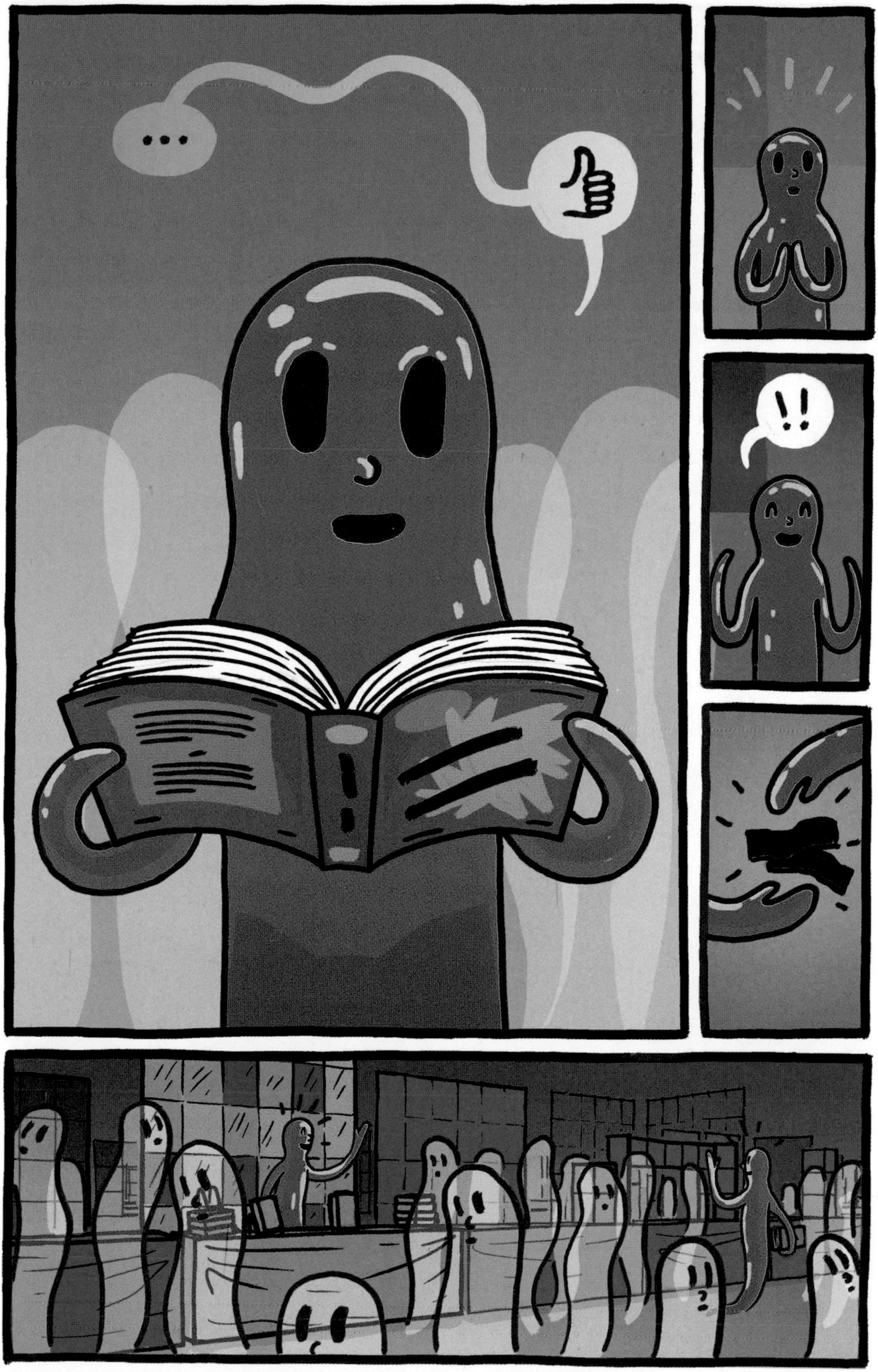
...
!!

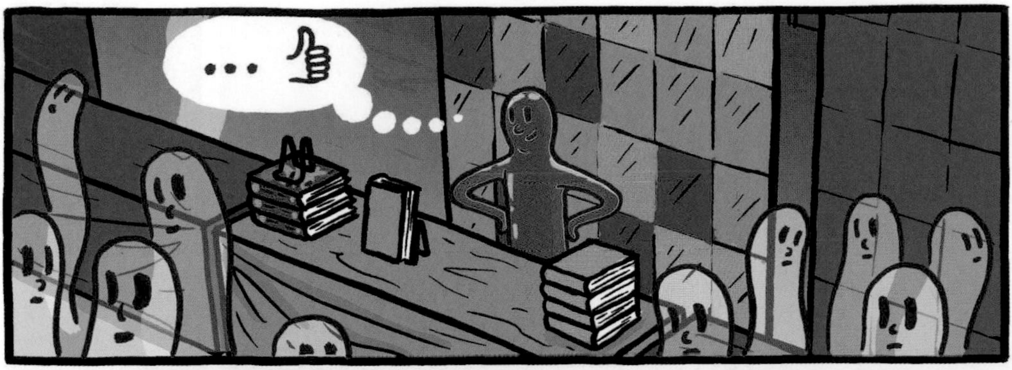

...

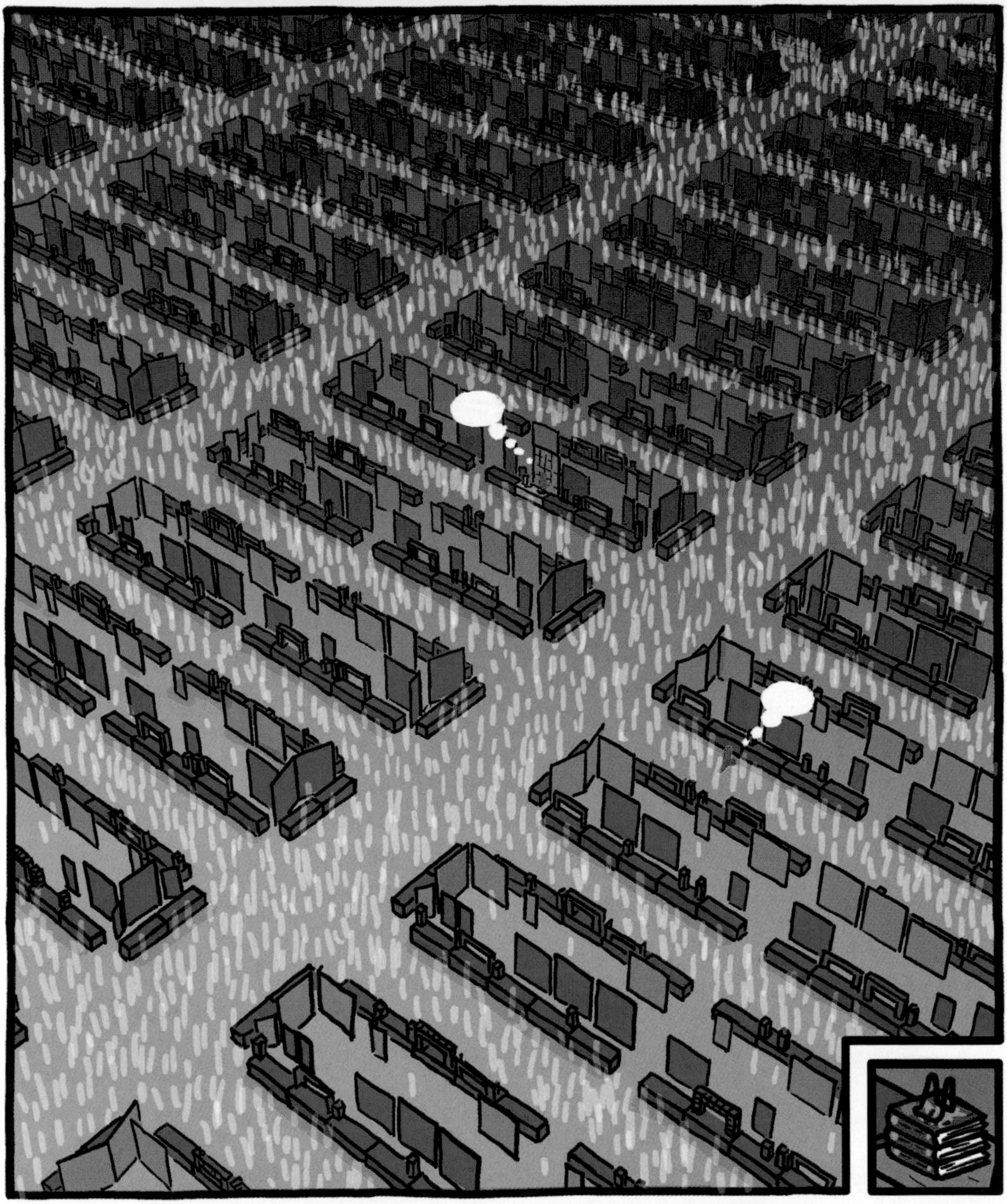

A FIRST TIME MODERATOR'S WORST NIGHTMARE

Morgan Hoffman

I worked as a host on a show called *InnerSpace,* which aired on the Space Channel across Canada. I hosted the show with two other co-hosts for five years and we covered everything from movies to television, comics, games and technology. We basically covered all things genre. When I first got hired at *InnerSpace,* I didn't have a lot of experience as a TV host. Before this, I had hosted a couple of cooking shows on a local television station and I had some acting experience, but that was about it. Becoming a host on a national television show was amazing and overwhelming all at once. I had to learn so many new skills immediately. I learned how to interview people, how to interact with my co-hosts on air, how to read the teleprompter, which I swear is harder than it looks, and how to host panels at conventions. I'm also a perfectionist. I put a lot of pressure on myself to perfect everything I do, so that first year was tough for me, but I loved my job and I was determined to be good at it.

A few months after becoming a host, I was told that *InnerSpace* was going to cover Fan Expo Canada, which is the largest genre convention in Canada and one of the largest in North America. I'd never been to a convention before, so I had no idea what to expect. My co-hosts filled me in on what a moderator does and warned me that they usually are asked to host a lot of panels at this convention. The whole thing sounded terrifying. They wanted me to interview someone live on stage in front of hundreds of people? Are you kidding me? I was still getting used to having sit-down interviews in front of a producer and a cameraman.

Moderating panels sounded like a nightmare, but I was reassured that they wouldn't feed me to the wolves and make me host one by myself. The plan was for me to share moderating duties with my co-hosts so that I could ease my way into the convention scene. It wasn't until a few weeks before Fan Expo that my executive producer called me into his office to tell me that I was going to moderate my own panel. He thought it was the best way for me to learn the ropes. I thought he was joking. When I realized he wasn't, my heart sank. I'd only been a TV host for four months and I was still overwhelmed with my daily hosting duties on the show. I didn't want anyone to think I couldn't handle my job, so I reluctantly agreed, hoping for a small panel. When my producer told me that I was going to be moderating the David Hasselhoff panel, something told me this wasn't going to be small. I tried to be happy about it, after all I grew up watching *Baywatch* and I knew my parents loved *Knight Rider* but I had an uneasy feeling.

I did a lot of research to prepare for this panel. I spent several days learning everything I could about Hasselhoff. I still had to host the show every day and I was really busy going out on shoots, so I didn't have a lot of time to research at work. I ended up doing most of it at home. I remember making dinner and then spending the rest of the night reading articles and interviews. I did this for several nights in a row, which I know sounds a little intense and unnecessary, but I wanted to make sure I was really prepared for my first panel. Plus, I wanted to be ready for The Hoff.

I couldn't sleep the night before. I just remember laying in bed picturing the worst possible scenario. What if I mess up my introduction? What if I trip and fall on the stage? What if I ask the wrong questions? I barely had any experience writing questions for interviews so I didn't feel very confident about the ones I had prepared.

It was the morning of the panel and my nerves were worse than ever, so I went to work and tried to act as normal as possible. Everyone was talking about the convention and a few people brought up my panel with David Hasselhoff, so I lied and told them I was really excited. I wasn't excited at all. I actually felt like crying. I'd worked myself up so much over this panel and I just wanted to run home and hide under the covers. Side note, while all of this was happening, my roommate of over a year was moving out of our apartment to live with her boyfriend. I don't even remember saying goodbye to her. She moved out the same weekend as the convention and I barely noticed. That's how overwhelmed I was.

When it was just a few hours before the panel, I went into the wardrobe room at work to pick out my outfit. All of a sudden I was lying on the floor, crying uncontrollably. I didn't know what to do so I called my mom. Whenever I felt overwhelmed at work or I thought I messed up an interview, I usually called her in that wardrobe room. It was the only place I could hide without anyone knowing I was upset, but this felt different. I was having a hard time breathing and I could barely get my words out. I was having a panic attack. There had been so much fear and stress leading up to this convention that I reached my breaking point. I remember telling my mom I would rather quit my job than have to go through with the panel. I didn't want to spend another second worrying about it. Thank God, my mom knows how to handle these situations. She calmly talked me through my panic attack and reminded me how prepared I was and that the skills I learned through years of theatre were going to help me more than I realized. She also pointed out how disappointed I would be with myself if I didn't end up moderating the panel. She was right. I eventually calmed down and was able to get up off the floor. I walked over to the mirror and saw the streaks of mascara down my face and how puffy my eyes were. I quickly fixed my makeup and got dressed, just in time to rush to the panel.

The Metro Toronto Convention Centre is just down the street from where I worked so I decided to walk over. I didn't feel 100% better, but the walk cleared my head. As soon as I got to the convention, my nerves started back up again. I found out that I was hosting my first panel in the biggest room at Fan Expo. I immediately wanted to walk out of there, but I knew I had to stay. I spotted my producer and cameraman near the stage, and slowly walked over to them. They were there to record my intro and to hopefully get an interview with The Hoff backstage after the panel. I told my producer how nervous I was and asked if she could go over my questions. She added a few questions of her own and told me everything look great. I can't tell you how relieved I felt. I realized I probably should have asked someone to look over my questions sooner and that asking for help was much easier than I thought. Now all I had to do was wait for the panel to start.

There was this giant hallway backstage where I was told to wait for the guest. I was also given two microphones. I was told that one was for me and the other was for The Hoff and that I was supposed to give it to him after I introduced him on stage. I kept pacing up and down the hallway as I practiced my intro. The start time for the panel had come and gone and still no David Hasselhoff. I popped my head out of the curtains to look around and immediately saw a packed house. Seeing this giant room when it was empty was one thing, but seeing it full of people was another. Someone working at the convention walked over to me to find out what was going on. It seemed like no one knew were he was so I walked back to the hallway to look for him. Then, all of a sudden I heard the audience go crazy. I ran back to the curtains and looked out at the audience and there was David Hasselhoff. He was walking through the crowd as people were cheering and clapping. I realized then that he'd come through the front doors of the room instead of backstage like everyone was expecting. So I jumped up on stage and waited for him to make his way through the room. The panel hadn't started off the way I expected, but I prepared myself to start moderating as soon as he joined me on stage.

However, Hasselhoff continued to entertain the crowd from the floor for the next twenty to thirty minutes. He walked up and down the rows of seats while telling stories about his time on set and at one point he started singing to everyone. Sure, he had a great voice but I was so confused. What was happening? Why did he come through the front door, and when should I start asking him questions? So here I was, standing by myself in the middle of this big stage in front of hundreds of people looking like the most awkward person ever. I didn't know what to do. The longer I stood on that stage the more embarrassed I started to feel. A few people looked up at me from the audience but mostly everyone was glued to The Hoff and for good reason. This guy was hilarious. You just didn't know what he was going to say next. If I was sitting in that audience, I would have thought this was the best panel ever.

After what felt like forever, he started making his way to the stage. I thought this is it. I'm going to hand him the microphone and we're going to take our seats on stage and I'm going to ask him the questions I prepared. Wrong. He walked on to the stage, looked over at me and asked, "who are you?" My face went beet-red. I could hear someone giggling in the audience. I wanted to crawl in a hole and die. I told him that I was his moderator. I remember he looked confused but immediately turned back to the audience and continued talking. I'd never been so embarrassed in my life. I made eye contact with one of my friends sitting in the audience and she just looked mortified for me. I knew my producer and cameraman were sitting nearby, but I couldn't look at them. I didn't know if I should start laughing or crying.

Hasselhoff started walking up and down the stage with the same energy he displayed while entertaining everyone on the floor and I was still standing in the middle of the stage, holding my microphone and feeling like the biggest dork ever. At some point Hasselhoff did get a microphone but I don't even remember giving it to him. It was obvious to everyone, including me, that he didn't need a moderator so I started slowly walking backwards towards the curtains until I could slide behind them. I'm pretty sure everyone saw that graceful exit, but I was just relieved to be off that stage. Now that I was backstage, all I wanted to do was run away but I knew I couldn't go anywhere because my producer and cameraman were meeting there for that interview. I sat down on a chair and waited for the panel to be over.

I couldn't believe what had just happened. The panel I'd done so much research for, the one I had sleepless nights over, the one I had shed tears over, just blew up in my face. When the audience started clapping again, I knew the panel was over. The curtains literally blew open and out came David Hasselhoff with the biggest smile. I knew I had to catch him before he left so I gathered my nerve and walked right up to him and asked for an interview. To my surprise, he said yes. I'd been warned ahead of time that a lot of guests don't like doing interviews backstage after a panel and I was relieved when he agreed. Then, everything happened so quickly. My cameraman gave me the mic and I started asking all the questions that I didn't get a chance to ask during the panel. He still had so much energy as he talked about his love for the fans, and I couldn't get over how animated he was. The interview lasted about five minutes and then it was over. I thanked Mr. Hasselhoff and watched him and his team walk down that giant hallway. After everyone left, I looked over at my producer, and we both started laughing. The whole thing felt so surreal. I'd never been through such a rollercoaster of emotions before and I was just happy it was over.

Looking back on all of this, I recognize that my emotions were unusually heightened. I was still a new host and I'd never moderated a panel before. Had all of this happened a year later, I would have just jumped off the stage and enjoyed the show with the rest of the audience. I recently found some clips of this panel online. I was reluctant to watch them because I didn't know how embarrassing they were going to be, but I watched them with my boyfriend and we couldn't stop laughing. The clips clearly show me standing on the stage looking super awkward while The Hoff is having the time of his life entertaining everyone by himself.

It's nice to be able to laugh at all of this now, but the whole experience slightly traumatized me for a couple of years. I didn't enjoy going to conventions for the longest time but after gaining more experience and confidence as a moderator, I started loving them. I've been lucky enough to moderate some great panels over the years like the big *Harry Potter* reunion panel a few years ago at Fan Expo, which was Ron Weasley a.k.a. Rupert Grint's first convention ever which made it extra special. Other panels that stand out include the cast of *Stranger Things, Orphan Black, The Expanse*, Matt Smith, Hayley Atwell, Stephen Amell, Ian Somerhalder, Ming-Na Wen and Margaret Atwood.

I learned a very valuable lesson after that panel. I learned that not all guests want moderators, even if you've been assigned to their panels. For example, William Shatner and Mark Hamill do not need moderators. They perform these entertaining one-man type shows with great stories and insight about their time spent on iconic sets. I've introduced them both on stage before, but they definitely don't need moderators and neither did The Hoff. After that first convention, I learned to always ask guests before every panel if the wanted a moderator. I didn't want to have any repeats of that first panel and you know what, I never did. I can tell you now that I never had another panel quite like the one I moderated, or rather didn't moderate, for David Hasselhoff. That one was definitely unique and although I didn't have the best time, I do have a lot of fun telling this story now to my friends and family over a few glasses of wine.

ON REFLECTION

BY DYLAN EDWARDS • STUDIONDR.COM © Dylan NDR

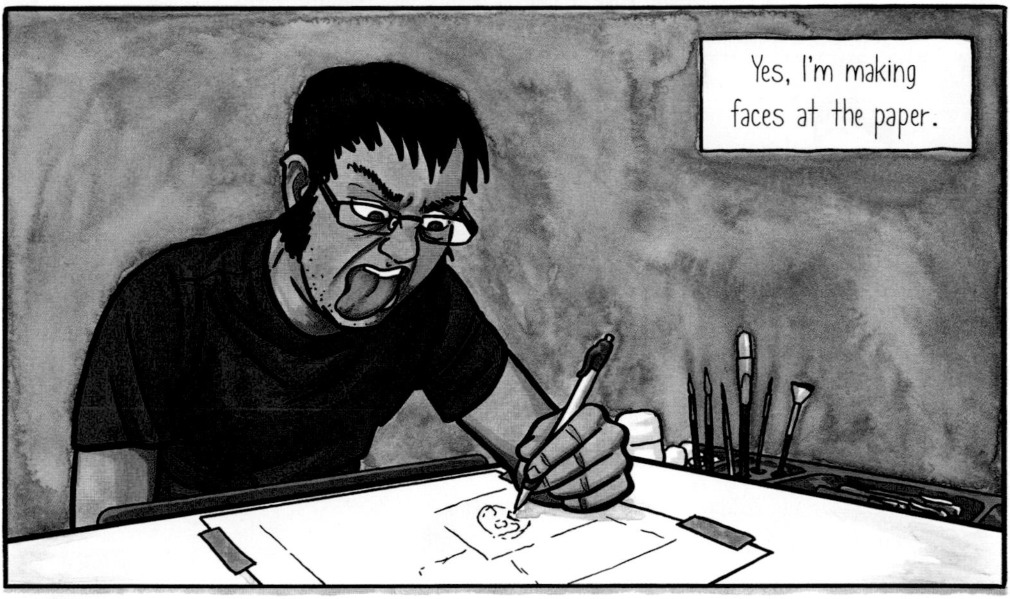

Yes, I'm making faces at the paper.

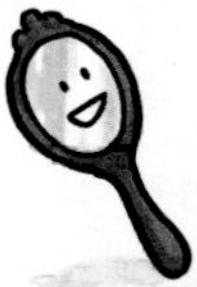

Humans subconsciously mimic each others' facial expressions. This behavior, known as mirroring, plays an important role in our ability to empathize with one another.

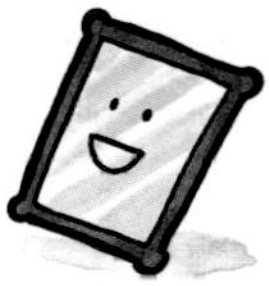

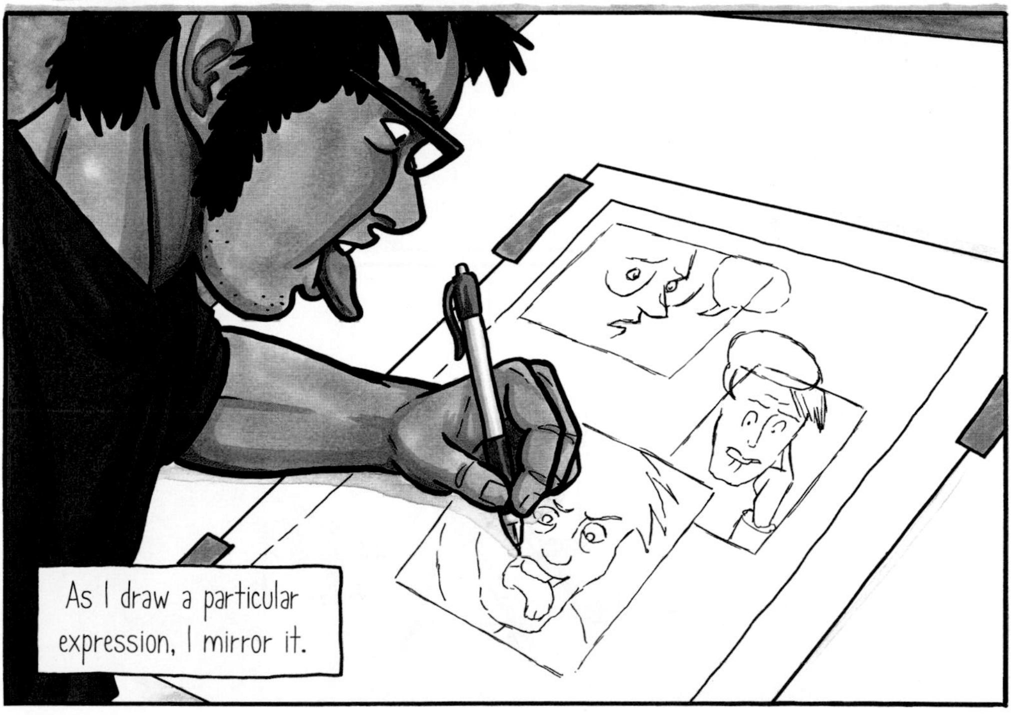

As I draw a particular expression, I mirror it.

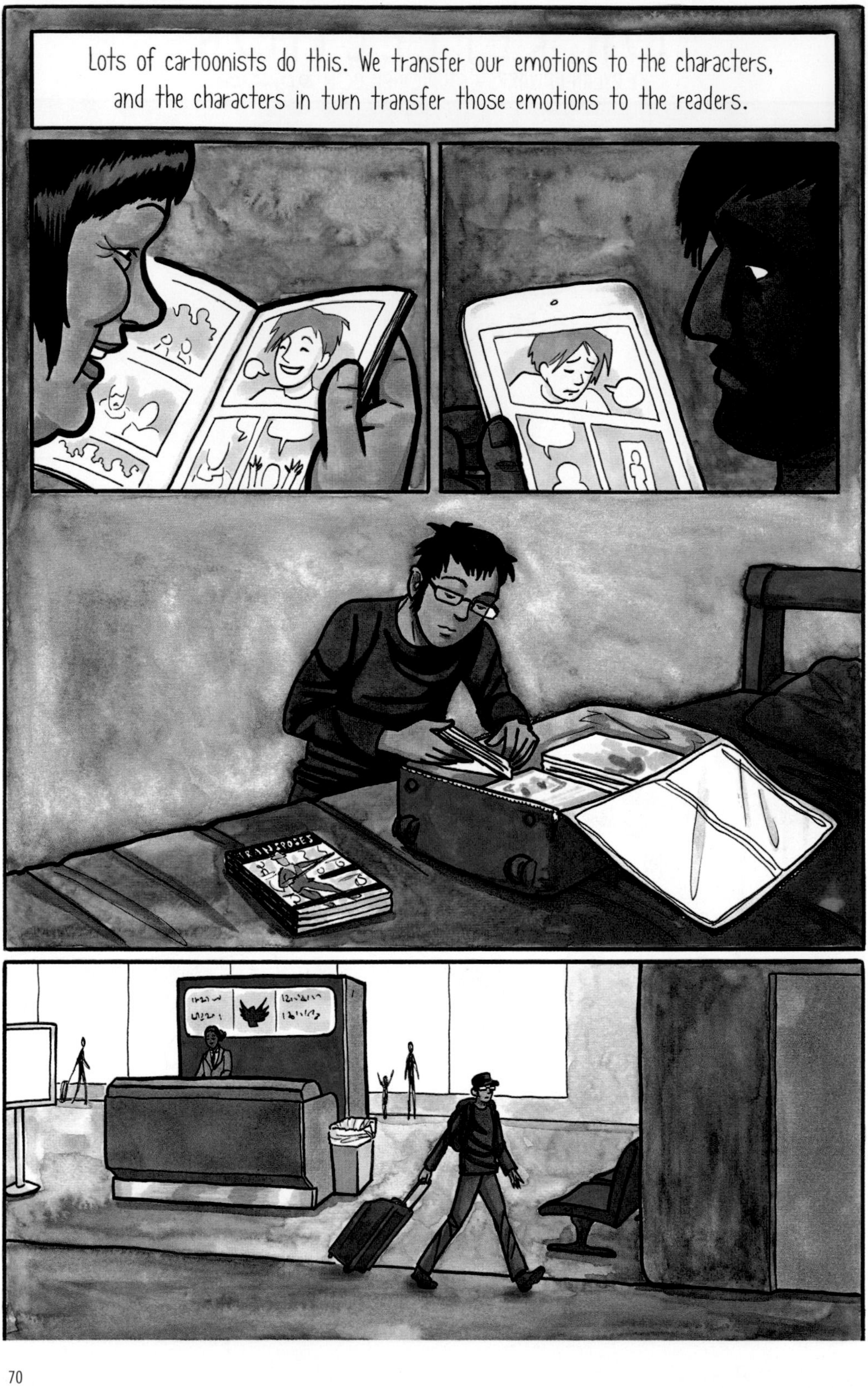
Lots of cartoonists do this. We transfer our emotions to the characters, and the characters in turn transfer those emotions to the readers.

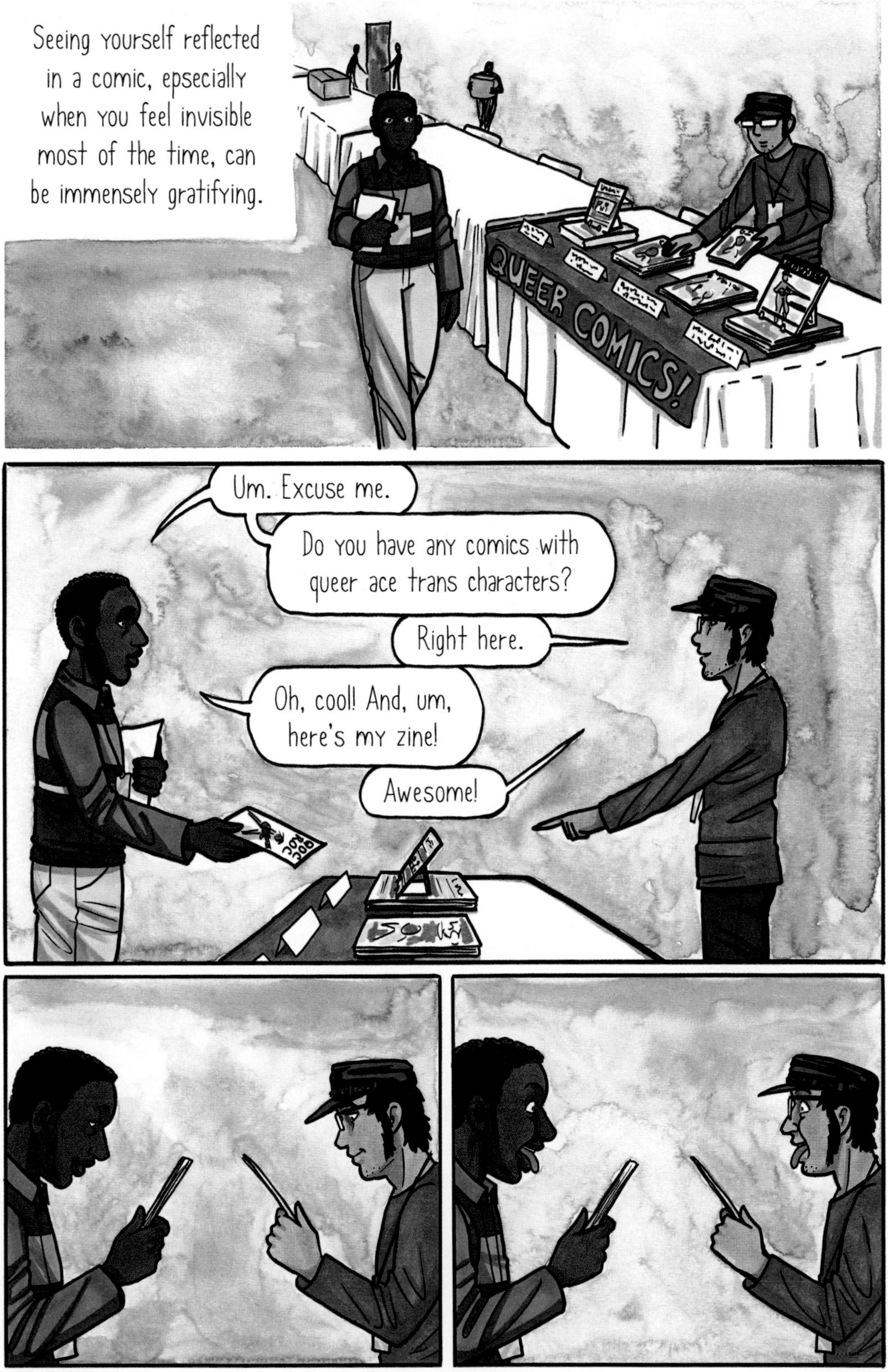

Seeing yourself reflected in a comic, epsecially when you feel invisible most of the time, can be immensely gratifying.
QUEER COMICS!
Um. Excuse me.
Do you have any comics with queer ace trans characters?
Right here.
Oh, cool! And, um, here's my zine!
Awesome!

CONS CONNED ME (BUT I GOT TO KEEP MY WALLET)

Marlene Bonnelly

There are a hundred-odd eager faces turned up to stare at me when my turn comes. I slide the microphone in from the left, lean forward, blink. My stomach churns—not because of the stale pretzel I'd had in the food court, but because of nerves— and I feel like I can't get *quite* enough air in my lungs when I inhale, but the words still come.

"I'm Marlene."

I'm relieved when the sound of my own voice is tolerable and I'm equally surprised that my heart beats at an even pace, though the sound feels exaggerated in my chest. Somehow, I can actually look at the faces in the crowd and maintain eye contact for half a second at a time. "I make videos, write about comics and play dress up," I say. The temptation to fiddle with the paper placard in front of me is overwhelming.

Still, I think I'm *supposed* to be on this stage. I think I'm *supposed* to be in this blissfully air-conditioned room, sheltered from the San Diego sun, on this panel, at an event I'd dreamed of experiencing since shortly before I hit puberty.

And then there's that tiny, tinny voice in the back of my head, cutting through my confidence, sharp and swift: what am I *doing* here?

A lot of it is luck, honestly; that's how these things generally go. Outside of calling in a favor with Lady Fortune, though, there's an element of effort—and hey! I'm proud of the work I did. I put real elbow grease into editing my videos, keeping up a presence on social media and building out a spread of articles and reviews. Still, there's a little more to marketing yourself for the convention scene, or at least I like to think so. Generally speaking, you have better chances if you're personable, sociable, confident, able to network in a way that means you'd be great on a stage with your peers. Think, oh, Superman: chest out, self-assured, capable. I was more on the *Clark Kent* side of things: hesitant, awkward, the kind of person who went for a handshake when someone tried to fist bump, and then we both tried to switch but it was too late so our hands would kind of collide and . . . unlike Clark, I wasn't putting on a show; that was actually who I was. (I was also browner. And in a training bra.) Being (a browner, training-bra-clad) Clark isn't a bad thing at all, mind you. It's just not what I wanted. I wanted to fit in.

See, and bear with me here, I've never watched nor read Shōnen Jump's *Prince of Tennis*. Seriously, I couldn't tell you the name of even one character; my knowledge of the series is limited to an understanding that it takes place in a school and that it involves tennis. Despite this, I dressed as a *Prince of Tennis* character for my first convention more than a decade ago, borrowing a cheap costume from a friend-of-a-friend in my desperation to fit in with what I (rightly) assumed was destined to be a colorful menagerie of cosplay. Other attendees gushed about the anime and asked questions about my favorite scenes, while I enthusiastically bobbed my head and pretended I knew more than the exactly zero percent I actually did.

It was weird. It was *fun*, but it was weird. I went in feeling like the odd man out, like I wasn't into fandom enough to deserve a ticket through the doors. Hungry for the authentic convention experience, I dutifully waited in endless lines and watched creators I idolized dish out business and life advice alike, all of which I drank in. Still, I was walking around in an itchy polyester lie. Worst of all, I was doing it alone. Embarrassed and buckling under the weight of social anxiety, I barely summoned the courage to ask other attendees for a handful of photos, let alone sustain a reasonable conversation or make new friends.

I remember with painful clarity the moment I realized just how socially inept I really was. You know that one pesky gnat of a memory so wholly embarrassing that you successfully manage to keep it buried in your subconscious 364 out of 365 days a year? The one that inevitably rears its ugly head just to remind you of how poorly you can make life decisions?

When I'm staring up at the ceiling at night, fighting back the goblins that keep my eyelids peeled back, this is the memory that unfurls:

He was looking at keychains. I was reading the sign on his back from a distance. The booth attendant had just finished chatting with him when I approached, sneakers thudding on the carpet as I gained momentum. He spread his fingers across the table, delicately fussing with a charm, and I launched myself with a battle cry that still makes my soul shudder in hindsight. The keychains rattled furiously as my chest met his 100% unprepared spine.

Now, for the young'uns, "glomp" might be a foreign term. Lucky you. For those of us raised in the age of dial-up Internet, however, it was right up there with "random" and "penguin" in the common vernacular. To "glomp" someone means to hug someone, *with force*. To an excitable little Marlene, a *Kingdom Hearts* Axel cosplayer with a crude "Glomp Me" sign stuck to his back was essentially an open invitation for friendship. And disaster, as it turned out.

It would've been better if Axel had actually jerked away and yelled. Instead, he sort of slowly straightened his spine and answered with an expression so icy that I felt my stomach drop into my shoes, and I abruptly found the stretch of floor between them to be the most fascinating thing at the venue. A prankster had placed that sign on his back, he said. No one "glomped" strangers in real life, he said. At least, not without asking first.

Noted.

Everyone experiences a learning curve with what might be obvious social dynamics; I just happened to experience mine at conventions. I didn't really *do* social calls outside of school and family functions, mostly because I felt too awkward to try, which fed into a vicious cycle. High school and college were conquered by the two saving graces of polite laughter and sturdy walls to imitate flowers against. Conventions . . . helped, though. At cons, I was a nobody in the masses and, generally, easily forgettable. Aside from the Axel incident, a situation I'm still not sure how I escaped from without a security escort, my faux-pas were small and momentarily painful but quickly dismissed despite serving as great teaching moments. It was freeing to be no one.

Shake hands firmly, conventions taught me. Ask before touching, even for hugs. When hugs are out of the question there are alternatives, like air high fives and waves. Look artists, writers and fellow fans in the eye when I talk to them. When I do talk to them, I should talk to them like they're people instead of the idealized characters or idols in my head. Open with "How are you?" and "How's your day been?" instead of "How do I get a job at Marvel?" or "Can you sketch in my book?" Know that the way I express enthusiasm may not be easily digestible by others— so match energy levels with theirs and tone it down if appropriate. Mind my volume, even in busy spaces like a convention, because being the loudest person in the room does not prove I'm the biggest fan.

On that note, I quickly learned that I didn't have to *be* the biggest fan. At my first convention, I dressed up because I thought I had to. Real fans went in costume, surely. Real fans knew their favorite character's first appearance in a comic and could name every writer or artist who had ever put them on a published page. Conventions were spaces for those real fans and only for those real fans; attendees would know if you weren't one of them and you risked being set upon by the judging gazes of a thousand disgruntled nerds. But . . . that's not really the case, is it?

There is no such thing as a "real fan." Sure, we can find different levels of passion just like in every hobby, but I came to realize that anyone at any of those levels is still a fan and deserves to set foot on a convention floor. That variety is actually what makes conventions so enjoyable! If I'm a fan of *Overwatch*, for example, I can queue up for an *Overwatch* panel and find myself between someone who's never played the game but might be interested in the characters because of fanart they'd seen and a Twitch affiliate who plays the game professionally each and every day. The latter has an opportunity to share something they love, while the former has the opportunity to learn something new. By the end of their chat, a new *Overwatch* player may have emerged and know just who to main.

I'll say it again to make sure this concept hits home: *there is no such thing as a "real fan."* When I started on the convention circuit, I was sure there was an invisible barrier to entry that could only be unlocked with enough "cred." Maybe I had to own a minimum number of single comic issues before the community respected me or I had to be able to answer trivia on the fly. Maybe, if someone approached while I was dressed as a character from *Prince of Tennis*, I had to be able to engage in a complex conversation about the series. Shoot, *and* I'm a girl. Did that mean I had to try extra hard to prove I belonged? Maybe some of the other attendees thought I only pretended to like comics or anime or video games for attention? Maybe I had to prove otherwise?

The answer is: I didn't. If I liked that itchy costume just because it looked interesting, then I had every right to wear it. I didn't—*don't* have to answer questions from anyone. I don't have to own a vast collection. I don't have to prove anything. Neither do you.

Let me be clear in pointing out that there might be convention attendees who have yet to learn this lesson. And that's fine! I was fortunate enough to learn it after a few rodeos, but maybe some still believe in the invisible barrier even after their second, third or one hundredth time around. They may never understand otherwise and may try to reinforce the idea of that barrier, but experience has taught me that I'm perfectly all right with going my own way. Conventions are unique personal experiences, and how I enjoy them is up to me to determine.

So, conventions offered me a few tutorials that YouTube couldn't: how to make small talk and how to find my place in a community. Not too shabby. What I was missing, though, was confidence. A friend recently described me as "an introvert who fakes being an extrovert" and that sounds about right. I could go through the motions of engaging with strangers politely, making new friends and networking but I continued to find those motions challenging and, more importantly, I didn't believe that I could reach any sort of professional capacity in the industry despite those motions and the obvious element of hard work. Even after I interned at Marvel and had my byline on the company website, I couldn't shake a nasty case of imposter syndrome. Fans new and old would come to me for advice and I wouldn't think myself capable of giving it. Creators would e-mail me books for review and I wouldn't think my opinion worthy of disclosing. I was a fan, and I deserved to be on the convention floor with everyone else, but any day now someone would call me out on trying to pass as something more.

Conventions conned me out of that mindset. I reached a point where faking it until I made it no longer *felt* like faking it, and sheer repetitive practice (plus encouragement from some very lovely professionals and fans) convinced me that I just *could*. When I started, I channeled the characters I dressed as just to summon enough courage to follow through with the basics I'd learned. If I was head-to-toe America Chavez, then surely I could channel some of *her* confidence, right? WWACD turned out to be an excellent motto; it lent me the strength to market myself as capable in the professional sphere. After a while, I didn't need the costume anymore.

Another while after that, I didn't even need to ask myself WWACD. I could stand on a stage on my own two feet, and even went as far as moderating panels—as Marlene, not America—instead of just talking on them alongside my peers.

The tiny, tinny voice is still there. I don't know if it ever goes away entirely. A touch of self-doubt is healthy, though, because it pushes me to be the best version of myself I can be and do fun things like rewrite the story you're reading about half a dozen times until it earns a *chef's kiss*. The difference now, compared to when I first began my convention journey, is that I can answer the voice. When I sit in front of a panel room and glance at all those faces, get a DM from a fan asking for advice, read an e-mail from a creator requesting a review of their work or skim the comments under my latest videos, the voice will ask me "What am I *doing* here?" And I'll put down the paper placard or stretch my typing fingers and feel comfortable answering, "Exactly what I want."

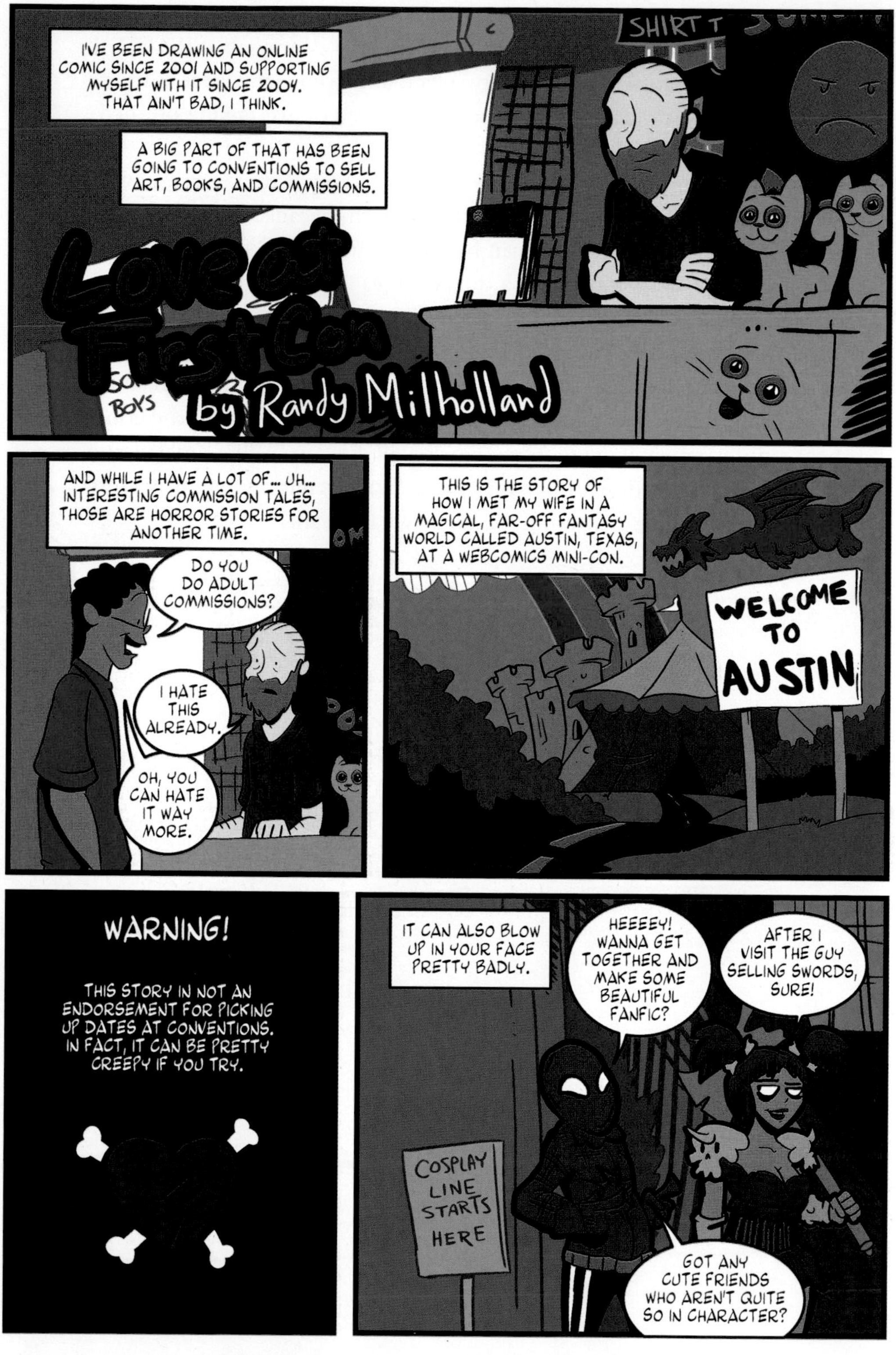
I'VE BEEN DRAWING AN ONLINE COMIC SINCE 2001 AND SUPPORTING MYSELF WITH IT SINCE 2004. THAT AIN'T BAD, I THINK.
A BIG PART OF THAT HAS BEEN GOING TO CONVENTIONS TO SELL ART, BOOKS, AND COMMISSIONS.
SHIRT
Love at First Con
by Randy Milholland
BOYS
AND WHILE I HAVE A LOT OF... UH... INTERESTING COMMISSION TALES, THOSE ARE HORROR STORIES FOR ANOTHER TIME.
DO YOU DO ADULT COMMISSIONS?
I HATE THIS ALREADY.
OH, YOU CAN HATE IT WAY MORE.
THIS IS THE STORY OF HOW I MET MY WIFE IN A MAGICAL, FAR-OFF FANTASY WORLD CALLED AUSTIN, TEXAS, AT A WEBCOMICS MINI-CON.
WELCOME TO AUSTIN
WARNING!
THIS STORY IN NOT AN ENDORSEMENT FOR PICKING UP DATES AT CONVENTIONS. IN FACT, IT CAN BE PRETTY CREEPY IF YOU TRY.
IT CAN ALSO BLOW UP IN YOUR FACE PRETTY BADLY.
HEEEEY! WANNA GET TOGETHER AND MAKE SOME BEAUTIFUL FANFIC?
AFTER I VISIT THE GUY SELLING SWORDS, SURE!
COSPLAY LINE STARTS HERE
GOT ANY CUTE FRIENDS WHO AREN'T QUITE SO IN CHARACTER?

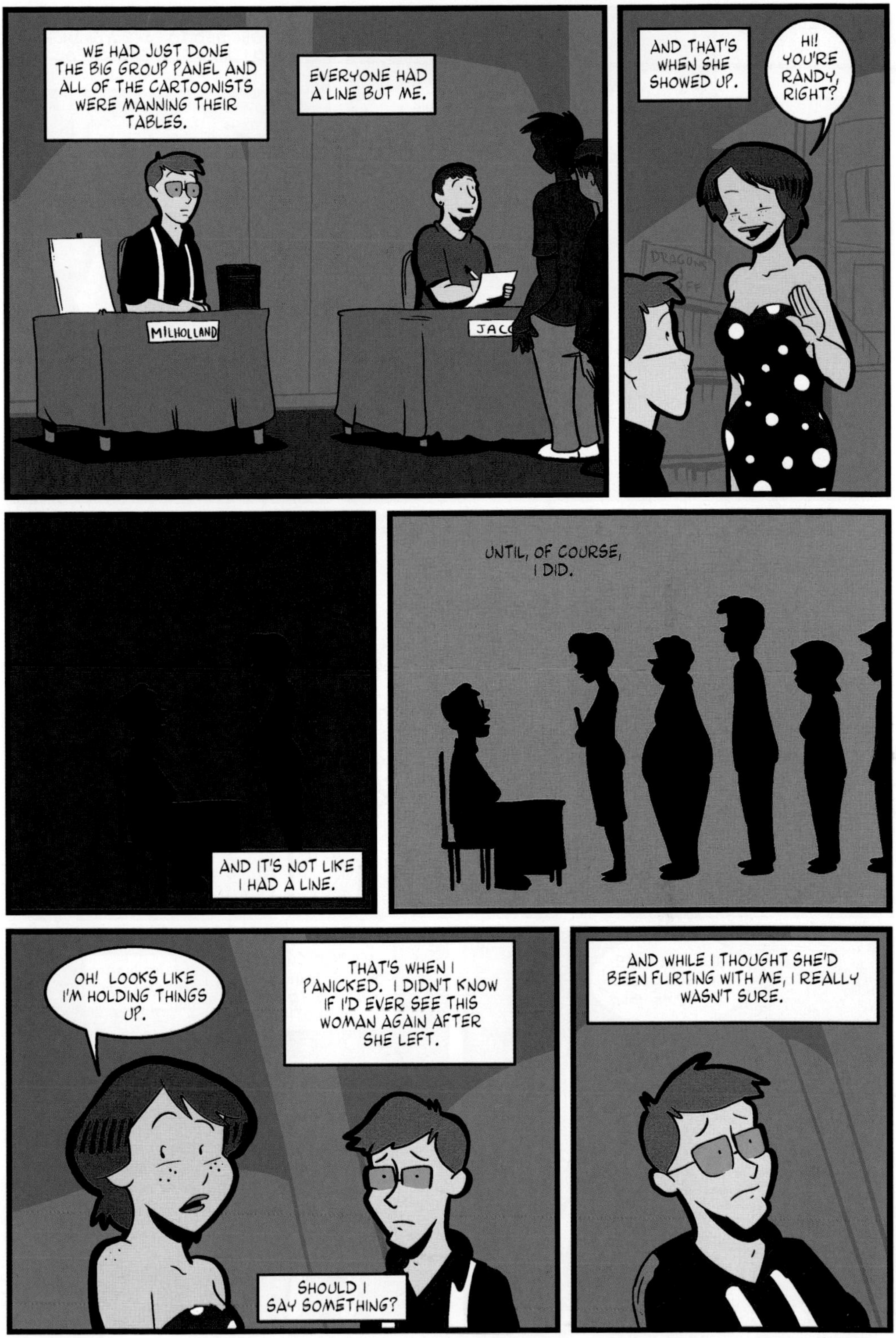
WE HAD JUST DONE THE BIG GROUP PANEL AND ALL OF THE CARTOONISTS WERE MANNING THEIR TABLES.
EVERYONE HAD A LINE BUT ME.
MILHOLLAND
JAC
AND THAT'S WHEN SHE SHOWED UP.
HI! YOU'RE RANDY, RIGHT?
AND IT'S NOT LIKE I HAD A LINE.
UNTIL, OF COURSE, I DID.
OH! LOOKS LIKE I'M HOLDING THINGS UP.
THAT'S WHEN I PANICKED. I DIDN'T KNOW IF I'D EVER SEE THIS WOMAN AGAIN AFTER SHE LEFT.
SHOULD I SAY SOMETHING?
AND WHILE I THOUGHT SHE'D BEEN FLIRTING WITH ME, I REALLY WASN'T SURE.

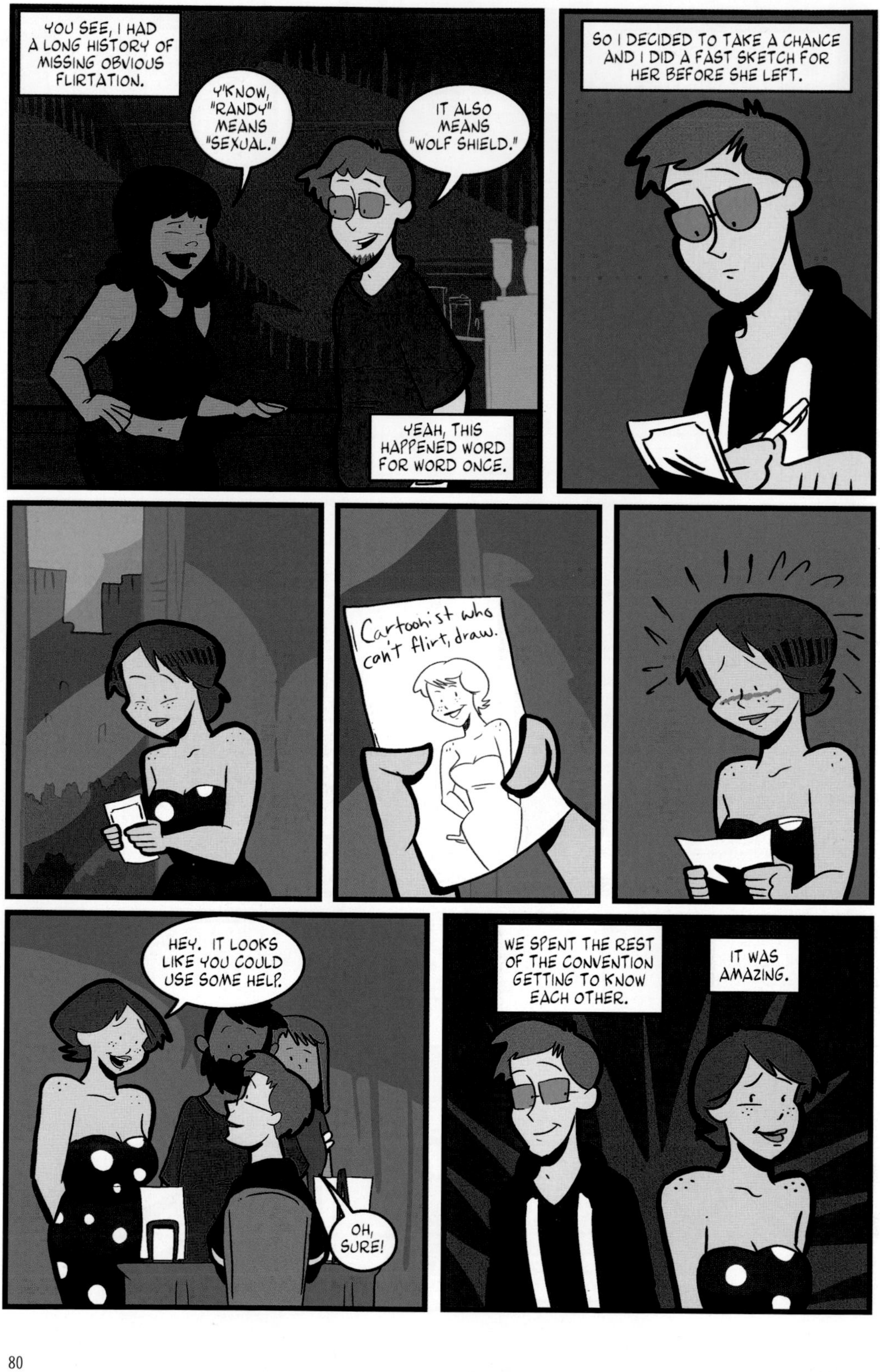
YOU SEE, I HAD A LONG HISTORY OF MISSING OBVIOUS FLIRTATION.
Y'KNOW, "RANDY" MEANS "SEXUAL."
IT ALSO MEANS "WOLF SHIELD."
YEAH, THIS HAPPENED WORD FOR WORD ONCE.
SO I DECIDED TO TAKE A CHANCE AND I DID A FAST SKETCH FOR HER BEFORE SHE LEFT.
Cartoonist who can't flirt, draw.
HEY. IT LOOKS LIKE YOU COULD USE SOME HELP.
OH, SURE!
WE SPENT THE REST OF THE CONVENTION GETTING TO KNOW EACH OTHER.
IT WAS AMAZING.

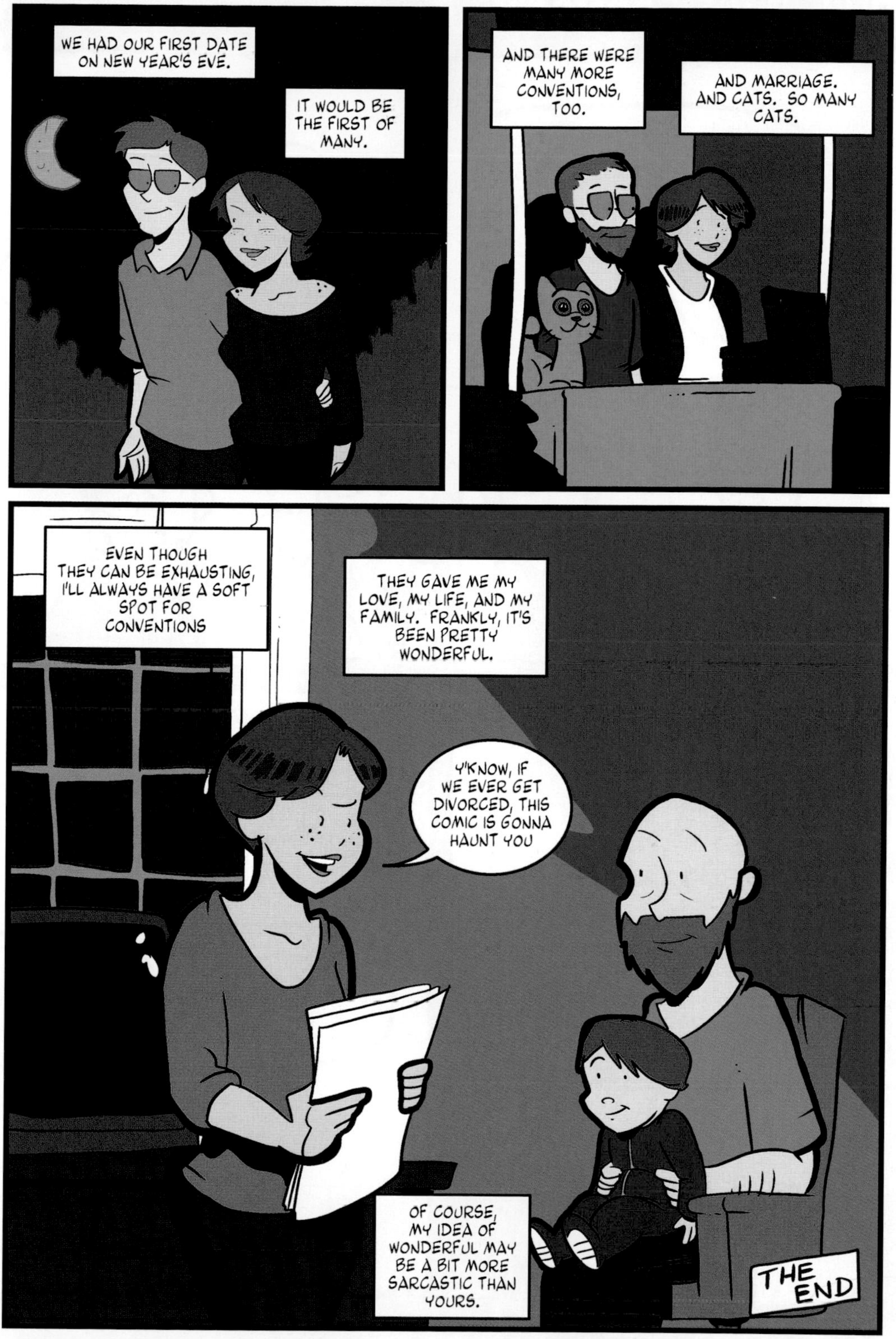
WE HAD OUR FIRST DATE ON NEW YEAR'S EVE.
IT WOULD BE THE FIRST OF MANY.
AND THERE WERE MANY MORE CONVENTIONS, TOO.
AND MARRIAGE. AND CATS. SO MANY CATS.
EVEN THOUGH THEY CAN BE EXHAUSTING, I'LL ALWAYS HAVE A SOFT SPOT FOR CONVENTIONS
THEY GAVE ME MY LOVE, MY LIFE, AND MY FAMILY. FRANKLY, IT'S BEEN PRETTY WONDERFUL.
Y'KNOW, IF WE EVER GET DIVORCED, THIS COMIC IS GONNA HAUNT YOU
OF COURSE, MY IDEA OF WONDERFUL MAY BE A BIT MORE SARCASTIC THAN YOURS.
THE END

OUR OWN ECONOMY

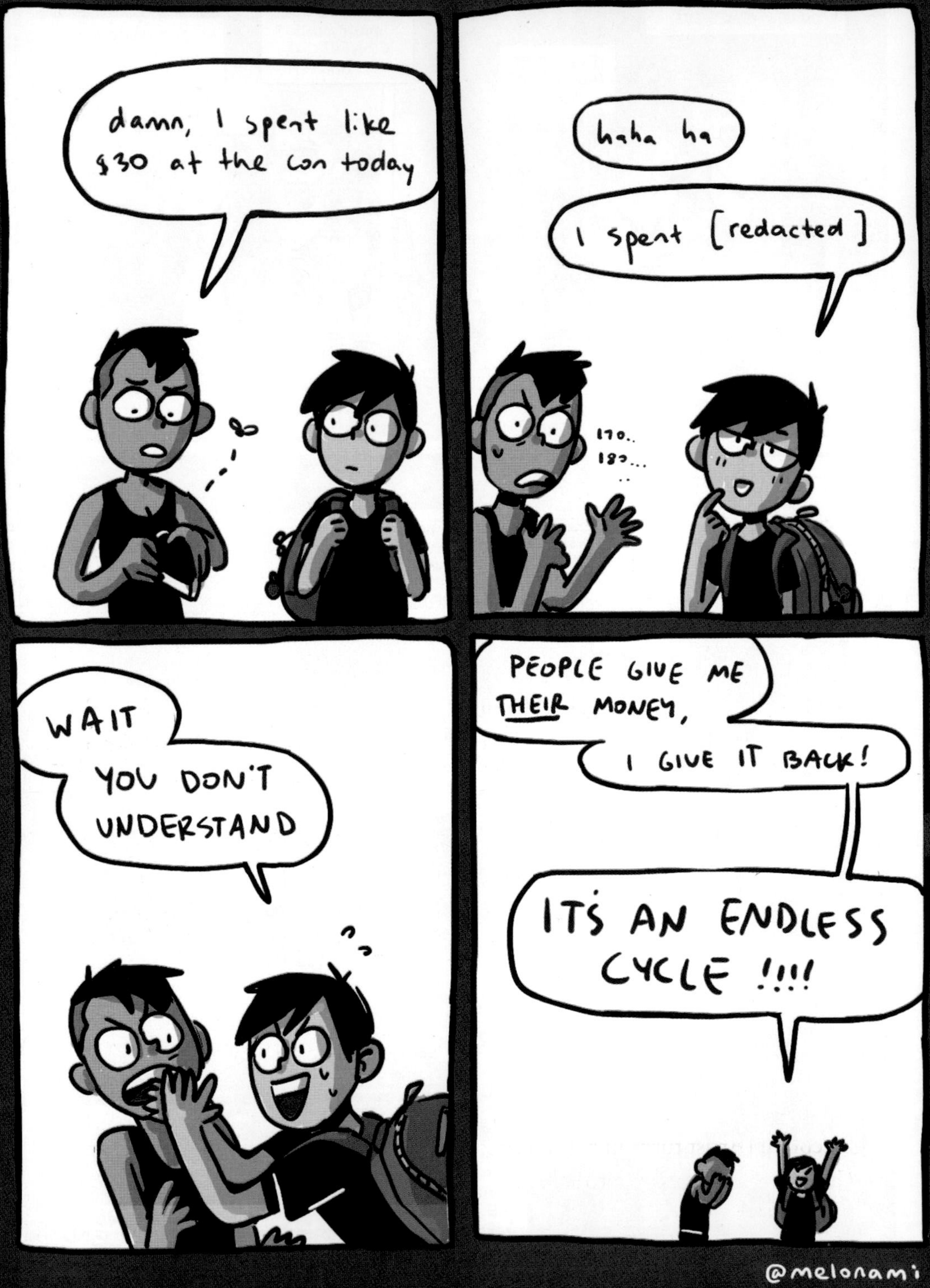

damn, I spent like $30 at the con today
haha ha
I spent [redacted]
170..
180...
WAIT
YOU DON'T UNDERSTAND
PEOPLE GIVE ME THEIR MONEY,
I GIVE IT BACK!
IT'S AN ENDLESS CYCLE !!!!
@melonami

A LONELY PLACE OF TRYING

Erik Radvon

Table cloth. Banner stand. Cash box. Pens. Hand sanitizer. Don't forget the hand sanitizer.

Is my phone charged? Will the convention center have WiFi? On the offhand chance someone wants to buy my books, will they be able to, or will I watch them walk away, muttering pleasantries about ATMs and coming back later.

"Writer" is a loaded term. It means a lot of different things to a lot of different people. It's changing rapidly. With Twitter and Facebook, everyone qualifies. "I'm a writer too, I have a book I'm working on," they say, casually flipping through a comic you spent the last year pulling together. Early mornings. Late nights. Time. Money. Anxiety. Fear. Doubt. Euphoria. Emptiness. "What makes you so special?" all over their face. "Is this free?" they ask, this time out loud, before shuffling away to look at Venom prints.

First convention, filled with eagerness and misplaced enthusiasm. "Look out world, I am HERE!" A self-stapled ashcan of bad prose and script fragments, pushed upon familiar names with unfamiliar faces. "There's nothing I can do for you," one finally says back, breaking the spell of naivety. Long hours walking row upon row. Cosplayers. Back issues. Wafting odors. By day's end, it's clear—nobody cares about you. Get to work.

Nose to the grindstone, writing, writing, writing. An anthology pitch accepted! (Artist turns in half-finished work.) Another anthology accepted! (Editor removes all your dialogue.) Self-publishing time! (You can only afford black and white.)

A few conventions later, a routine takes form. Your primary goal—creating stories and bringing them into the world—is now covered in logistical barnacles. Arrival at door such and such, setup at this time, breakdown at that time, bring your own chair, no power outlets, the AC broke and it's ninety-seven degrees, the heat broke and it's fifty degrees.

Writer, now publisher, now clerk, now carny/stagehand. Whatever it takes. Just get your name out there. It takes ten years of this.

Sitting behind the table, the banner overhead shouting "WRITER" to the world seeming more ridiculous by the minute. The scorn visible in their eyes as they walk past, seeking out celebrity autographs and action figures. "Do you draw these?" someone asks, someone who looks like the type of person you desperately want reading your stories. It takes longer to explain than it should. "Cool," they say as they back away.

Artists are awesome. They have bespoke clothing and tasteful tattoos, like edgy magicians. Their craft is a form of elaborate illusion, conjuring dreams onto paper in real time. "That's so sick," a kid says as my neighbor cranks out a commission.

What am I doing here? Opening up a Word doc and dumping my bullshit dreams into it, that's a skill? The world has enough Neil Gaimans and Chris Claremonts. Look, Marv Wolfman is sitting there eating a salad. Marv fucking Wolfman! Who do I think I am?

"You guys wanna check out some COMICS?" booms the carnival barker next to me. This guy hangs in front of his booth, roping them in like stray cattle. Inexplicably, they leave with handfuls of his books. I check my watch. Four hours left.

Bitter and forlorn, avoiding eye contact. Suddenly, someone who seems slightly medicated grabs one of each book from my little setup and opens up their wallet. "Uh, do you want me to sign them?" I stammer as I grab a barely-used Sharpie. We talk, they laugh, I sign. Am I for real? Is this real?

I start a tally list. Some conventions, book A sells. Others, it's this collection. I learn to talk, but not too much. I drink a lot of water. Stretch. It's a marathon, not a sprint.

The table grows, the books now spreading end-to-end in tidy little piles. Something for everyone. Look at me, the dynamic and eclectic writer.

Stan Lee and Jack Kirby worked this as their JOB, I think. They would never have spent their weekends, their free time, their own money, to do this. They went to work in New York City to pay their mortgage. This is insane!

"It's like everyone is waiting in line and working really hard to get into a restaurant that serves only bologna sandwiches," my wife says, as we work the booth. "But you can just go to the grocery store and buy bologna yourself."

It's the best summation of trying to "break in" to the modern comics industry that I've ever heard.

And yet I go on. New series, new formats, gloriously expensive color, new artists, new friends, perhaps a few enemies—each convention a gauntlet of experience. "I'm done!" I tell her as we sneak in a bite to eat, bad convention food doing damage to already damaged arteries. "This is definitely my last one."

The weekend ends and the show wraps up, laughter and manic exhaustion swirling around the half-empty warehouse space as fellow miscreants pack up the circus. The relief of home. The return to normal life.

Then the digestion. The faces. The conversations. That one guy, he really liked that story, didn't he? And that lady who didn't have cash on Saturday, she actually came back on Sunday! I wonder what they would think of this story I've been carrying around. I should reach out to that artist I met. I just got a bonus at work. I could probably do one hundred copies in full color with that money.

And just like that, the itch takes hold again. The multitude of visceral horrors presented by comic conventions melt away into a vague memory of grunge. You forget the nagging cough. You check the calendar. There's another one coming up next month . . .

CON SKETCH

STORY & ART

ANDY KUHN

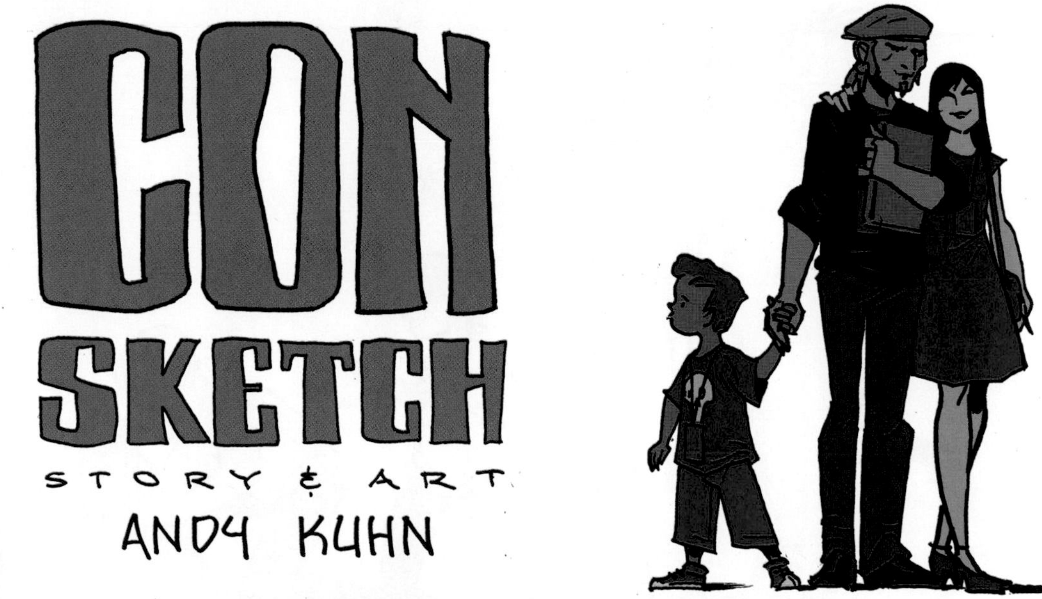

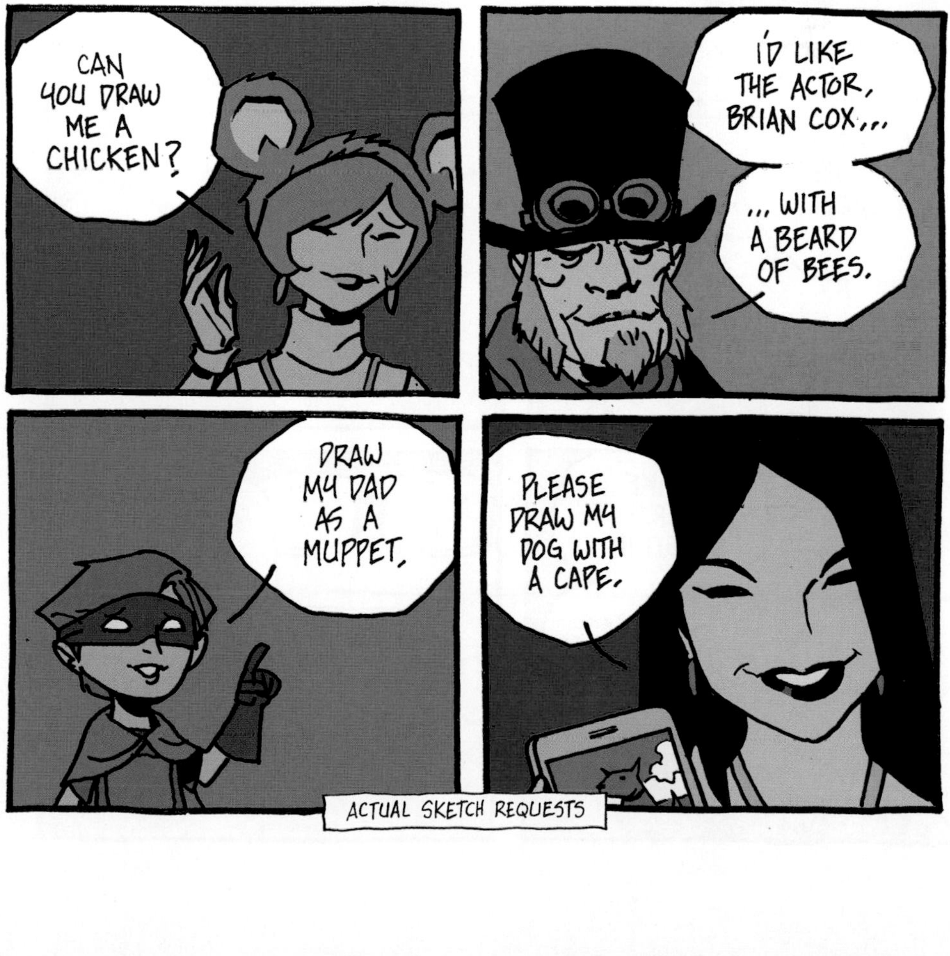
CAN YOU DRAW ME A CHICKEN?
I'D LIKE THE ACTOR, BRIAN COX...
... WITH A BEARD OF BEES.
DRAW MY DAD AS A MUPPET.
PLEASE DRAW MY DOG WITH A CAPE.
ACTUAL SKETCH REQUESTS

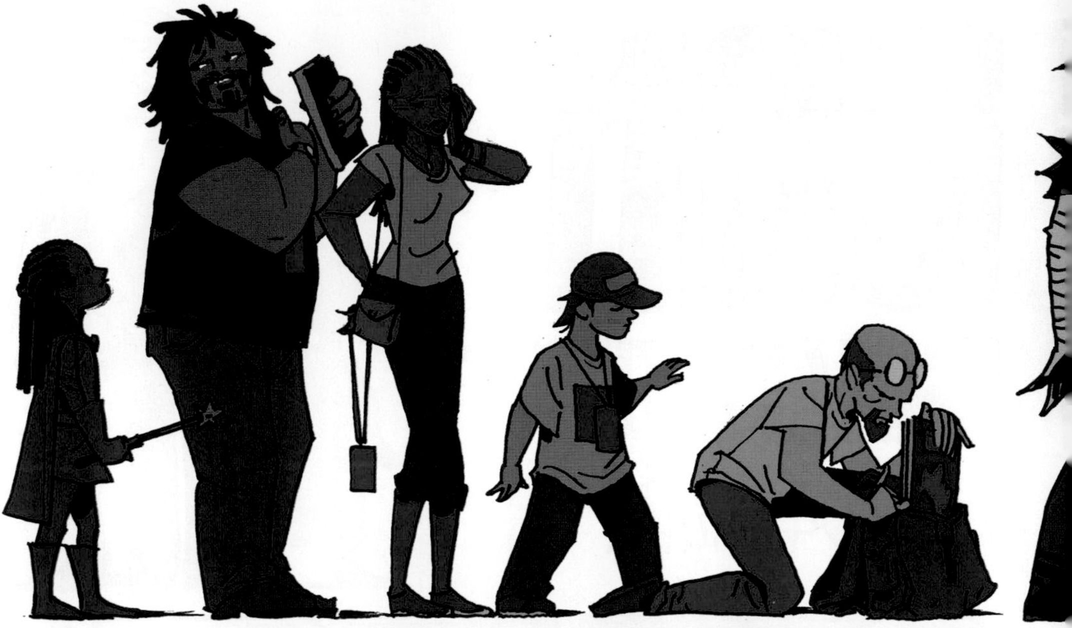

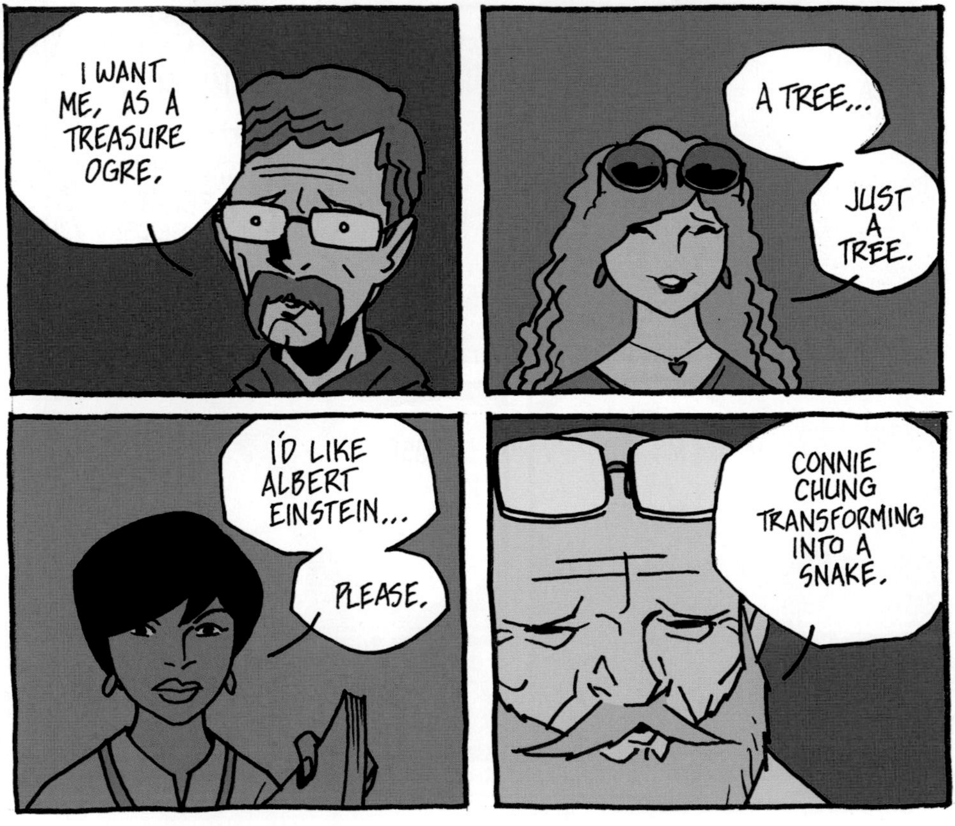
I WANT ME, AS A TREASURE OGRE.
A TREE...
JUST A TREE.
I'D LIKE ALBERT EINSTEIN...
PLEASE.
CONNIE CHUNG TRANSFORMING INTO A SNAKE.

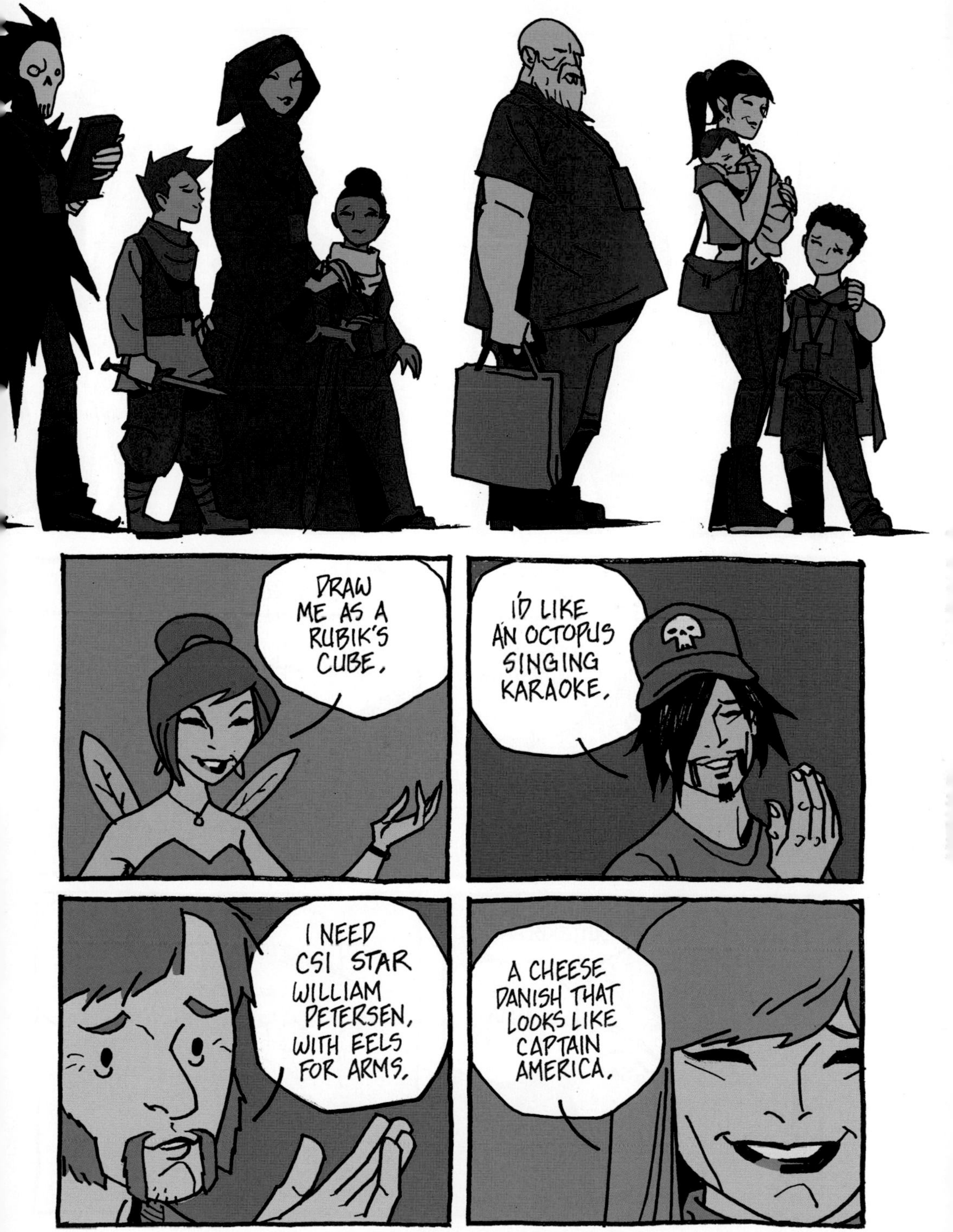
DRAW ME AS A RUBIK'S CUBE.
I'D LIKE AN OCTOPUS SINGING KARAOKE.
I NEED CSI STAR WILLIAM PETERSEN, WITH EELS FOR ARMS.
A CHEESE DANISH THAT LOOKS LIKE CAPTAIN AMERICA.

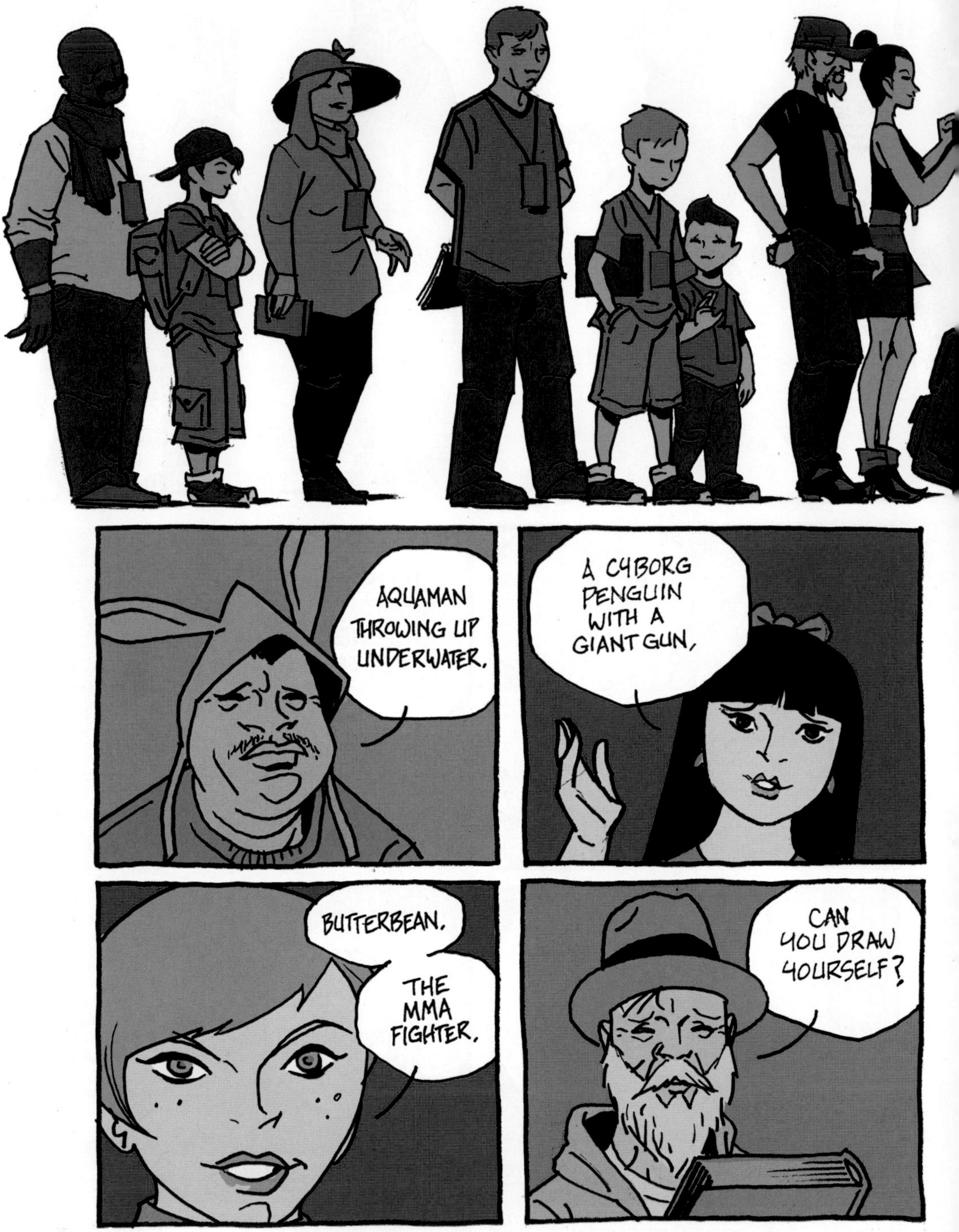
AQUAMAN THROWING UP UNDERWATER.
A CYBORG PENGUIN WITH A GIANT GUN,
BUTTERBEAN.
THE MMA FIGHTER.
CAN YOU DRAW YOURSELF?

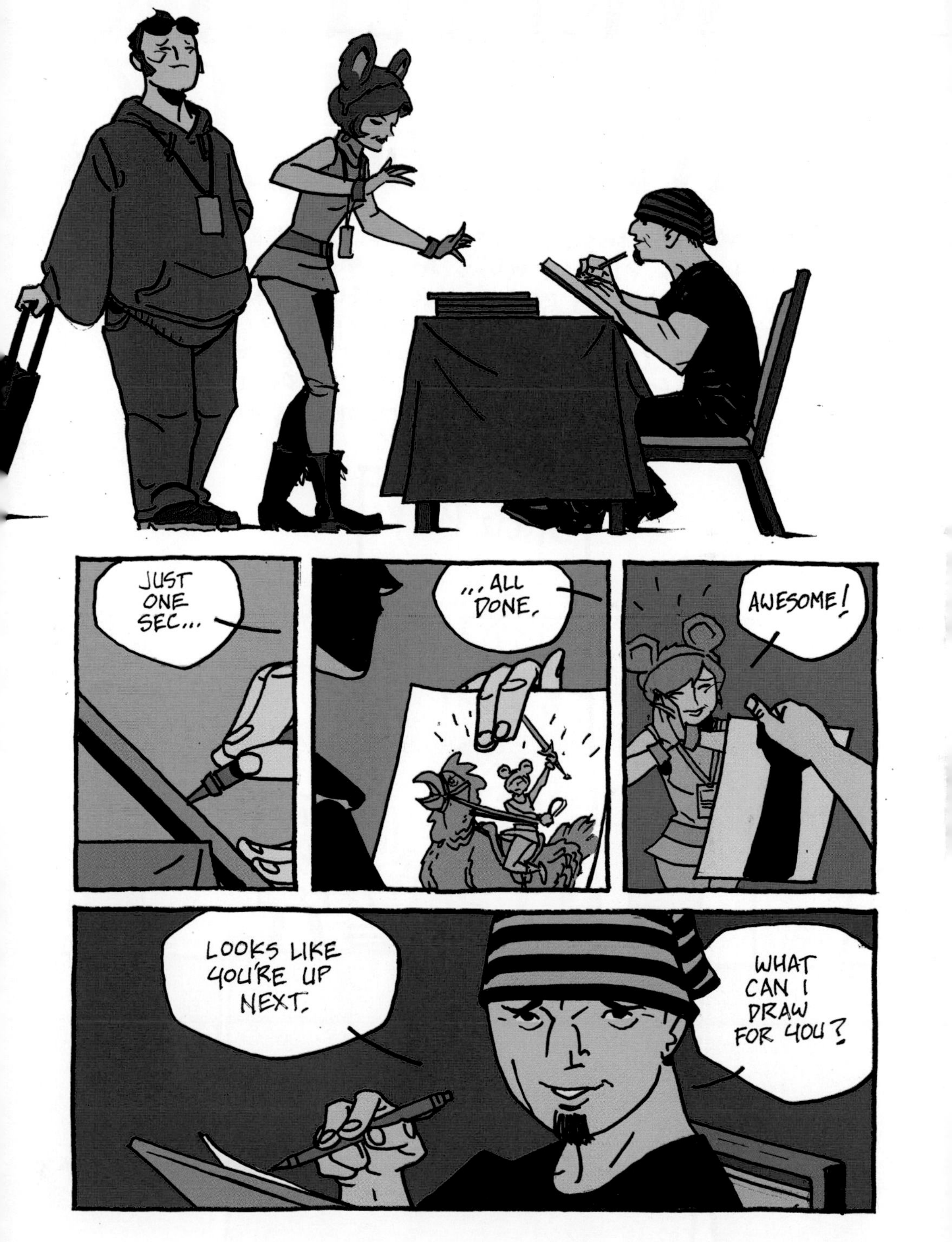
JUST ONE SEC...
...ALL DONE.
AWESOME!
LOOKS LIKE YOU'RE UP NEXT.
WHAT CAN I DRAW FOR YOU?

A WRITER IN ARTIST ALLEY

HEY, I'M GREG PAK, A COMIC BOOK WRITER BEST KNOWN FOR PLANET HULK AND MECH CADET YU AND A CHILDREN'S BOOK CALLED THE PRINCESS WHO SAVED HERSELF. I'VE BEEN TABLING IN ARTIST ALLEYS OF COMIC BOOK CONVENTIONS FOR 12 YEARS. HERE'S JUST A LITTLE TASTE OF WHAT IT'S BEEN LIKE. (SPOILER ALERT: PRETTY AWESOME!)

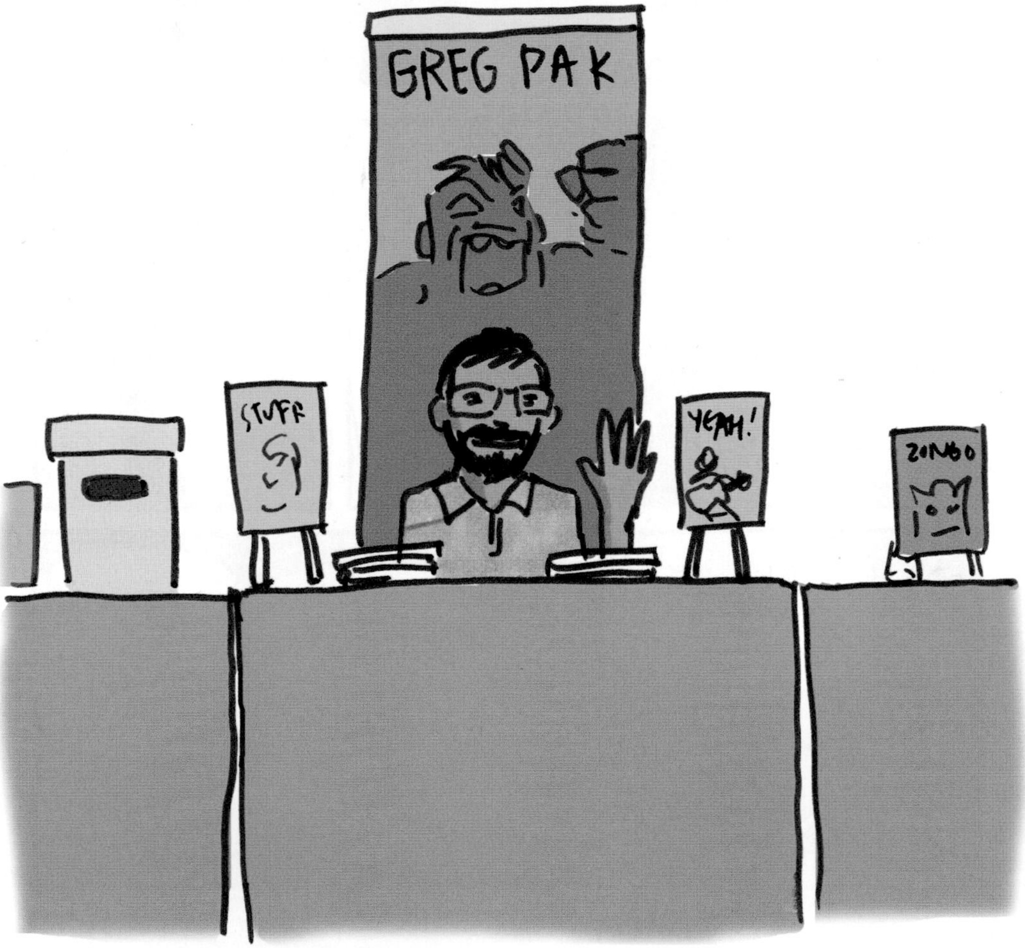

GREG PAK
STUFF
YEAH!

JUST THE WRITER

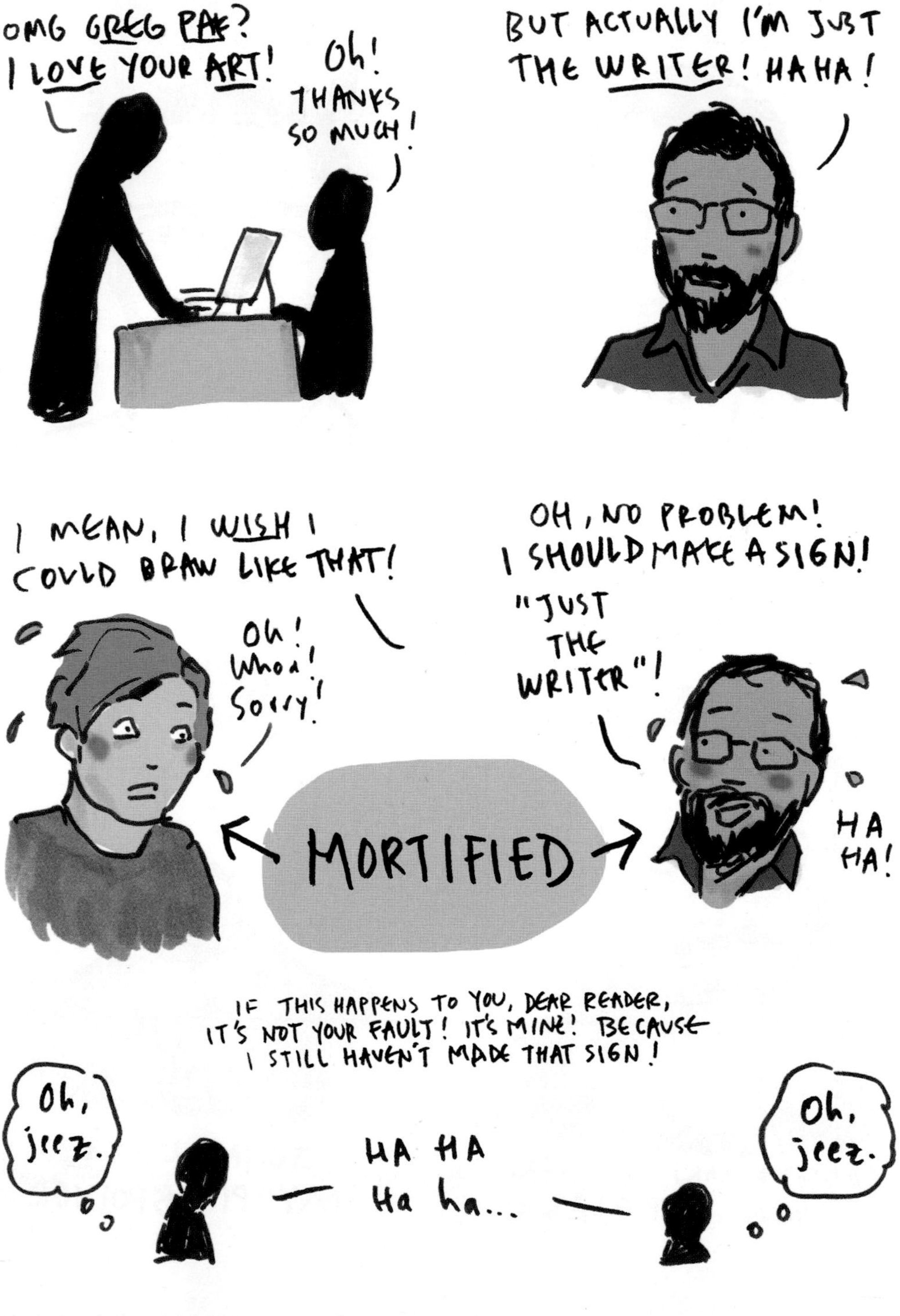
OMG GREG PAK? I LOVE YOUR ART!
Oh! THANKS SO MUCH!
BUT ACTUALLY I'M JUST THE WRITER! HAHA!
I MEAN, I WISH I COULD DRAW LIKE THAT!
Oh! Whoa! Sorry!
OH, NO PROBLEM! I SHOULD MAKE A SIGN!
"JUST THE WRITER"!
HA HA!
MORTIFIED
IF THIS HAPPENS TO YOU, DEAR READER, IT'S NOT YOUR FAULT! IT'S MINE! BECAUSE I STILL HAVEN'T MADE THAT SIGN!
Oh, jeez.
HA HA
Ha ha...
Oh, jeez.

HOW I COSPLAY

BEARDED HALF-ASIAN
BRUCE BANNER

BEARDED HALF-ASIAN
CLARK KENT

HALF-ASIAN STEPHEN
STRANGE WITH GLASSES

JOHN WICK'S
MYOPIC BROTHER

WHY I MIGHT STOP DOING CONS

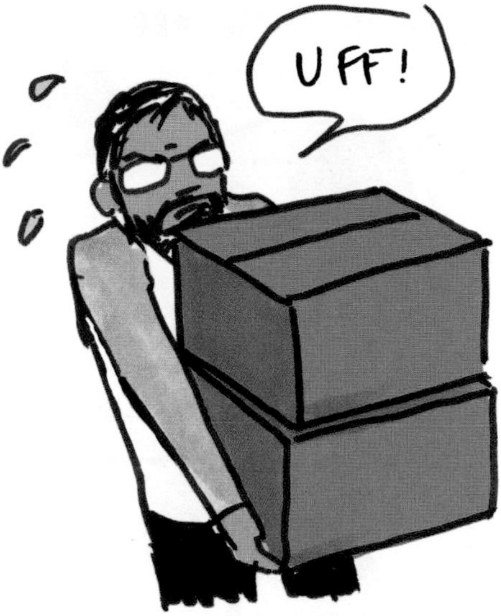
UFF!

BOOKS ARE SO HEAVY.

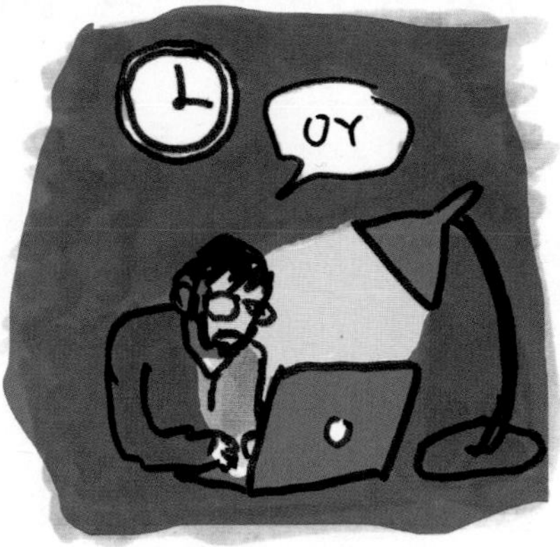
OY

DEADLINES NEVER STOP.

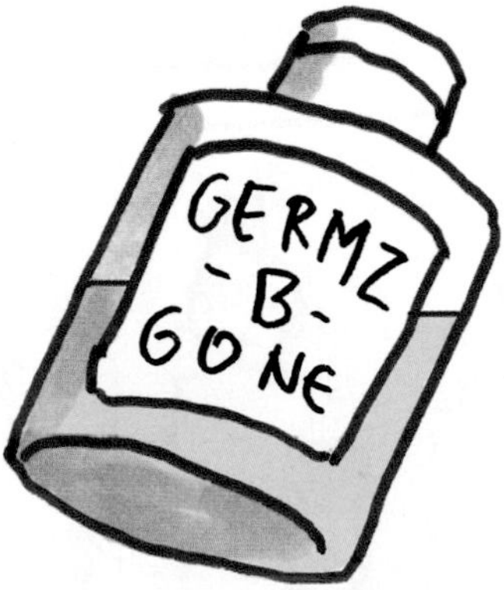
GERMZ
-B-
GONE

HAND SANITIZERS NO LONGER KILL THE MOST VIRULENT BACTERIA.

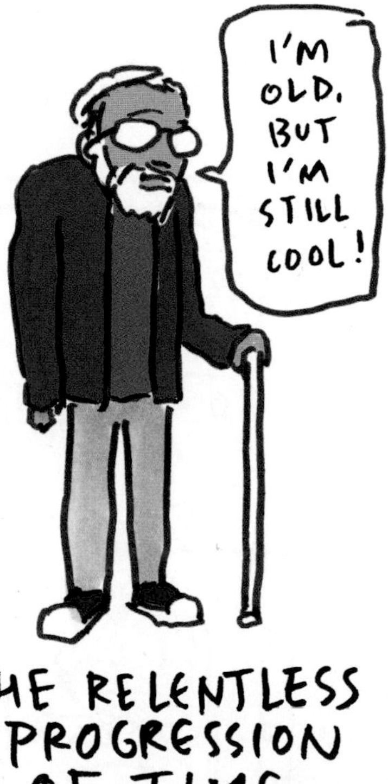
I'M OLD. BUT I'M STILL COOL!

THE RELENTLESS PROGRESSION OF TIME.

WHY I'LL NEVER STOP DOING CONS

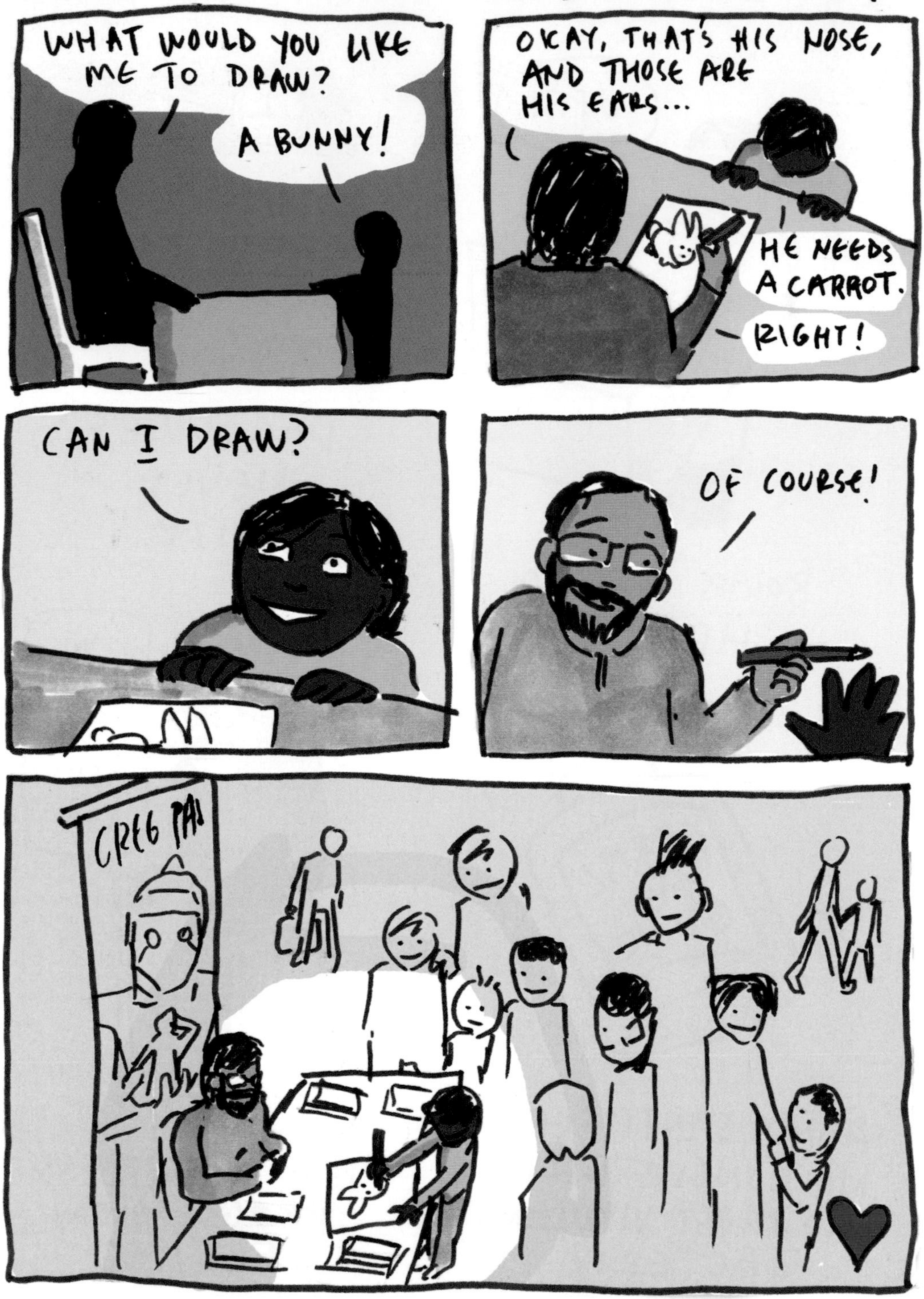
WHAT WOULD YOU LIKE ME TO DRAW?
A BUNNY!
OKAY, THAT'S HIS NOSE, AND THOSE ARE HIS EARS...
HE NEEDS A CARROT.
RIGHT!
CAN I DRAW?
OF COURSE!
GREG PAK

COMIC CONversations: HOW CONS BRING CREATORS TOGETHER

Chris Arrant

How often do you see your co-workers? In most cases, I can bet you'd say every day that you go to work. But if you work in the comics industry, you often go for weeks, months, and sometimes even years between seeing the people you work with every day.

Virtually every comic creator, except for those lucky enough to share studio space, works from home; speaking to their collaborators, editors, and publishers by email, chat, and the occasional voice call. It isn't uncommon for comic creators to have never met the people they work with—or work for; and in some cases, they may not even know what their collaborators look or sound like.

The rise of mass communication has allowed people to create comics from all over the world, without the need to even be in the same country as their publisher, but that same globalization of comics has also inadvertently made face-to-face interactions more and more rare.

How rare? When I asked writer Greg Pak (*Incredible Hulk, Mech Cadet Yu*) about it, he parsed it out in exact numbers: "95% via email, 4% via text, 1% on the phone."

While those numbers may vary to a degree, in large part Pak's experiences are the same that other writers, artists, colorists, and letterers around the world have. Editors and publishing staff might have a shared office they work out of, but when it comes to meeting the freelance creators they work with—it's usually not in-person.

Which is where comic conventions come in.

Comic conventions have become a *de facto* place for comic pros to meet one another, hash out collaborations, and in many cases, sign very important business deals. While the primary goal of creators are comic conventions is to meet fans and sell their work, face-time with their co-workers—from business-related networking down to just informal camaraderie—is an integral undercurrent at comic conventions.

"It's true, I do cons to meet fans, sell my work, and appear on panels—but a *massive* part of it is to meet other creators. It's a lesson I learned early," says Irish writer/artist Declan Shalvey (*Return of Wolverine, Injection*). "I come from a small country that had little to no comics in the culture. If I was to make a career doing this I soon found out that I had to go to the places where comics creators were, in order to get better feedback and make contacts."

Many creators—especially artists—have had great success in making their first inroads into the comics industry by going to conventions, meeting publishers and fellow artists, and participating in portfolio reviews.

When DC Entertainment's Chief Creative Officer/co-Publisher Jim Lee first tried to break into comics in the late eighties, he received rejection letters from all the top publishers—ones he kept and has recently shared on social media. It wasn't until a fellow artist convinced Lee to attend a New York comic convention did he get his foot in the door with then-Marvel editor Archie Goodwin. Jim Lee left New York a few days later with his first assignment—a fill-in issue of *Alpha Flight*.

That opportunity existed then, and continues to flourish now.

"Meeting the talent I hire makes the work relationship far stronger," says Lion Forge Comics editor Christina "Steenz" Stewart, who is also an artist on Oni Press' *Archival Quality*.

As Steenz balances editing and being an artist, she says the big reason she attends conventions is to meet other people in the industry.

"I'm there to talk on panels, meet all the friends I only see at cons, and find new talent."

Conventions aren't just for new talent, as they can also be for established talent to parse online conversations they've had with potential and current publishers and collaborators.

"A huge benefit of meeting people in-person can be the thing that cuts through a lot of freelancer anxiety," says Shalvey. "'Why didn't that editor email me back?' 'Were they angry with me in that email?' 'Does this person really want to work with me?' These are questions we've all asked ourselves at the other end of a computer screen. In person, people will be far more straight up with you and you can have a much better idea of where you stand and often realize you were worried about nothing."

The opportunity to have face-to-face meetings with collaborators as well as would-be business partners is something that comics pros take advantage of with conventions. I have heard several stories where a high-profile creator working exclusive for one company "bumped" into someone from a rival company at a convention and ended up switching teams either later on—or in one case that same weekend—breaking the news to their soon-to-be-former-publisher on the convention floor.

In other cases, creators might meet up in person to pitch a new series to a publisher—doing it in-person, in some cases, to negotiate a particular point that might have been brushed off online.

"The first time I met Nick Spencer was at Comic-Con International: San Diego in 2009, and we had just completed our pitch for *Morning Glories*," says Joe Eisma, the comic's artist/co-creator. "He was going to pitch it at the show, and I went to one of his signings beforehand and he was very gracious and told me that he was going to Image Comics with the ultimatum that he couldn't do this book unless it was ongoing. Back then, trying to do an ongoing was a risky move, and I had a mild panic attack that there was no way Image would go for it. I needn't have worried!"

Image went for it, with *Morning Glories #1* hitting stands in 2010, and was an ongoing for six years.

"It's a great thing to meet a collaborator face-to-face. It's not essential—I've worked with dozens of folks I've never met in person. But it absolutely helps," Pak says. "Aaron Lopresti and I met at a con right before we started working together on *Incredible Hulk*'s 'Planet Hulk' story-arc back in the day. We just talked for a little while, but it was great to put a face to the name and have some sense of each other as we dove into the work. Meeting a person face-to-face can also give you a sense of how they talk and communicate, which can help understand the tone of the emails you exchange later."

"If we've met and bonded in person, we don't have to fret quite so much about misunderstandings of tone in emails or texts."

While meeting in-person doesn't always end up creating high-profile comics like *Planet Hulk* or *Morning Glories*, it does help establish a bond that can go a long way.

"You tend to forge new relationships that will carry on further into your career at conventions," says Shalvey. "Also, sometimes these are the places where ideas for comics come from, or inspire a creator to work with another creator."

While meeting in person isn't necessary, it can often strengthen the bond between two creators who go on to do very different projects away from one another.

"I'd been close friends with writer Kelly Thompson for years before we worked on *Jem & The Holograms* together and we've hung out a few times," says Sophie Campbell. "And I think having that as part of relationship made for an interesting dynamic. It was a much closer and constant relationship than I usually have with writers; we were always sending things back and forth and chatting."

"Luckily, I've never had a collaborator who seems cool at first but then I'm irritated with them after I meet them in person," she says laughingly.

In the realm of creator-owned comics, the bonds between writer, artist, colorist, and letterer is often more than just as co-workers—it's as business partners and co-owners in a promising new venture. Meeting in person helps to flesh out just who they're getting into business with, because if successful the partnership could go on for years—or even decades.

"It doesn't mean that the work automatically becomes amazing or anything, but I think you can't help but feel invested when you genuinely *know* the person you're making a comic with," Shalvey says. "Spending some quality time with co-creators isn't compulsory by any means, but genuinely knowing the person you're working with creates a level of respect and understanding. Making a comic is like being in a marriage of sorts; there can be stresses and strains but if you really have a partner you know you can rely on that you have someone who supports your artistic process. You know they're not going to ignore your emails. I think you can maintain that relationship online, but it's generated far more sincerely in person.

"As a general rule from now on, I really only want to work with people I've met in person first."

One of the most popular facets of comic conventions after-hours for comics pros is what's familiarly known as "BarCon." After the convention floor closes, comics pros spread out to the convention hotel(s) bars and restaurants to eat, drink—and more importantly, meet other professionals.

"It's one of my favorite parts of any show. Sitting around with your peers and catching up and talking shop," says Dennis Culver. "There's one show in particular I do every single year because I know it will be a good crowd after the show ends each day."

Conversations at BarCon range wildly. They might be about the sales and pace of business on the convention floor that day, current events in the industry, or talking about craft from one creator to another.

But given an average convention day is an hour of prep and then eight to ten hours working at a booth or table on the convention floor, BarCon isn't for everyone—and that's before even mentioning the bar environment.

"BarCon is exhausting. But it's gotten my alcohol tolerance through the roof. And honestly, it's great for creators but after-hours stuff is even better for publishers and professionals," Stewart says.

The first time I visited Comic-Con International: San Diego, I made a point to check out the after-hours BarCon at the nearby Hyatt—and it was eye-opening. Creators from different areas of the industry mingling; high-profile executives catching up with colleagues from other companies; newer creators being welcomed into a tight-knight circle of colleagues huddled in a corner. I learned that a Big Two editor was hosting meetings in a nearby hotel room, with the BarCon acting as a "waiting room" of sorts with their assistants and the creators or company staff they would be meeting with.

BarCon isn't the only after-hours event for comics pros during conventions, however. For many creators, they're in a new city with lots of event and dining options to explore—and they want to explore it with their colleagues.

"I don't drink, so I don't generally end up at the hotel bar for any length of time. I'm also old and don't really love parties or any very loud environment," Pak says. "I do most of my socializing with fellow pros over smaller gatherings at breakfasts, lunches, or dinners. Or karaoke! I'm always in for karaoke."

Some creators split off from the convention floor and BarCon to their individual rooms for smaller gatherings—card games have been a frequent after-hours pastime for comics pros at conventions for decades. That continues to this day, but has expanded to include board games, tabletop gaming, and other communal activities.

"Seeing your creator friends at shows tends to feel like a high school reunion, so there's quite a bit of partying that goes on post-show," says Eisma. "It can get pretty wild, or it can be pretty chill, depending on who you're with!"

Whether it's on the convention floor, at a panel, or after-hours at the bar or hotel rooms, conventions serve a vital purpose in the bonding between creators and comics staff—whether you're just breaking in or already established.

"Now that I'm a few years into a respectable career, it's not something I *need* to do, but I think it's wise to keep those face-to-face contacts, especially in an age where online interactions are so prevalent," Shalvey explains. "If anything, I think people take in-person interactions for granted; so many creators are available online, and that's great, but we're in an age where everyone is dehumanizing each other on those platforms. In-person interaction is the glue that holds us together."

And while comic creators come to conventions to do work, they're still fans themselves, and some of their most memorable encounters are with their creative heroes.

"I'm still looking forward to meeting Denys Cowan and Bill Sienkiewicz; they have been working on *Wild Storm: Michael Cray* with me," says writer Bryan Edward Hill. "Of course, I'd be meeting them as a fan as much as I am a fellow professional. We would talk about the work aspect though, of course."

In this respect, however, comic creators are just like the fans who come to comic conventions—to see the spectacle, to buy unique products, and to meet the creators that interest them.

"When I go to a convention," Hill said, "I tend to look at who's going to be there and then try to find them in a quiet moment to have a real conversation."

While the modern comic industry has creators working all over the globe, conventions have grown to be the crossroads for comic creators—and yes, for fans too—to meet other comic creators: to share notes, to blow off steam, and sometimes just to be a fan once again themselves.

MURDER! MAYHEM! ME?

WRITTEN BY B. CLAY MOORE ART BY CHRIS GRINE

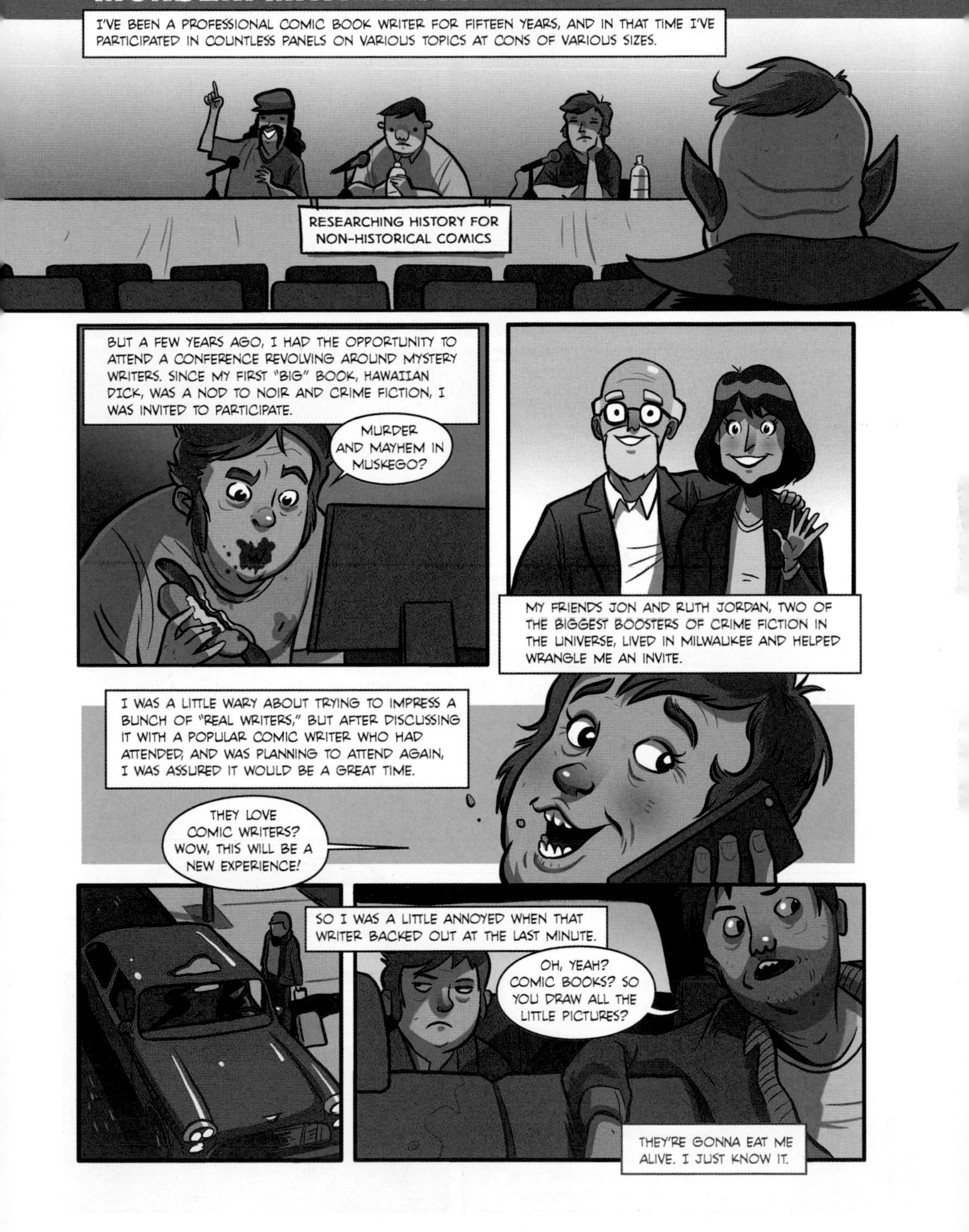

I'VE BEEN A PROFESSIONAL COMIC BOOK WRITER FOR FIFTEEN YEARS, AND IN THAT TIME I'VE PARTICIPATED IN COUNTLESS PANELS ON VARIOUS TOPICS AT CONS OF VARIOUS SIZES.
RESEARCHING HISTORY FOR NON-HISTORICAL COMICS
BUT A FEW YEARS AGO, I HAD THE OPPORTUNITY TO ATTEND A CONFERENCE REVOLVING AROUND MYSTERY WRITERS. SINCE MY FIRST "BIG" BOOK, HAWAIIAN DICK, WAS A NOD TO NOIR AND CRIME FICTION, I WAS INVITED TO PARTICIPATE.
MURDER AND MAYHEM IN MUSKEGO?
MY FRIENDS JON AND RUTH JORDAN, TWO OF THE BIGGEST BOOSTERS OF CRIME FICTION IN THE UNIVERSE, LIVED IN MILWAUKEE AND HELPED WRANGLE ME AN INVITE.
I WAS A LITTLE WARY ABOUT TRYING TO IMPRESS A BUNCH OF "REAL WRITERS," BUT AFTER DISCUSSING IT WITH A POPULAR COMIC WRITER WHO HAD ATTENDED, AND WAS PLANNING TO ATTEND AGAIN, I WAS ASSURED IT WOULD BE A GREAT TIME.
THEY LOVE COMIC WRITERS? WOW, THIS WILL BE A NEW EXPERIENCE!
SO I WAS A LITTLE ANNOYED WHEN THAT WRITER BACKED OUT AT THE LAST MINUTE.
OH, YEAH? COMIC BOOKS? SO YOU DRAW ALL THE LITTLE PICTURES?
THEY'RE GONNA EAT ME ALIVE. I JUST KNOW IT.

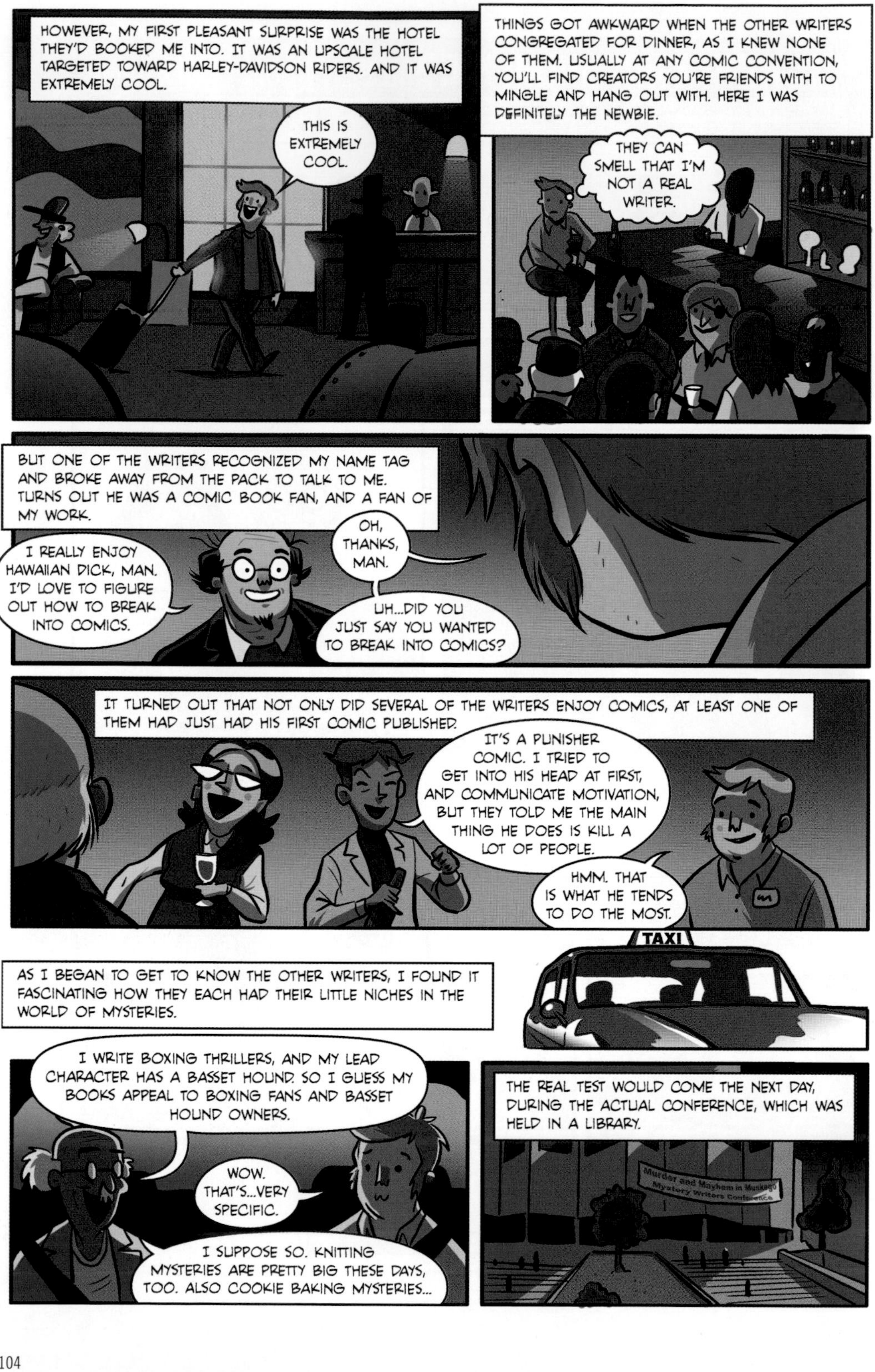
HOWEVER, MY FIRST PLEASANT SURPRISE WAS THE HOTEL THEY'D BOOKED ME INTO. IT WAS AN UPSCALE HOTEL TARGETED TOWARD HARLEY-DAVIDSON RIDERS. AND IT WAS EXTREMELY COOL.
THIS IS EXTREMELY COOL.
THINGS GOT AWKWARD WHEN THE OTHER WRITERS CONGREGATED FOR DINNER, AS I KNEW NONE OF THEM. USUALLY AT ANY COMIC CONVENTION, YOU'LL FIND CREATORS YOU'RE FRIENDS WITH TO MINGLE AND HANG OUT WITH. HERE I WAS DEFINITELY THE NEWBIE.
THEY CAN SMELL THAT I'M NOT A REAL WRITER.
BUT ONE OF THE WRITERS RECOGNIZED MY NAME TAG AND BROKE AWAY FROM THE PACK TO TALK TO ME. TURNS OUT HE WAS A COMIC BOOK FAN, AND A FAN OF MY WORK.
I REALLY ENJOY HAWAIIAN DICK, MAN. I'D LOVE TO FIGURE OUT HOW TO BREAK INTO COMICS.
OH, THANKS, MAN.
UH...DID YOU JUST SAY YOU WANTED TO BREAK INTO COMICS?
IT TURNED OUT THAT NOT ONLY DID SEVERAL OF THE WRITERS ENJOY COMICS, AT LEAST ONE OF THEM HAD JUST HAD HIS FIRST COMIC PUBLISHED.
IT'S A PUNISHER COMIC. I TRIED TO GET INTO HIS HEAD AT FIRST, AND COMMUNICATE MOTIVATION, BUT THEY TOLD ME THE MAIN THING HE DOES IS KILL A LOT OF PEOPLE.
HMM. THAT IS WHAT HE TENDS TO DO THE MOST.
AS I BEGAN TO GET TO KNOW THE OTHER WRITERS, I FOUND IT FASCINATING HOW THEY EACH HAD THEIR LITTLE NICHES IN THE WORLD OF MYSTERIES.
TAXI
I WRITE BOXING THRILLERS, AND MY LEAD CHARACTER HAS A BASSET HOUND. SO I GUESS MY BOOKS APPEAL TO BOXING FANS AND BASSET HOUND OWNERS.
WOW. THAT'S...VERY SPECIFIC.
I SUPPOSE SO. KNITTING MYSTERIES ARE PRETTY BIG THESE DAYS, TOO. ALSO COOKIE BAKING MYSTERIES...
THE REAL TEST WOULD COME THE NEXT DAY, DURING THE ACTUAL CONFERENCE, WHICH WAS HELD IN A LIBRARY.
Murder and Mayhem in Muskogee
Mystery Writers Conference

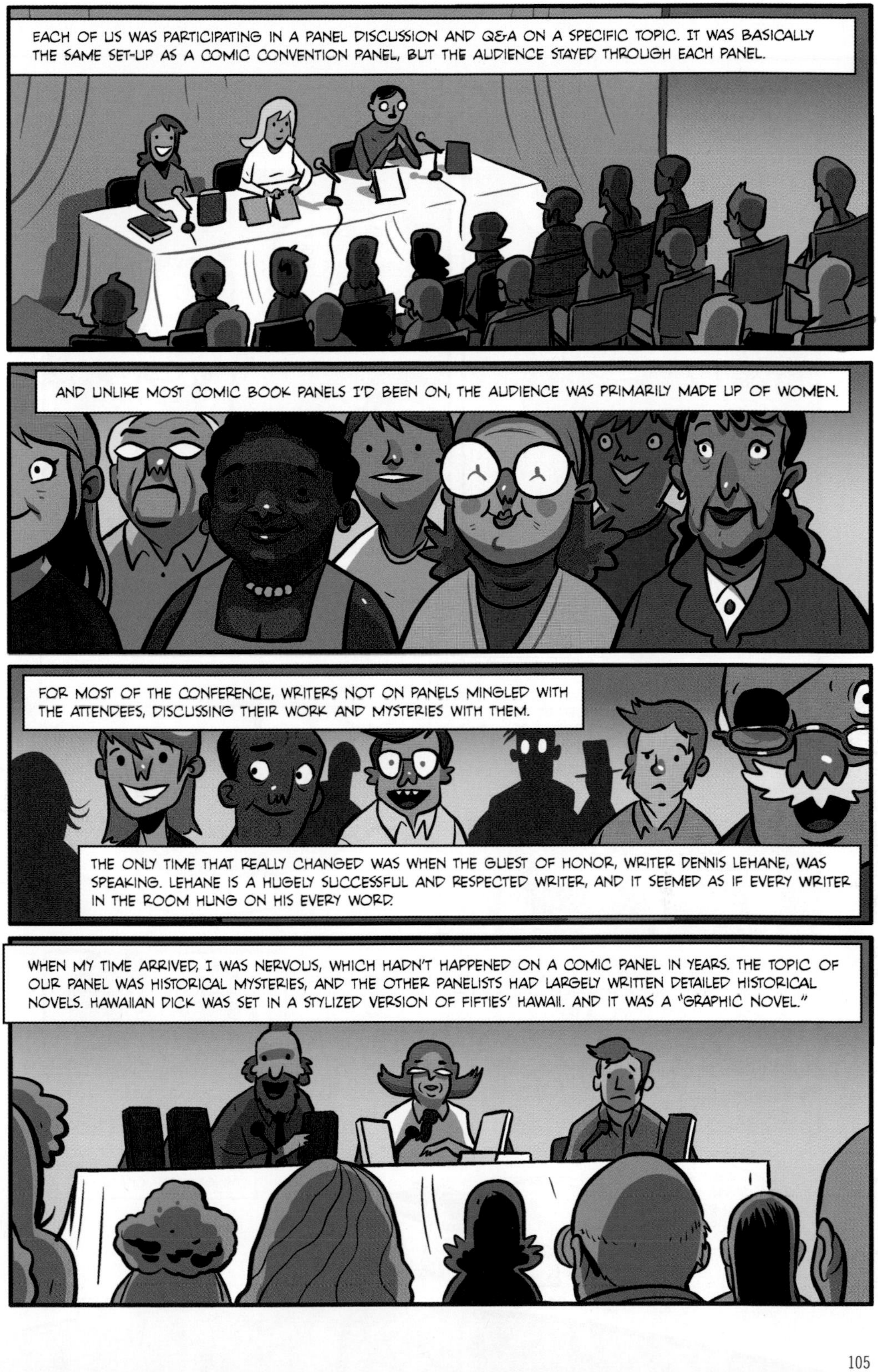
EACH OF US WAS PARTICIPATING IN A PANEL DISCUSSION AND Q&A ON A SPECIFIC TOPIC. IT WAS BASICALLY THE SAME SET-UP AS A COMIC CONVENTION PANEL, BUT THE AUDIENCE STAYED THROUGH EACH PANEL.
AND UNLIKE MOST COMIC BOOK PANELS I'D BEEN ON, THE AUDIENCE WAS PRIMARILY MADE UP OF WOMEN.
FOR MOST OF THE CONFERENCE, WRITERS NOT ON PANELS MINGLED WITH THE ATTENDEES, DISCUSSING THEIR WORK AND MYSTERIES WITH THEM.
THE ONLY TIME THAT REALLY CHANGED WAS WHEN THE GUEST OF HONOR, WRITER DENNIS LEHANE, WAS SPEAKING. LEHANE IS A HUGELY SUCCESSFUL AND RESPECTED WRITER, AND IT SEEMED AS IF EVERY WRITER IN THE ROOM HUNG ON HIS EVERY WORD.
WHEN MY TIME ARRIVED, I WAS NERVOUS, WHICH HADN'T HAPPENED ON A COMIC PANEL IN YEARS. THE TOPIC OF OUR PANEL WAS HISTORICAL MYSTERIES, AND THE OTHER PANELISTS HAD LARGELY WRITTEN DETAILED HISTORICAL NOVELS. HAWAIIAN DICK WAS SET IN A STYLIZED VERSION OF FIFTIES' HAWAII. AND IT WAS A "GRAPHIC NOVEL."

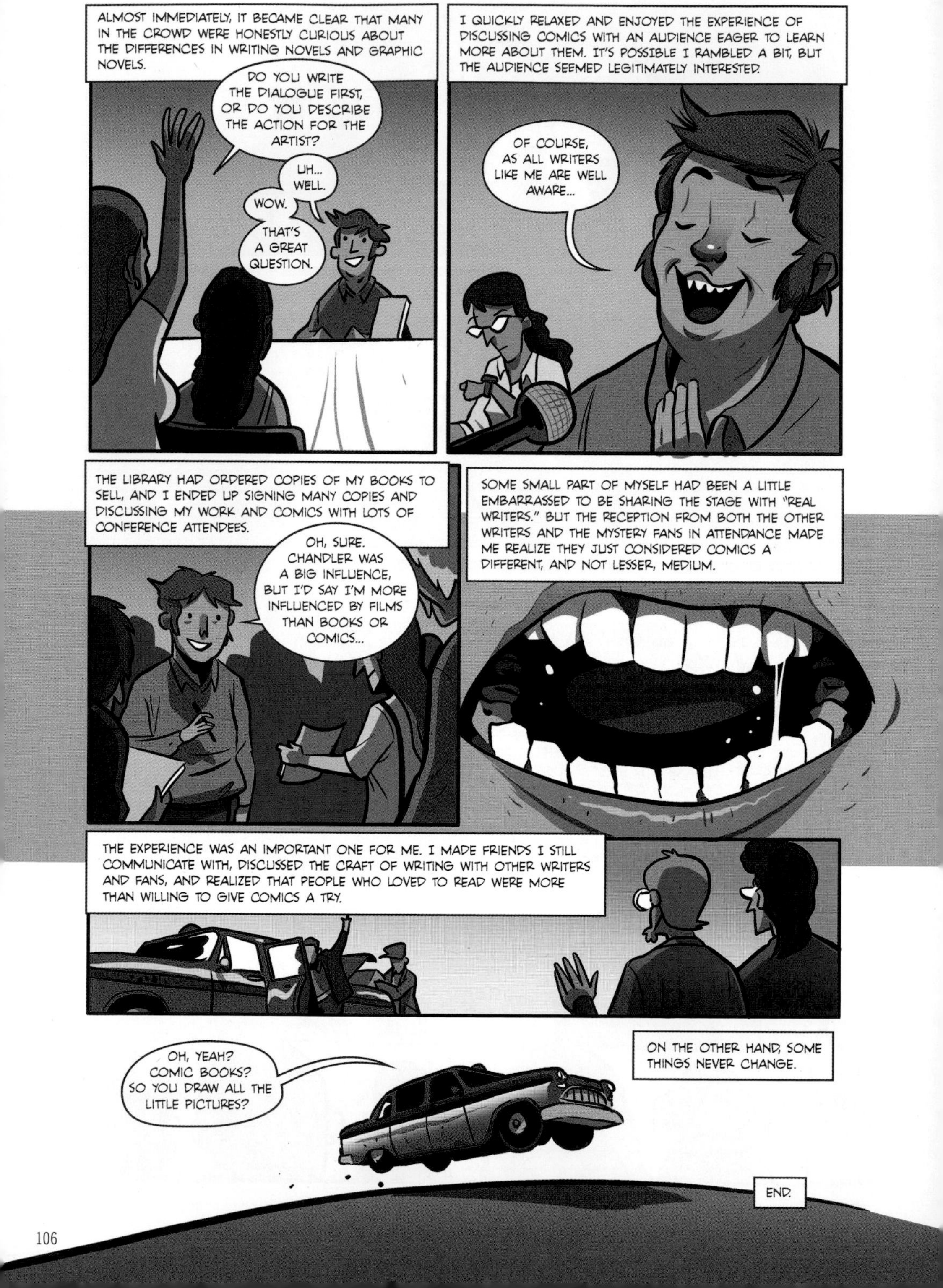
ALMOST IMMEDIATELY, IT BECAME CLEAR THAT MANY IN THE CROWD WERE HONESTLY CURIOUS ABOUT THE DIFFERENCES IN WRITING NOVELS AND GRAPHIC NOVELS.
DO YOU WRITE THE DIALOGUE FIRST, OR DO YOU DESCRIBE THE ACTION FOR THE ARTIST?
UH... WELL.
WOW.
THAT'S A GREAT QUESTION.
I QUICKLY RELAXED AND ENJOYED THE EXPERIENCE OF DISCUSSING COMICS WITH AN AUDIENCE EAGER TO LEARN MORE ABOUT THEM. IT'S POSSIBLE I RAMBLED A BIT, BUT THE AUDIENCE SEEMED LEGITIMATELY INTERESTED.
OF COURSE, AS ALL WRITERS LIKE ME ARE WELL AWARE...
THE LIBRARY HAD ORDERED COPIES OF MY BOOKS TO SELL, AND I ENDED UP SIGNING MANY COPIES AND DISCUSSING MY WORK AND COMICS WITH LOTS OF CONFERENCE ATTENDEES.
OH, SURE. CHANDLER WAS A BIG INFLUENCE, BUT I'D SAY I'M MORE INFLUENCED BY FILMS THAN BOOKS OR COMICS...
SOME SMALL PART OF MYSELF HAD BEEN A LITTLE EMBARRASSED TO BE SHARING THE STAGE WITH "REAL WRITERS." BUT THE RECEPTION FROM BOTH THE OTHER WRITERS AND THE MYSTERY FANS IN ATTENDANCE MADE ME REALIZE THEY JUST CONSIDERED COMICS A DIFFERENT, AND NOT LESSER, MEDIUM.
THE EXPERIENCE WAS AN IMPORTANT ONE FOR ME. I MADE FRIENDS I STILL COMMUNICATE WITH, DISCUSSED THE CRAFT OF WRITING WITH OTHER WRITERS AND FANS, AND REALIZED THAT PEOPLE WHO LOVED TO READ WERE MORE THAN WILLING TO GIVE COMICS A TRY.
OH, YEAH? COMIC BOOKS? SO YOU DRAW ALL THE LITTLE PICTURES?
ON THE OTHER HAND, SOME THINGS NEVER CHANGE.
END.

SAN DIEGO 1977

SCRIPT
TRINA ROBBINS

ART
LAURA NEUBERT & CHRIS CHUCKRY

LETTERS
RYAN FERRIER

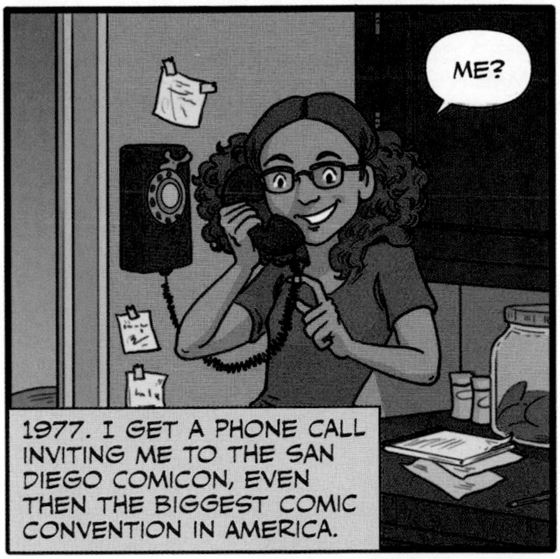
ME?
1977. I GET A PHONE CALL INVITING ME TO THE SAN DIEGO COMICON, EVEN THEN THE BIGGEST COMIC CONVENTION IN AMERICA.

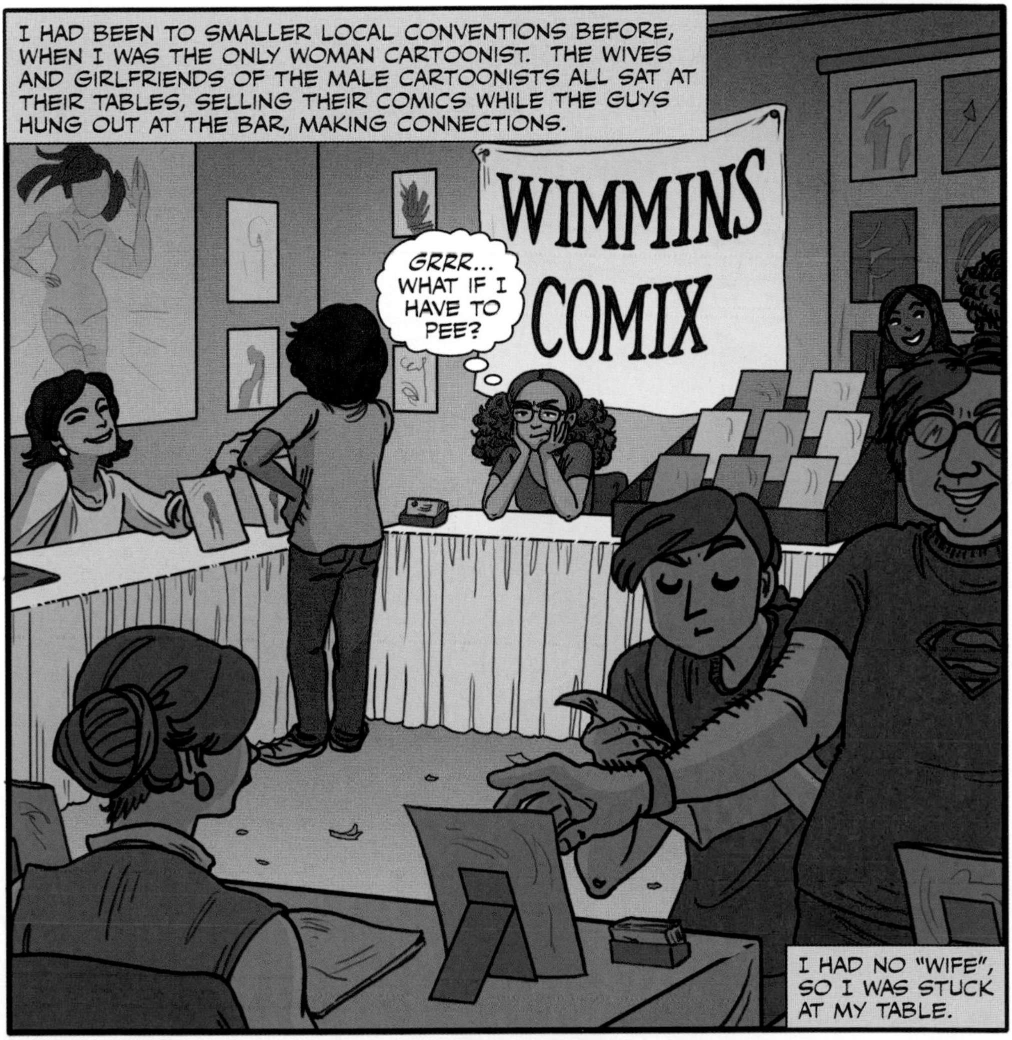
I HAD BEEN TO SMALLER LOCAL CONVENTIONS BEFORE, WHEN I WAS THE ONLY WOMAN CARTOONIST. THE WIVES AND GIRLFRIENDS OF THE MALE CARTOONISTS ALL SAT AT THEIR TABLES, SELLING THEIR COMICS WHILE THE GUYS HUNG OUT AT THE BAR, MAKING CONNECTIONS.
WIMMINS COMIX
GRRR... WHAT IF I HAVE TO PEE?
I HAD NO "WIFE", SO I WAS STUCK AT MY TABLE.

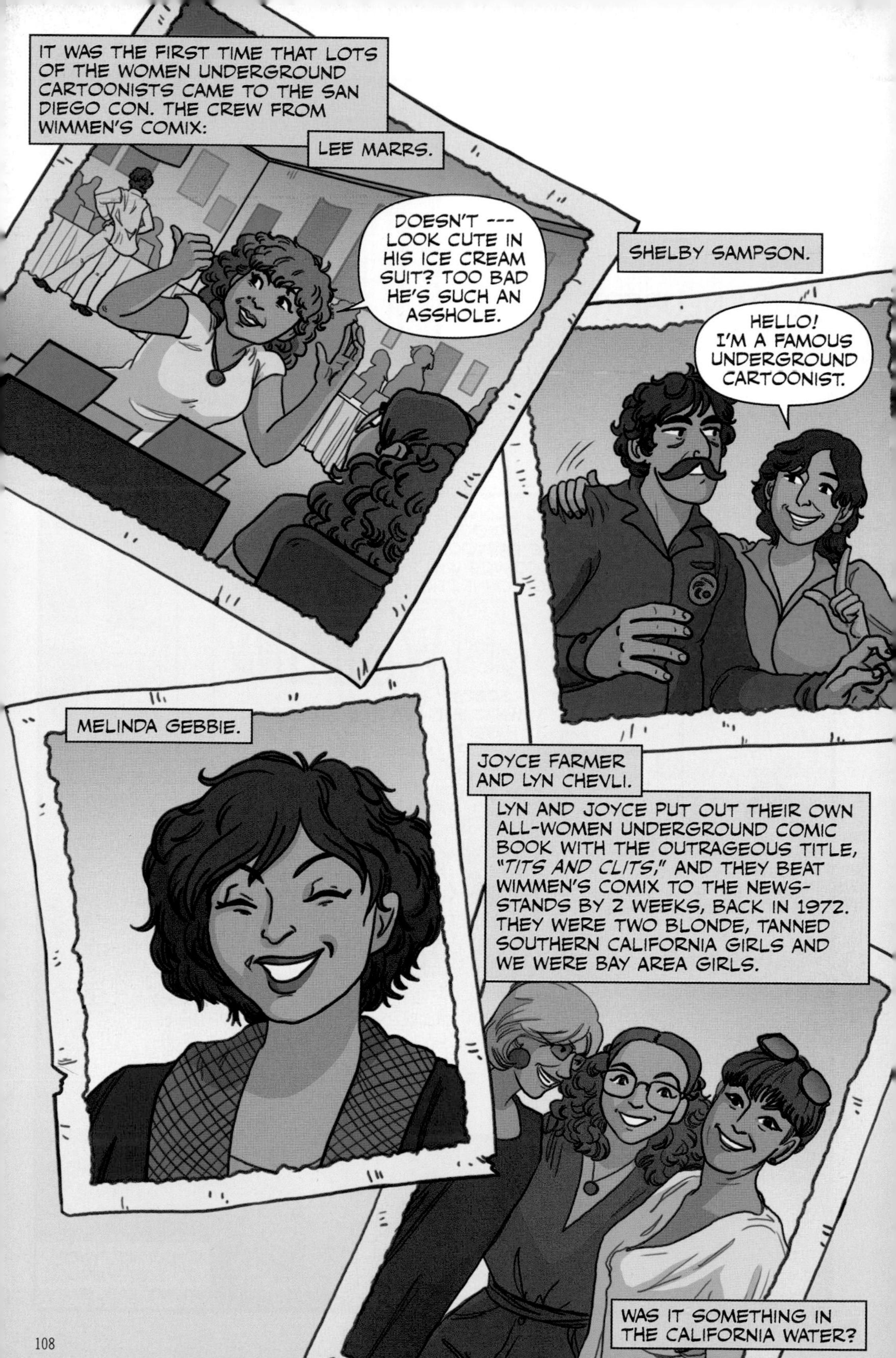

IT WAS THE FIRST TIME THAT LOTS OF THE WOMEN UNDERGROUND CARTOONISTS CAME TO THE SAN DIEGO CON. THE CREW FROM WIMMEN'S COMIX:
LEE MARRS.
DOESN'T --- LOOK CUTE IN HIS ICE CREAM SUIT? TOO BAD HE'S SUCH AN ASSHOLE.
SHELBY SAMPSON.
HELLO! I'M A FAMOUS UNDERGROUND CARTOONIST.
MELINDA GEBBIE.
JOYCE FARMER AND LYN CHEVLI.
LYN AND JOYCE PUT OUT THEIR OWN ALL-WOMEN UNDERGROUND COMIC BOOK WITH THE OUTRAGEOUS TITLE, "TITS AND CLITS," AND THEY BEAT WIMMEN'S COMIX TO THE NEWS-STANDS BY 2 WEEKS, BACK IN 1972. THEY WERE TWO BLONDE, TANNED SOUTHERN CALIFORNIA GIRLS AND WE WERE BAY AREA GIRLS.
WAS IT SOMETHING IN THE CALIFORNIA WATER?

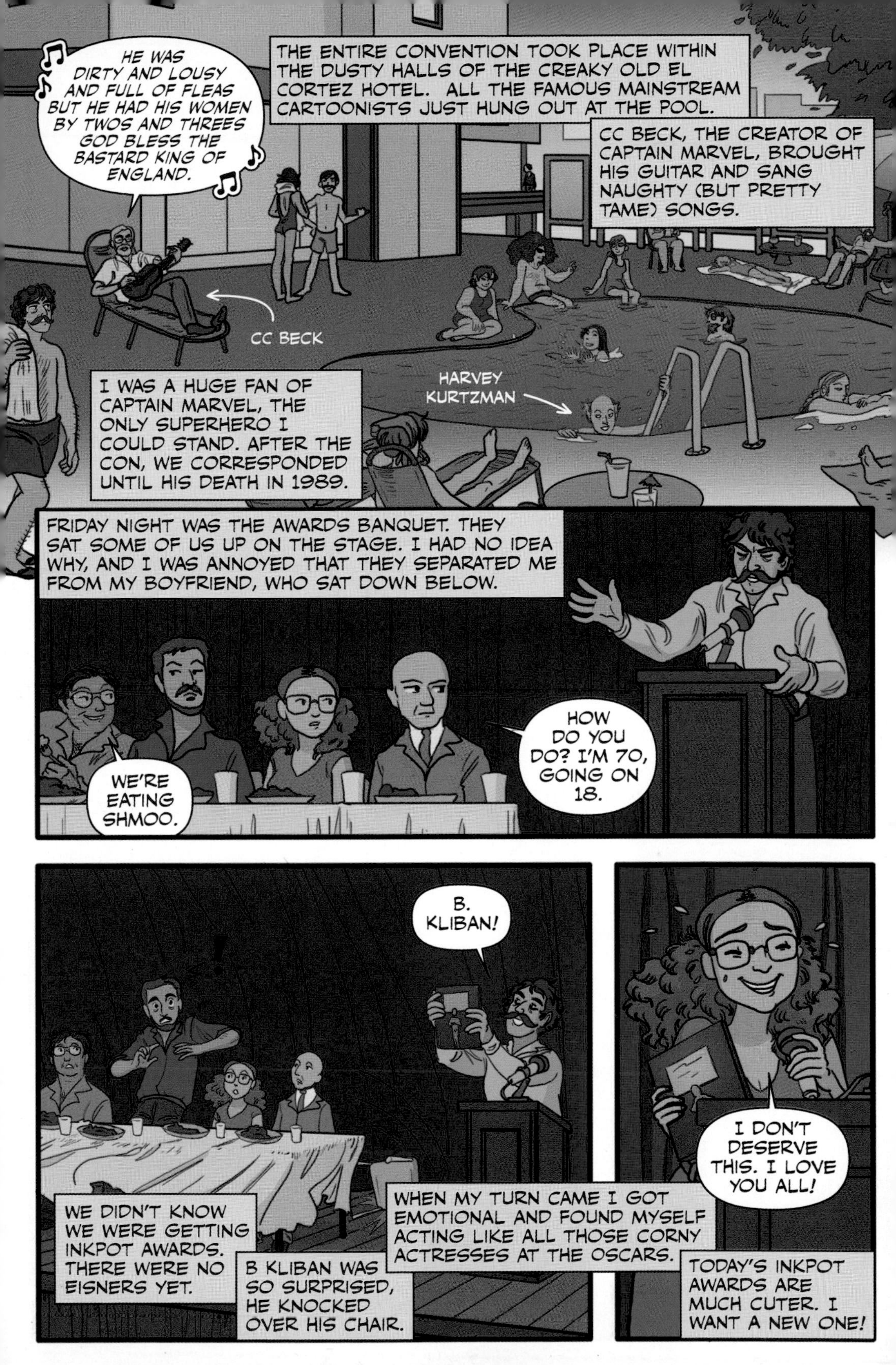
THE ENTIRE CONVENTION TOOK PLACE WITHIN THE DUSTY HALLS OF THE CREAKY OLD EL CORTEZ HOTEL. ALL THE FAMOUS MAINSTREAM CARTOONISTS JUST HUNG OUT AT THE POOL.
HE WAS DIRTY AND LOUSY AND FULL OF FLEAS BUT HE HAD HIS WOMEN BY TWOS AND THREES GOD BLESS THE BASTARD KING OF ENGLAND.
CC BECK, THE CREATOR OF CAPTAIN MARVEL, BROUGHT HIS GUITAR AND SANG NAUGHTY (BUT PRETTY TAME) SONGS.
CC BECK
HARVEY KURTZMAN
I WAS A HUGE FAN OF CAPTAIN MARVEL, THE ONLY SUPERHERO I COULD STAND. AFTER THE CON, WE CORRESPONDED UNTIL HIS DEATH IN 1989.
FRIDAY NIGHT WAS THE AWARDS BANQUET. THEY SAT SOME OF US UP ON THE STAGE. I HAD NO IDEA WHY, AND I WAS ANNOYED THAT THEY SEPARATED ME FROM MY BOYFRIEND, WHO SAT DOWN BELOW.
WE'RE EATING SHMOO.
HOW DO YOU DO? I'M 70, GOING ON 18.
B. KLIBAN!
!
WE DIDN'T KNOW WE WERE GETTING INKPOT AWARDS. THERE WERE NO EISNERS YET.
B KLIBAN WAS SO SURPRISED, HE KNOCKED OVER HIS CHAIR.
WHEN MY TURN CAME I GOT EMOTIONAL AND FOUND MYSELF ACTING LIKE ALL THOSE CORNY ACTRESSES AT THE OSCARS.
I DON'T DESERVE THIS. I LOVE YOU ALL!
TODAY'S INKPOT AWARDS ARE MUCH CUTER. I WANT A NEW ONE!

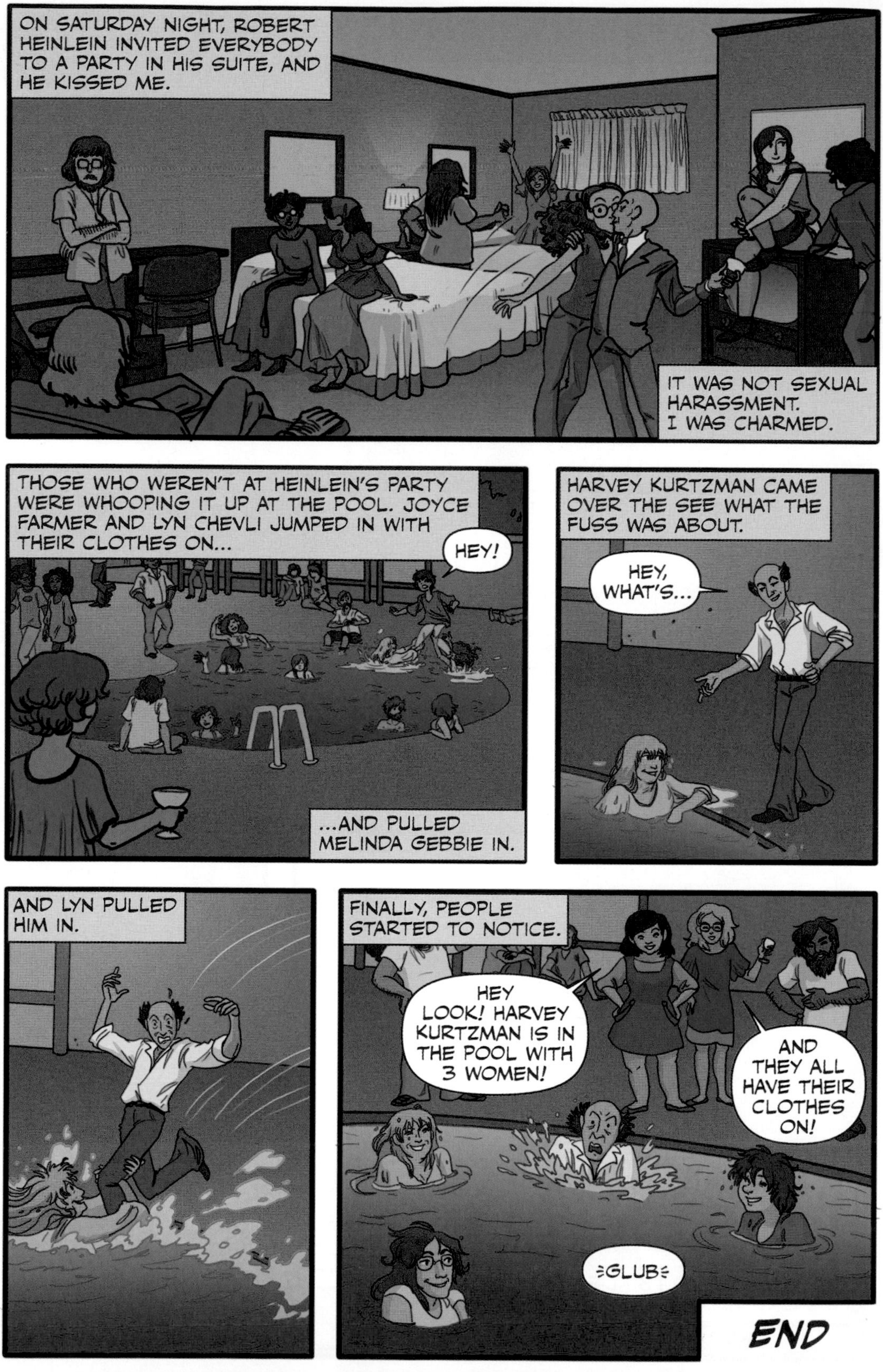
ON SATURDAY NIGHT, ROBERT HEINLEIN INVITED EVERYBODY TO A PARTY IN HIS SUITE, AND HE KISSED ME.
IT WAS NOT SEXUAL HARASSMENT. I WAS CHARMED.
THOSE WHO WEREN'T AT HEINLEIN'S PARTY WERE WHOOPING IT UP AT THE POOL. JOYCE FARMER AND LYN CHEVLI JUMPED IN WITH THEIR CLOTHES ON...
HEY!
...AND PULLED MELINDA GEBBIE IN.
HARVEY KURTZMAN CAME OVER THE SEE WHAT THE FUSS WAS ABOUT.
HEY, WHAT'S...
AND LYN PULLED HIM IN.
FINALLY, PEOPLE STARTED TO NOTICE.
HEY LOOK! HARVEY KURTZMAN IS IN THE POOL WITH 3 WOMEN!
AND THEY ALL HAVE THEIR CLOTHES ON!
GLUB
END

CRUNCH

Jackson Lanzing

No one told me about the crunch.

I'm twenty years old, on the tail end of my first Friday at San Diego Comic-Con and I'm packed together with at least two hundred people in an exit corridor, each of us hoping to escape into the Gaslamp after a day of full-scale geek revelry. It's a new kind of hell for me—not content to worry about my own safety, I'm now concerned with not breaking the deceptively flimsy wings of the Transformer I've been pinned against by the crowd. I think to turn back, to head the other direction and take some kind of refuge at the Hyatt, but those are nothing more than the dreams of a neophyte. There's no turning back. The crunch has swept me away.

This close to the rest of Comic-Con's denizens, I can see that San Diego for this weekend is home to a caste system. Single Day Badges look shell-shocked; these poor folks thought they could do this casually and are just now realizing that they shouldn't have made those dinner plans. Full Weekend Badges—like mine—indicate a full Kool-Aid drinker—a fan willing-and-excited to spend four days in this gauntlet. Press Badges, you would think, would have the good sense not to be stuck in this mess, and yet not five feet from me, pressed against three Predators, is a beard with a microphone. Most Exhibitor Badges are still inside the hall, preparing their booths for tomorrow's onslaught, though a few booth workers are unlucky enough to have walked into the crunch, from which they may never return.

I glimpse a single Professional Badge. Because this is my first show—and because I harbor aspirations to someday write comics of my own—I crane my neck to see who it might be. Are my heroes subject to this crunch as well? I run his face through a mental database fed by Wizard headshots and early internet photos. I don't know him and let him be.

Not that I have much choice. I can't move. Not a muscle. And this isn't my first rodeo either—though Comic-Con is a new, mindblowing experience, I have the benefit of having been raised at music festivals by my party animal of a mother. I'm equipped with all kinds of mechanisms for escaping this kind of crowd. The polite "excuse me, excuse me, excuse me" as you forge ahead like a snake through tall grass. The turtle-esque tuck-and-move. The crowdsurf.

Turns out, none of those work here. This is a place of equality in pain. This is the crunch. We will never feel the Gaslamp under our feet. The Transformer seems to turn its cold robotic eyes and whisper a truth I can't yet admit to myself.

We live here now.

The crunch has evolved.

I'm twenty-four years old, I'm selling my very first creator-owned comic book at San Diego Comic-Con, and I've unthinkingly walked into the oldest trap in Comic-Con history. This time, the crunch extends in both directions—meaning that even as I exit away from the Gaslamp, the sweat and smell and foam core closes in like a trash compactor and stops me right in my tracks before I can even see my hotel on the horizon. Moreover, because this is my first year with an Exhibitor Badge and it's a Sunday, I'm holding two huge boxes stacked with unsold copies of *Freakshow*. I cannot put them down. I cannot move forward.

The crunch has me in its clutches once again. But this time, it's got some tricks up its sleeve.

The first trick is a wisecracking dude stuck right next to me who has decided to use this very captive audience to make some very bad jokes. My arms may be dying but I can at least make a play to engage him at my own expense, saving others from dealing with his heckling. It's only after I've started our back-and-forth that I notice that the letters on his chest.

Professional Badge. I don't know him. But when he figures that out, that my conversation doesn't come from idolatry, dude manages to push through the crunch by sheer force of will. How dare I, who do I think I am, etc., etc.

The crunch seems to part for him, just enough to give him space from me. Even here, the caste system is apparent.

A few moments later, I find myself standing next to an old-school movie star. He is kind and courteous. He asks me for a copy of my comic, which I freely give, just as the crunch breaks and disposes us all out onto the chaotic streets of San Diego.

Over the course of that week, I've been told over and over again all the things I'm doing wrong. My logo's too illegible. My printing's on the wrong stock. Our lettering isn't professional. Our storytelling instincts are off. Though I can hold my book in my hands, it feels a million miles from where my ambition wants to take me. But a little kindness from a stranger, famous or not, reminds me that we're all in this weird crunch together—and I promise myself quietly that I'll never get pissed at someone for not knowing who I am.

Even if it's clear that no one will ever know who I am.

The crunch knows who I am.

I'm twenty-eight and with my age has come experience. Turns out, this whole time, there's been a bridge beyond Hall H, connecting across the main thoroughfare and heading into the Gaslamp from the back, near Petco Park. A secret hack for those in the know, a way to separate myself from the dregs of the con and allow myself room to breathe—and a near-zero chance at being stuck near a Star Lord cosplayer who won't stop playing his walkman. It'll add fifteen minutes to the walk back to my hotel, but it's worth it. I've beaten the crunch.

I'm experienced by this point, I don't even pause in my stride as I get as close to Hall H as possible from the inside of the convention center before bursting through the doors—past the main crunch nexus—and using my well-honed concert-navigation skills to find the freedom that lies beyond.

My ambition, a weight though it is, has paid off—I'm sporting a Pro Badge for the third time. I've sold through the stock of my new book and am not responsible for carrying a damn thing out of this convention except the signed Drew Struzan poster on which I spent all my money. I feel like a million bucks. I feel like a king. Maybe no one knows who I am . . .

. . . But I stayed out of the damn crunch.

The crunch knows. And it is unrelenting.

I'm thirty-two years old and though my words have graced the lips of Batman, no one knows who I am. And unlike the twenty-something kid who thought so highly of himself and his caste-climbing, I've managed to see beyond my ambition. The fun of these shows is no longer hoping the right person will buy my book, or let me pitch, or give me a pat on the back. It's become a once-a-year opportunity to see my friends in the comics community, to decompress from the bullshit. The Pro Badge no longer means anything—I still think of myself as a fan. I still walk around completely unrecognized. I've learned to love it.

Or at least I think I have. See, this day was a challenge. It's my one and only signing at the DC booth that year. My writing partner and I have our names in lights and videos showing our stupid faces, but the truth is there's not a person in line to get one of our many cancelled series signed. Instead, our line extends for ages in an effort to get time with one of DC's big guns, an awesome dude who's been driving these kids wild for years with capes and tights and big-budget adventure. We're the opening act. We're the amuse-bouche. And we know it.

And as much as I hate to admit it, it's a little sad. You made it. But it turns out, no one cares.

One by one, people pass by and chat with the guy seated directly next to us. One or two folks bring a copy of a random issue of ours they found, with a compliment or a hushed "thanks." Mostly, we just smile and wave and crack jokes with the fans who've come to see their favorite writer, who is absolutely definitely not us.

One fan in particular picks up on something I say and we go round and round with excitement about the new Green Lantern series. It's a nice moment. It's the only thing I remember from that signing. Just a couple folks laughing about space. As if the divide wasn't there. "At least there was that," I think to myself. "A moment of connection. I made a friend."

But that optimism is not to last, because I've got a lunch meeting off-site. In the middle of the Gaslamp. And there's no time to take the bridge.

If you want to make the crunch laugh, tell it your plans.

So once again, I'm packed with nearly two hundred people in an exit corridor trying to get to the Gaslamp. I don't recognize the cosplayer who body-checks me; my anime blind spot is showing. But I do manage a little joke about how no matter what planet we're from, we're all in this together. A meager way of making myself feel better. Which elicits exactly one laugh, from right behind me.

"Hey, wait, aren't you the guy who was just signing at DC?"

I look back and there he is—the fan who loved Green Lantern as much as me. His 4-Day pass hangs around his neck. My Pro Badge is rotated but the jig is up. My joke is more right than I know—we are, regardless of our position here at the con, in this together. As the crowd slowly moves, a shuffling snail of bodies oozing across the bottlenecked train tracks into San Diego, this dude and his friend realize they've got something of a captive Q&A—I'm in an impromptu spotlight panel for two fans who've never read my work. For a moment, I'm terrified. I think of shuffling away. Of hiding. Of being anywhere else.

And then I remember. I remember being them at twenty-four. I remember the look in that writer's eyes when I didn't know him. I remember being left alone in the crunch and the silent promise I made to myself. So instead of shutting down . . .

I just geek out.

We talk about Marvel, where I've never worked. We talk about Batman. We talk about how much we love our favorite books and what news broke this weekend and where we live and who we are. The crunch fades away and we're just three friends chatting about comics. Pretty soon, we're in the middle of the Gaslamp just talking—enjoying the things we love and sharing that love with each other. The crunch is a distant memory. I'm twenty minutes late to my lunch because I just want to keep gabbing with these folks. I'm not forced there. We're not arm-to-arm. We found friendship in the crunch and we used it to break through.

I thank them. I don't think they know why.

And as we part ways, them to their train and me to my lunch, I think back to my many years complaining about the crunch and marvel how I could've been so wrong. Because though our relationship felt so personal, me and the crunch, it was never a trap for me. Sure, it may have seemed like some monster lurking in the dark, tracking me until the next time my foot crossed over into its lair, waiting to pull me back in. But it wasn't after me. It was after everyone.

How many friends did I miss out on, just by being in my own head? How many great conversations did I miss while I let the wheels of anxiety turn? I promise myself that next year, I won't run from this inevitable disaster. I'll embrace it. Or at least, I'll try.

After all, we were all equal in the crunch.

And we always will be.

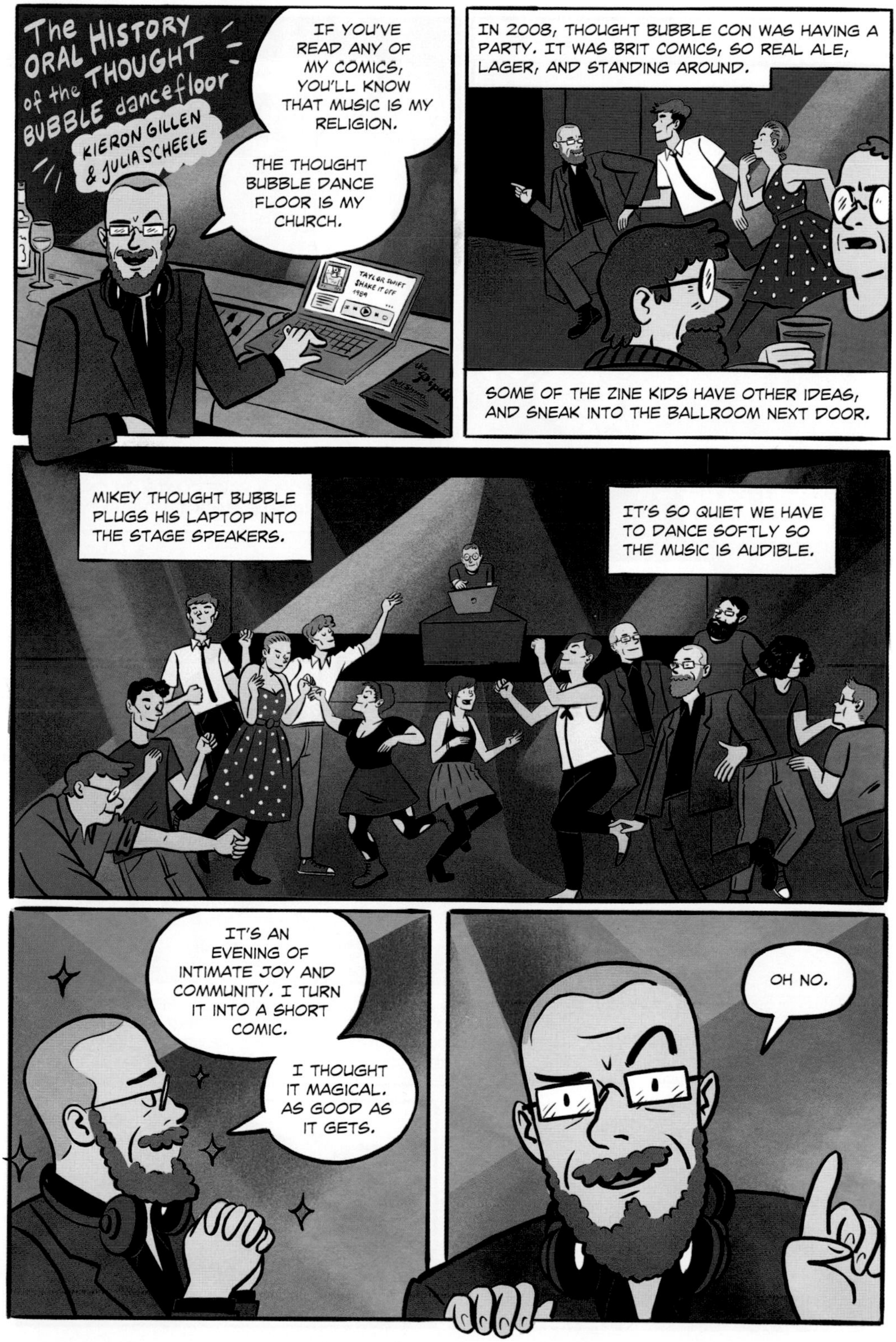
The Oral History of the Thought Bubble dancefloor
Kieron Gillen & Julia Scheele
IF YOU'VE READ ANY OF MY COMICS, YOU'LL KNOW THAT MUSIC IS MY RELIGION.
THE THOUGHT BUBBLE DANCE FLOOR IS MY CHURCH.
TAYLOR SWIFT SHAKE IT OFF 1989
IN 2008, THOUGHT BUBBLE CON WAS HAVING A PARTY. IT WAS BRIT COMICS, SO REAL ALE, LAGER, AND STANDING AROUND.
SOME OF THE ZINE KIDS HAVE OTHER IDEAS, AND SNEAK INTO THE BALLROOM NEXT DOOR.
MIKEY THOUGHT BUBBLE PLUGS HIS LAPTOP INTO THE STAGE SPEAKERS.
IT'S SO QUIET WE HAVE TO DANCE SOFTLY SO THE MUSIC IS AUDIBLE.
IT'S AN EVENING OF INTIMATE JOY AND COMMUNITY. I TURN IT INTO A SHORT COMIC.
I THOUGHT IT MAGICAL. AS GOOD AS IT GETS.
OH NO.

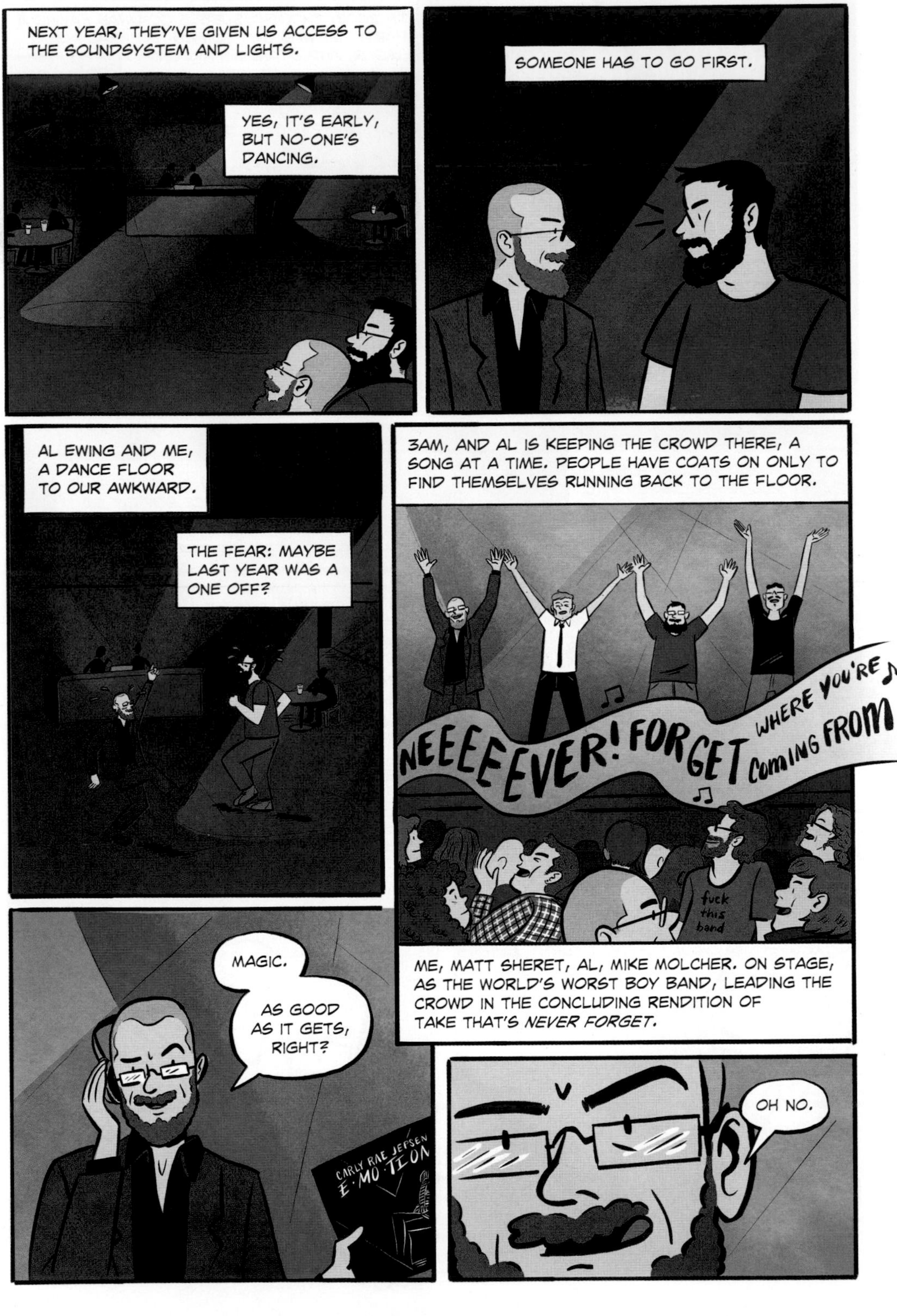
NEXT YEAR, THEY'VE GIVEN US ACCESS TO THE SOUNDSYSTEM AND LIGHTS.
YES, IT'S EARLY, BUT NO-ONE'S DANCING.
SOMEONE HAS TO GO FIRST.
AL EWING AND ME, A DANCE FLOOR TO OUR AWKWARD.
THE FEAR: MAYBE LAST YEAR WAS A ONE OFF?
3AM, AND AL IS KEEPING THE CROWD THERE, A SONG AT A TIME. PEOPLE HAVE COATS ON ONLY TO FIND THEMSELVES RUNNING BACK TO THE FLOOR.
NEEEEEVER! FORGET WHERE YOU'RE COMING FROM
fuck this band
ME, MATT SHERET, AL, MIKE MOLCHER. ON STAGE, AS THE WORLD'S WORST BOY BAND, LEADING THE CROWD IN THE CONCLUDING RENDITION OF TAKE THAT'S *NEVER FORGET*.
MAGIC.
AS GOOD AS IT GETS, RIGHT?
CARLY RAE JEPSEN E·MO·TION
OH NO.

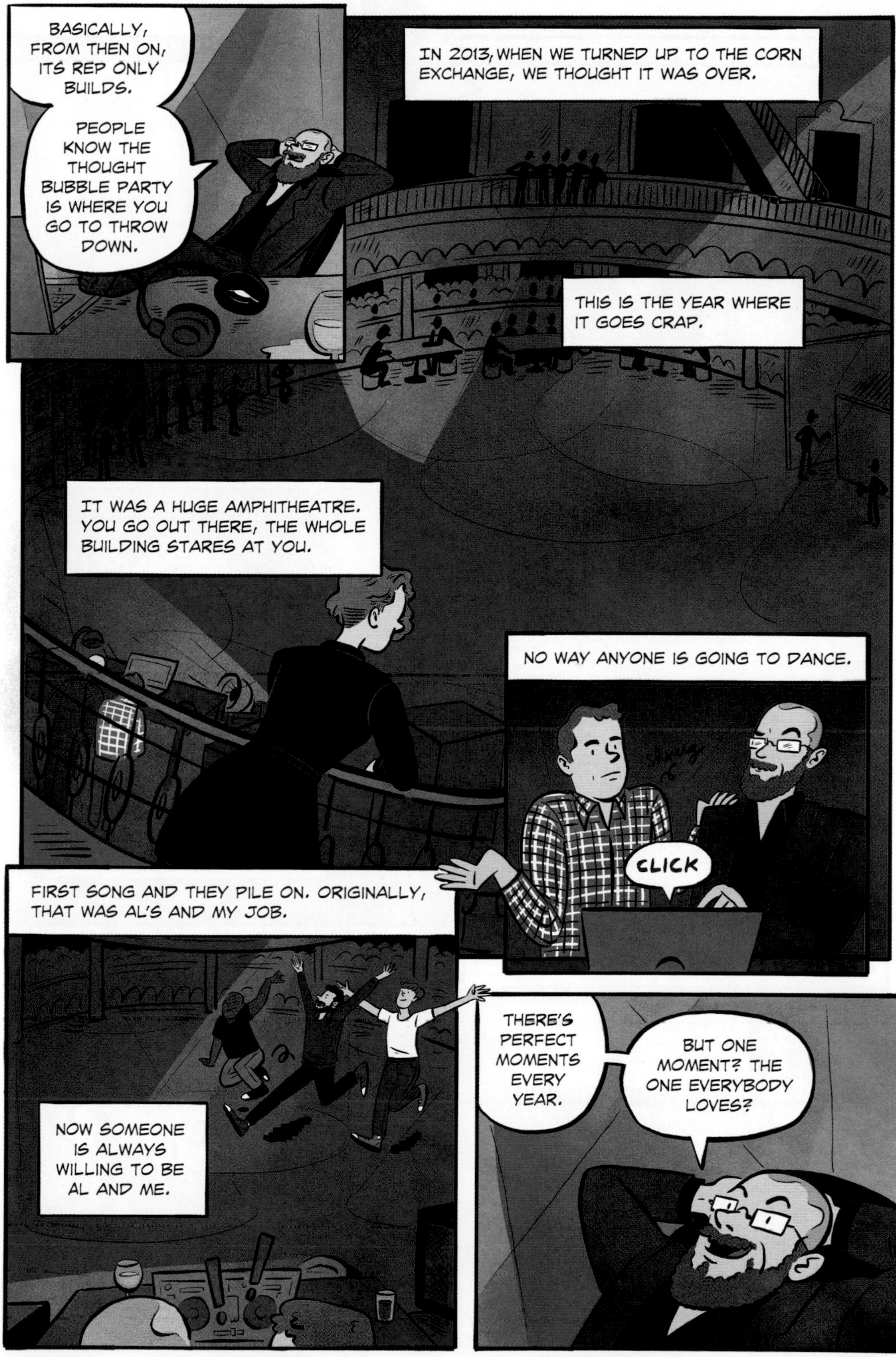
BASICALLY, FROM THEN ON, ITS REP ONLY BUILDS.
PEOPLE KNOW THE THOUGHT BUBBLE PARTY IS WHERE YOU GO TO THROW DOWN.
IN 2013, WHEN WE TURNED UP TO THE CORN EXCHANGE, WE THOUGHT IT WAS OVER.
THIS IS THE YEAR WHERE IT GOES CRAP.
IT WAS A HUGE AMPHITHEATRE. YOU GO OUT THERE, THE WHOLE BUILDING STARES AT YOU.
NO WAY ANYONE IS GOING TO DANCE.
CLICK
FIRST SONG AND THEY PILE ON. ORIGINALLY, THAT WAS AL'S AND MY JOB.
NOW SOMEONE IS ALWAYS WILLING TO BE AL AND ME.
THERE'S PERFECT MOMENTS EVERY YEAR.
BUT ONE MOMENT? THE ONE EVERYBODY LOVES?

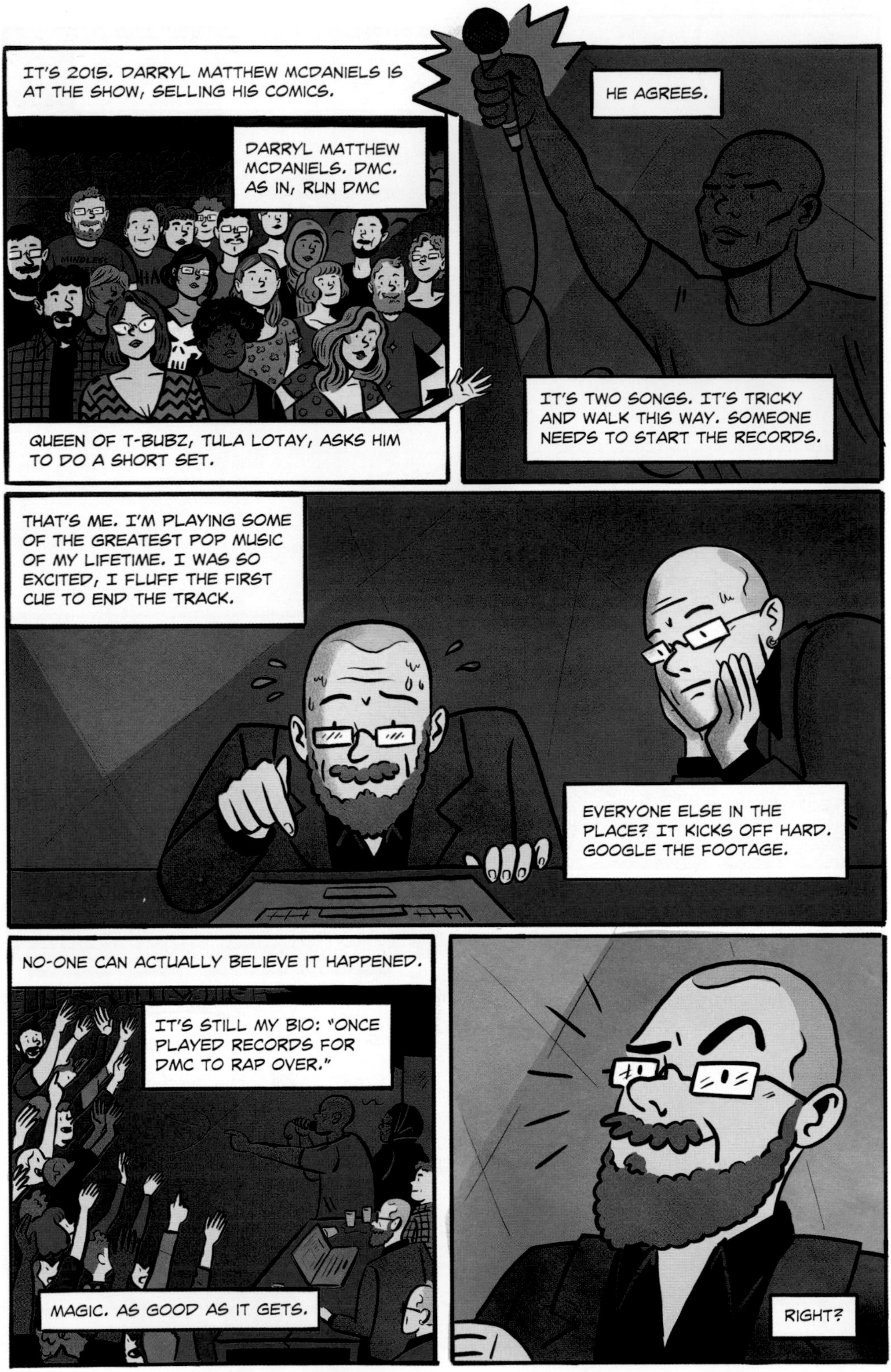
IT'S 2015. DARRYL MATTHEW MCDANIELS IS AT THE SHOW, SELLING HIS COMICS.
DARRYL MATTHEW MCDANIELS. DMC. AS IN, RUN DMC
QUEEN OF T-BUBZ, TULA LOTAY, ASKS HIM TO DO A SHORT SET.
HE AGREES.
IT'S TWO SONGS. IT'S TRICKY AND WALK THIS WAY. SOMEONE NEEDS TO START THE RECORDS.
THAT'S ME. I'M PLAYING SOME OF THE GREATEST POP MUSIC OF MY LIFETIME. I WAS SO EXCITED, I FLUFF THE FIRST CUE TO END THE TRACK.
EVERYONE ELSE IN THE PLACE? IT KICKS OFF HARD. GOOGLE THE FOOTAGE.
NO-ONE CAN ACTUALLY BELIEVE IT HAPPENED.
IT'S STILL MY BIO: "ONCE PLAYED RECORDS FOR DMC TO RAP OVER."
MAGIC. AS GOOD AS IT GETS.
RIGHT?

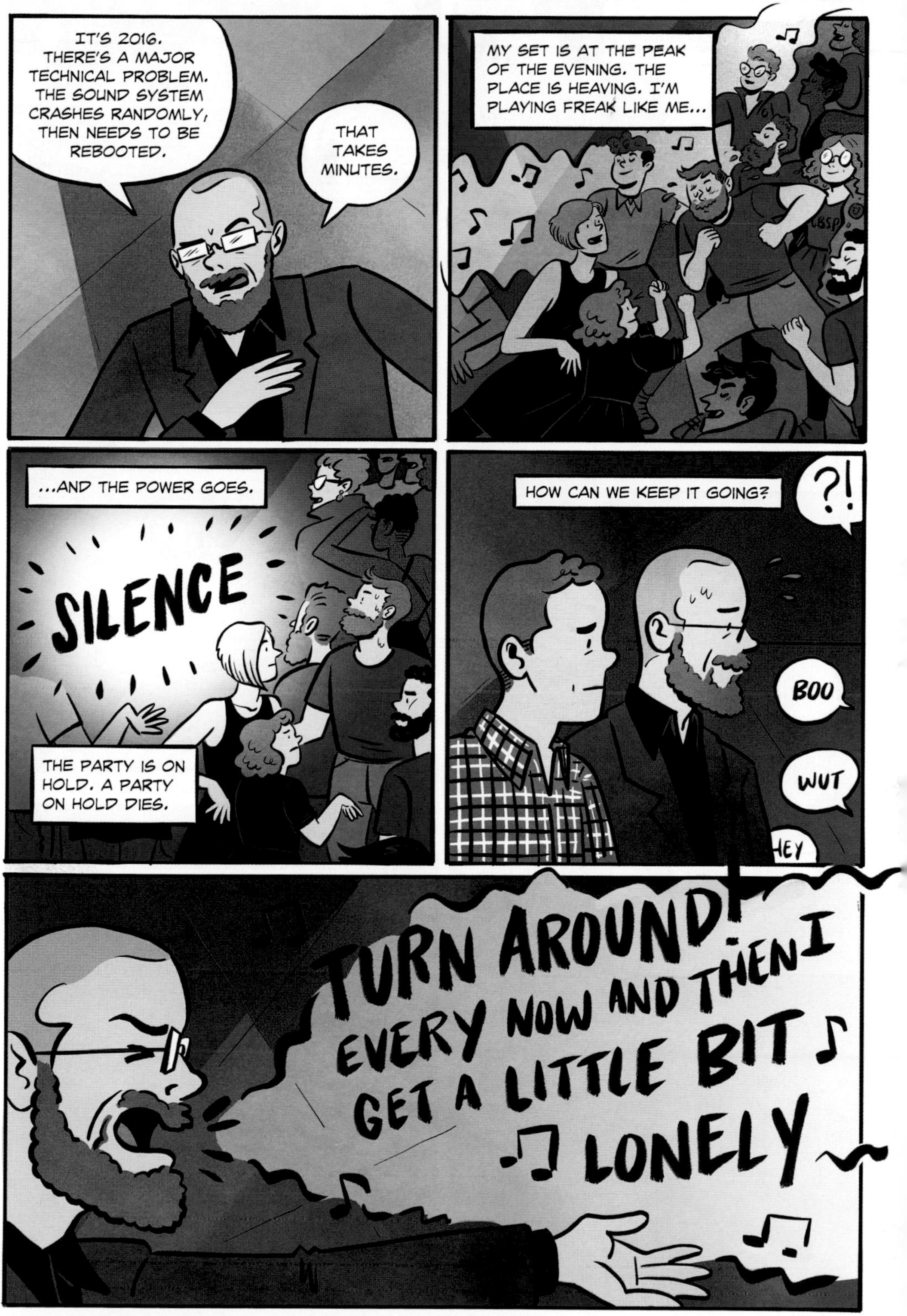
IT'S 2016. THERE'S A MAJOR TECHNICAL PROBLEM. THE SOUND SYSTEM CRASHES RANDOMLY, THEN NEEDS TO BE REBOOTED.
THAT TAKES MINUTES.
MY SET IS AT THE PEAK OF THE EVENING. THE PLACE IS HEAVING. I'M PLAYING FREAK LIKE ME...
...AND THE POWER GOES.
SILENCE
THE PARTY IS ON HOLD. A PARTY ON HOLD DIES.
HOW CAN WE KEEP IT GOING?
?!
BOO
WUT
HEY
TURN AROUND!
EVERY NOW AND THEN I
GET A LITTLE BIT
LONELY

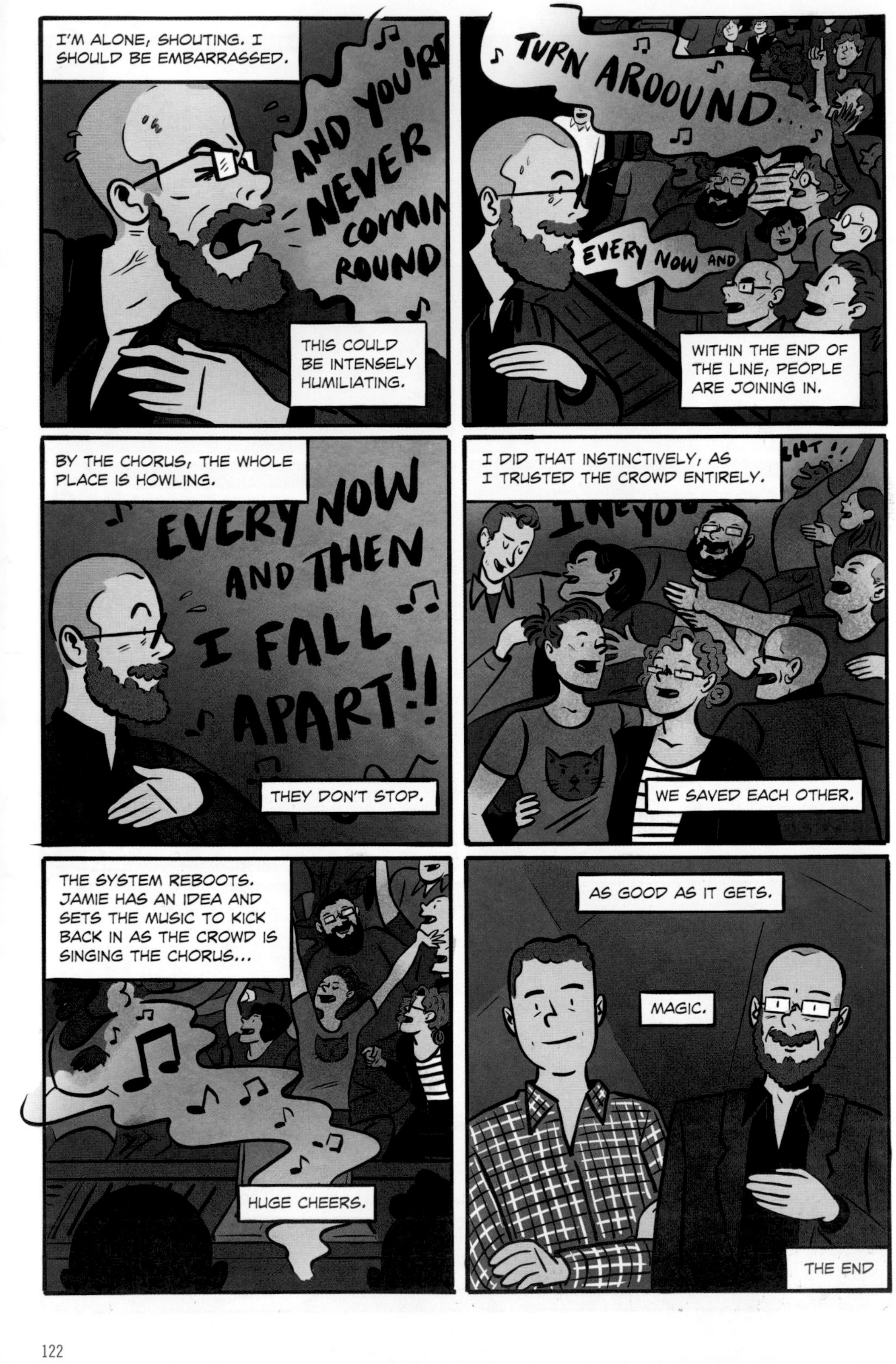
I'M ALONE, SHOUTING. I SHOULD BE EMBARRASSED.
AND YOU'R NEVER COMIN ROUND
THIS COULD BE INTENSELY HUMILIATING.
TURN AROOUND...
EVERY NOW AND
WITHIN THE END OF THE LINE, PEOPLE ARE JOINING IN.
BY THE CHORUS, THE WHOLE PLACE IS HOWLING.
EVERY NOW AND THEN I FALL APART!!
THEY DON'T STOP.
I DID THAT INSTINCTIVELY, AS I TRUSTED THE CROWD ENTIRELY.
WE SAVED EACH OTHER.
THE SYSTEM REBOOTS. JAMIE HAS AN IDEA AND SETS THE MUSIC TO KICK BACK IN AS THE CROWD IS SINGING THE CHORUS...
HUGE CHEERS.
AS GOOD AS IT GETS.
MAGIC.
THE END

FOLLOW THE GOTHS

Bonnie Burton

When you're a geek, there's nothing more exciting than getting lost at San Diego Comic-Con in the labyrinth of vendors selling everything from vintage *Star Wars* comic books to Batman codpieces. But when you have a deep-seated fear of crowds and you're stuck in a sea of sweaty collectors and Groot cosplayers, panic can set in almost immediately.

When I had my first panic attack at a comic convention, I was at a standstill in the middle of an irate swarm of Stormtroopers. I felt silly to be complaining to the group of guys who were probably even more uncomfortable than I was considering their stifling white armor and helmets.

But I felt helpless. The exit seemed like it was miles away and I really needed to escape the crowds, the noise, the stale air, the everything.

So, a helpful member of the 501st Legion—the official name of the *Star Wars* Stormtrooper cosplayer community—grabbed my hand and guided me through the crowd while yelling that he captured one of the Rebels who stole the Death Star plans.

My hero suddenly made me part of his *Star Wars* roleplaying act, and even though I looked more like a tired, nervous fangirl instead of Princess Leia, it worked. My Stormtrooper in white shining armor made the masses of attendees part like the Red Sea, and we were soon transported to a more secluded area where everyone in armor seemed to hang out.

Among the many Stormtroopers, everyone in this almost secret area of the convention was cosplaying as Darth Vader, Medieval knights, Vikings, *Halo* Master Chief, gladiators, Iron Man, Batman, and more. If there was a costume where heavy armor and helmets were required, this was the calm, cool oasis where they all hung out.

"What is this place?" I asked my Stormtrooper savior.

"Oh, all the cosplayers who have heavy costumes and armor hang out up here away from everyone," he answered. "We can relax, fix our costumes if they rip or need some sewing, and there's plenty of space to catch our breath. It's kind of a secret."

It was fascinating to see knights compare their metal swords with Darth Vader cosplayers who had glowing lightsabers. Vikings and Klingons were laughing with each other about having to pretend to get hurt in the fake battles they would put on for fans wanting the ultimate photo.

Seeing Iron Man and Batman high-five each other about getting extra cheese on their nachos just seemed surreal in the best, geekiest way.

But it wasn't just cosplayers, this remote rest area of the convention also seemed to attract every Goth kid attending Comic-Con. It made sense. This space was quieter, full of air-conditioned places to sit and even rarer— no lines for the tiny food court outside. I had found my geek mecca.

For years, I kept this nerd Narnia area of San Diego Comic-Con a secret from my friends. I didn't want to give away the fact that I knew the one spot at a crowded convention where I could finally stop freaking out after getting my feet run over from a baby stroller, or accidentally stomped on by a *T. Rex* cosplayer with too many blindspots.

Whenever I felt the pangs of dread from too many people surrounding me, I would sneak off to my Comic-Con safety zone for a cool-down break and the occasional churro.

Then I'd rejoin my friends and co-workers who all wanted to know where I disappeared to and why I suddenly looked so cool and collected. But, I never revealed my private trick to circumvent Comic-Con insanity.

Not all geek conventions have the same hideout areas as San Diego Comic-Con, so you have to be more diligent in discovering the safety zone where air conditioning, wide open spaces and easy-access nachos can be found.

Following Stormtroopers and Master Chiefs won't always get you quick access to the hidden sanctuary, especially since they often have to stop every five feet to take photos with fans on a mission for the ultimate geek selfie.

I once followed a Darth Vader around for almost an hour only to end up in the middle of a crowded mass of fans all trying to get a selfie with

Doctor Who actor David Tennant, who seemed as nervous as I was to be trapped in a mob.

That's where Goth kids come in handy. Anytime I was starting to feel a panic attack creep its way into my brain, I would frantically look for a very annoyed Goth. Granted, as a recovering Goth myself, I realize that our resting face is usually that of being perpetually perturbed. But, the more vexed a Goth looks, the more likely they are headed to the one place in the con they can be left alone to relax and silently judge everyone who rushes by.

My chance to test out my theory came one year at Emerald City Comic Con in Seattle. I was boxed in by a large gathering of Guardians of the Galaxy cosplayers who had suddenly swarmed the spot I was standing in to do a group meet-up. Large Groot cosplayers repeatedly bumped into me, accidentally smacked me with their arm branches and eventually pinned me to a wall as they snapped photo after photo.

I felt like that kid attacked by the demonic trees outside his bedroom window in the movie Poltergeist. There seemed to be no way out, and as I was panicking that my lifeless body would eventually be discovered with bits of foam and fake tree bark coming out of mouth, I spotted him—a Goth!

I squirmed out from behind a dancing Groot who was oblivious to my plight, and slowly made my way to the Goth. Dressed like he was the lovechild of Nine Inch Nails frontman Trent Reznor and the Death Note demon Ryuk, it was clear from his exasperated expression that he was fed up with being on the vendor floor of the convention and needed some space.

So I made a beeline for him and followed him through the crowds, up the stairs, past artist booths and to what looked like a Batman lair full of dark-clothed Goths all looking vaguely shell-shocked.

I found it! The Goth Oasis. And soon I realized I could find these secret destinations at every convention I attended just by finding the Goths in a crowd. I knew that panic attacks would be a thing of the past if I could always single out a Goth at a convention.

Other bonuses of following Goths include no sunburns. They hate direct sunlight—so there's zero threat of ending up outside in the path of the sun. Goths aren't too keen on loud noises either. I could be assured I wouldn't be stuck next to a speaker at a video game booth where techno and sounds of machine gun salvo would trigger convention PTSD.

And Goths love to sit and contemplate the world around them. That means plenty of comfy seating wherever they end up. This is key when you're tired from wandering from booth to booth for hours, and just want to take a load off.

No one likes sitting on the floor. You never know if you'll randomly sit in a wet spot of spilled soda or pierce your butt on a stray safety pin flung from a cosplayer's haphazardly fixed costume. The worst is accidentally sitting in a pile of glitter. That stuff is forever. It's not nicknamed the herpes of the craft world for nothing.

Goths understand that sitting on the floor is for amateurs. If you want a real chair—and not a rickety food court folding chair—then follow a Goth until he or she sits down.

This is how I found out that the Washington State Convention Center (where Emerald City Comic Con takes place) has hidden nooks and crannies with soft-upholstered arm chairs scattered throughout. Denver Comic Con has squishy, comfy chairs in the back area by scarcely attended comic book collecting panels. And Portland's Rose City Comic Con has chairs and sofas near the small bistros and cafes inside.

Perhaps it sounds silly to everyone who gets excited about flocking to their favorite comic book conventions every year, but when social anxiety hits you like a Hulk punch, there's nothing scarier than feeling like you're trapped without a way out.

Next time you're at a big convention, scan the faces of everyone around you. Among the throngs of happy, thrilled, and ecstatic fans, there will be plenty of others who look like a deer trapped in headlights. We are a proud but easily annoyed group of geeks. And even though we're as excited as you are to shop for our favorite collectibles and take selfies with Wonder Woman, we need places to sneak off to and recoup.

I know now that panic attacks, freak-outs, and an extreme sense of claustrophobia are my curse as a life-long nerd who still loves to go to conventions. But with the help of Goths who never need to stop and take photos with fans or do group shots in the middle of the convention floor, I know I will find salvation . . . or at least to shorter lines for snacks and an armchair directly under the air conditioning vent.

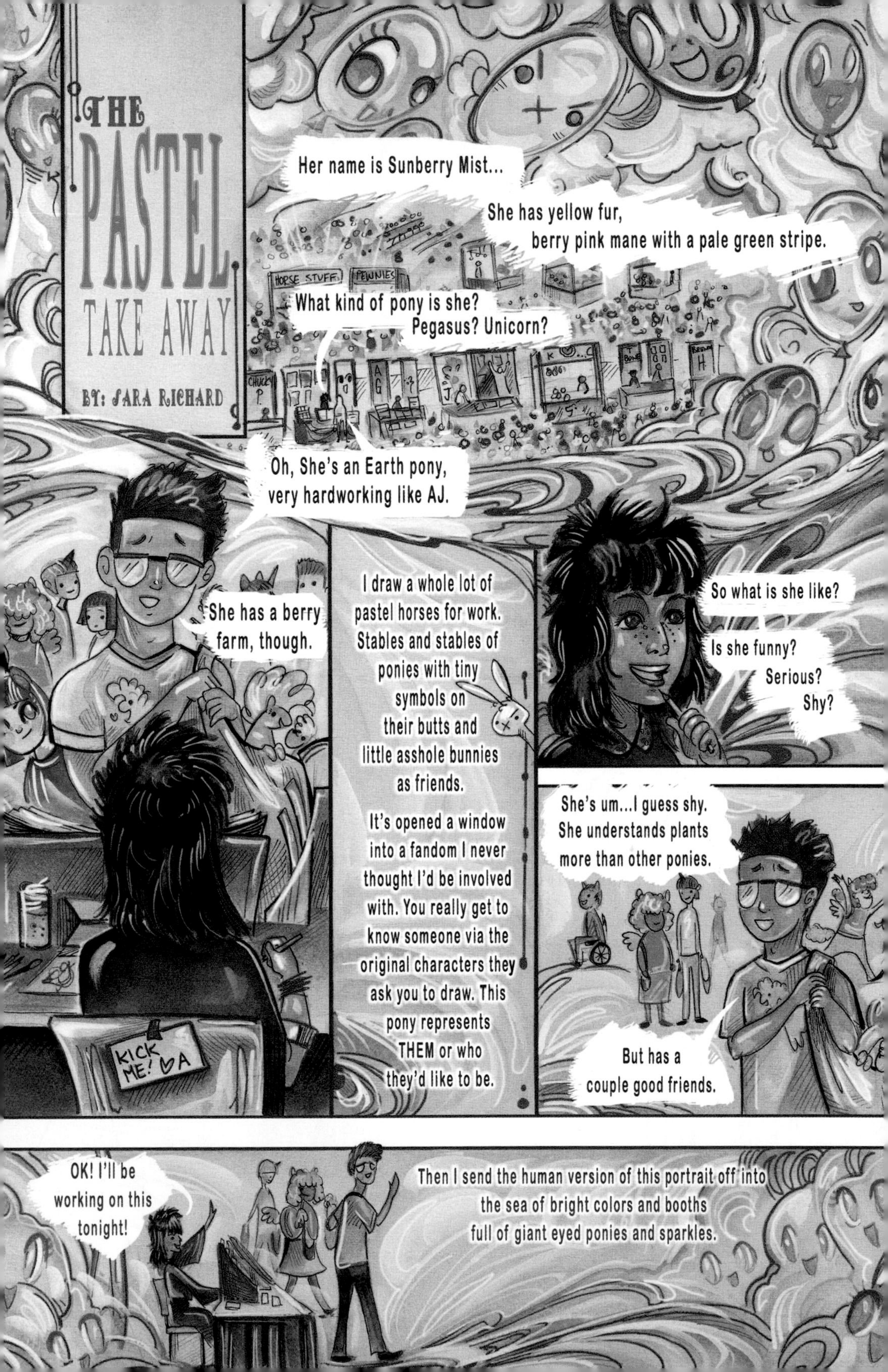
THE PASTEL TAKE AWAY
BY: SARA RICHARD
Her name is Sunberry Mist...
She has yellow fur, berry pink mane with a pale green stripe.
HORSE STUFF
PEWNIES
What kind of pony is she? Pegasus? Unicorn?
Oh, She's an Earth pony, very hardworking like AJ.
She has a berry farm, though.
I draw a whole lot of pastel horses for work. Stables and stables of ponies with tiny symbols on their butts and little asshole bunnies as friends.
It's opened a window into a fandom I never thought I'd be involved with. You really get to know someone via the original characters they ask you to draw. This pony represents THEM or who they'd like to be.
KICK ME! ♡A
So what is she like?
Is she funny? Serious? Shy?
She's um...I guess shy. She understands plants more than other ponies.
But has a couple good friends.
OK! I'll be working on this tonight!
Then I send the human version of this portrait off into the sea of bright colors and booths full of giant eyed ponies and sparkles.

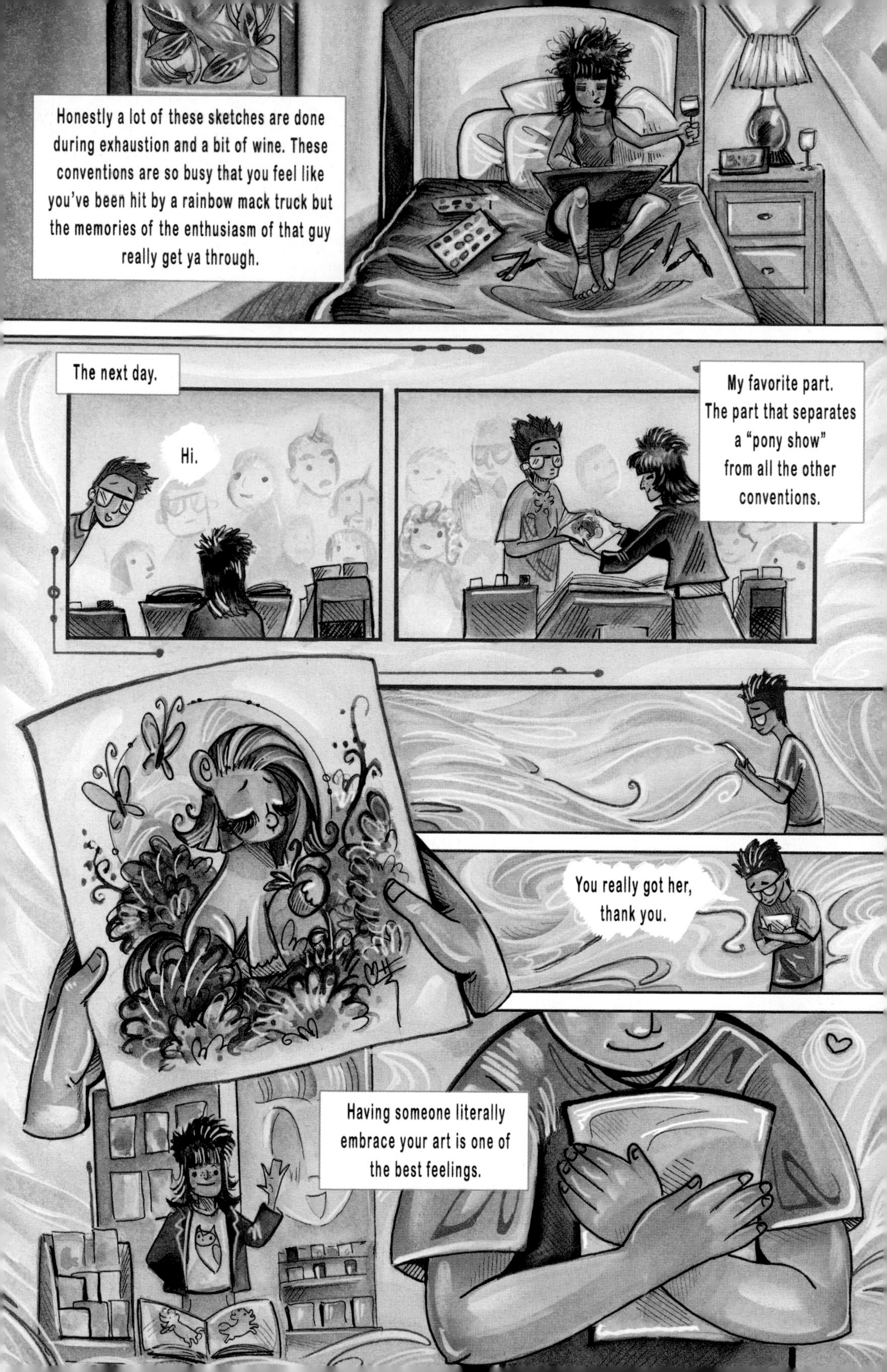

Honestly a lot of these sketches are done during exhaustion and a bit of wine. These conventions are so busy that you feel like you've been hit by a rainbow mack truck but the memories of the enthusiasm of that guy really get ya through.
The next day.
Hi.
My favorite part. The part that separates a "pony show" from all the other conventions.
You really got her, thank you.
Having someone literally embrace your art is one of the best feelings.

MY INEVITABLE DOOM

BY: BARBARA GUTTMAN

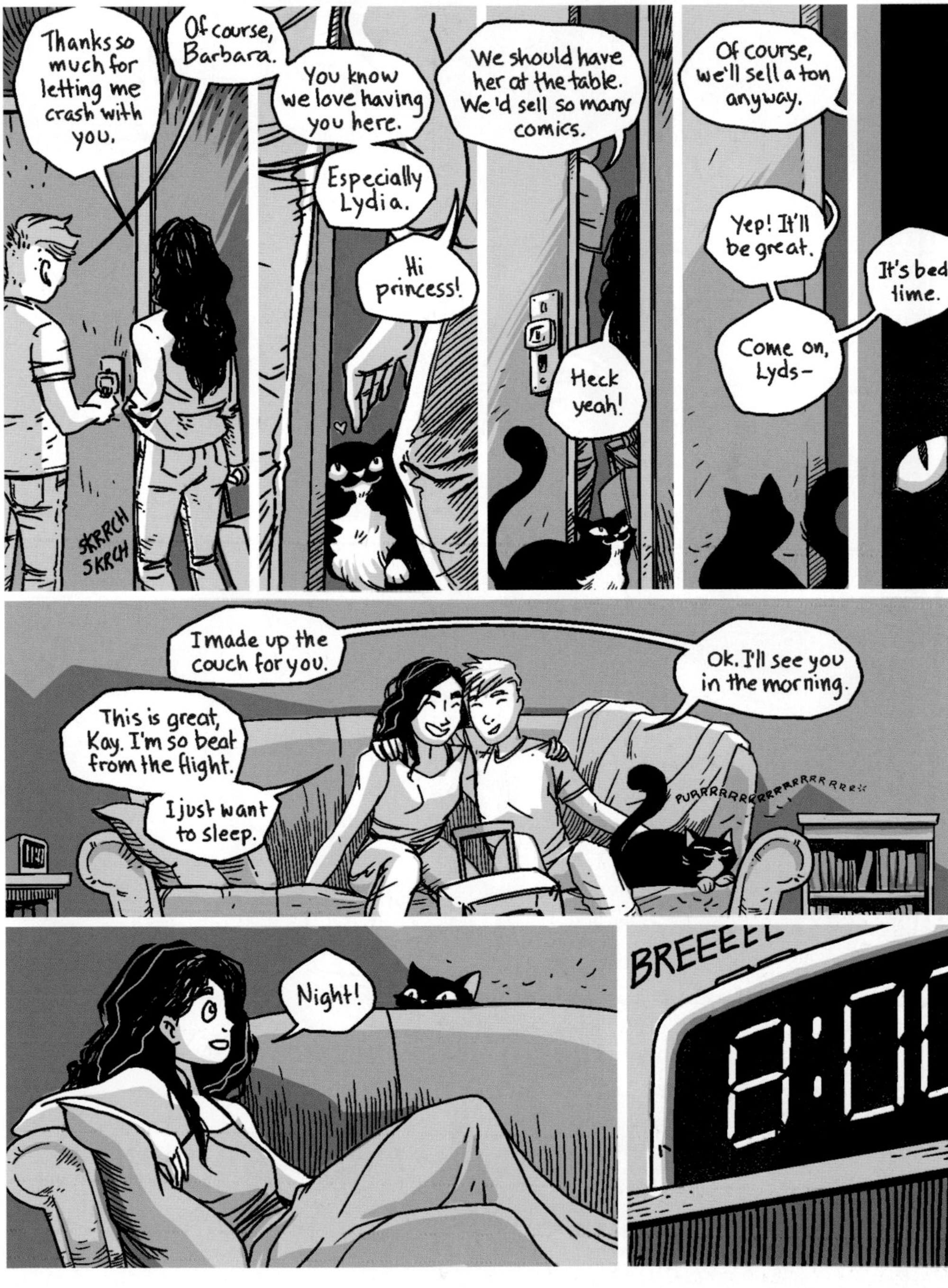

Thanks so much for letting me crash with you.
Of course, Barbara.
You know we love having you here.
Especially Lydia.
Hi princess!
SKRRCH SKRCH
We should have her at the table. We'd sell so many comics.
Heck yeah!
Of course, we'll sell a ton anyway.
Yep! It'll be great.
Come on, Lyds-
It's bed time.
I made up the couch for you.
Ok. I'll see you in the morning.
This is great, Kay. I'm so beat from the flight.
I just want to sleep.
PURRRRRRRRRRRRRRRRRRRRR
Night!
BREEEEE

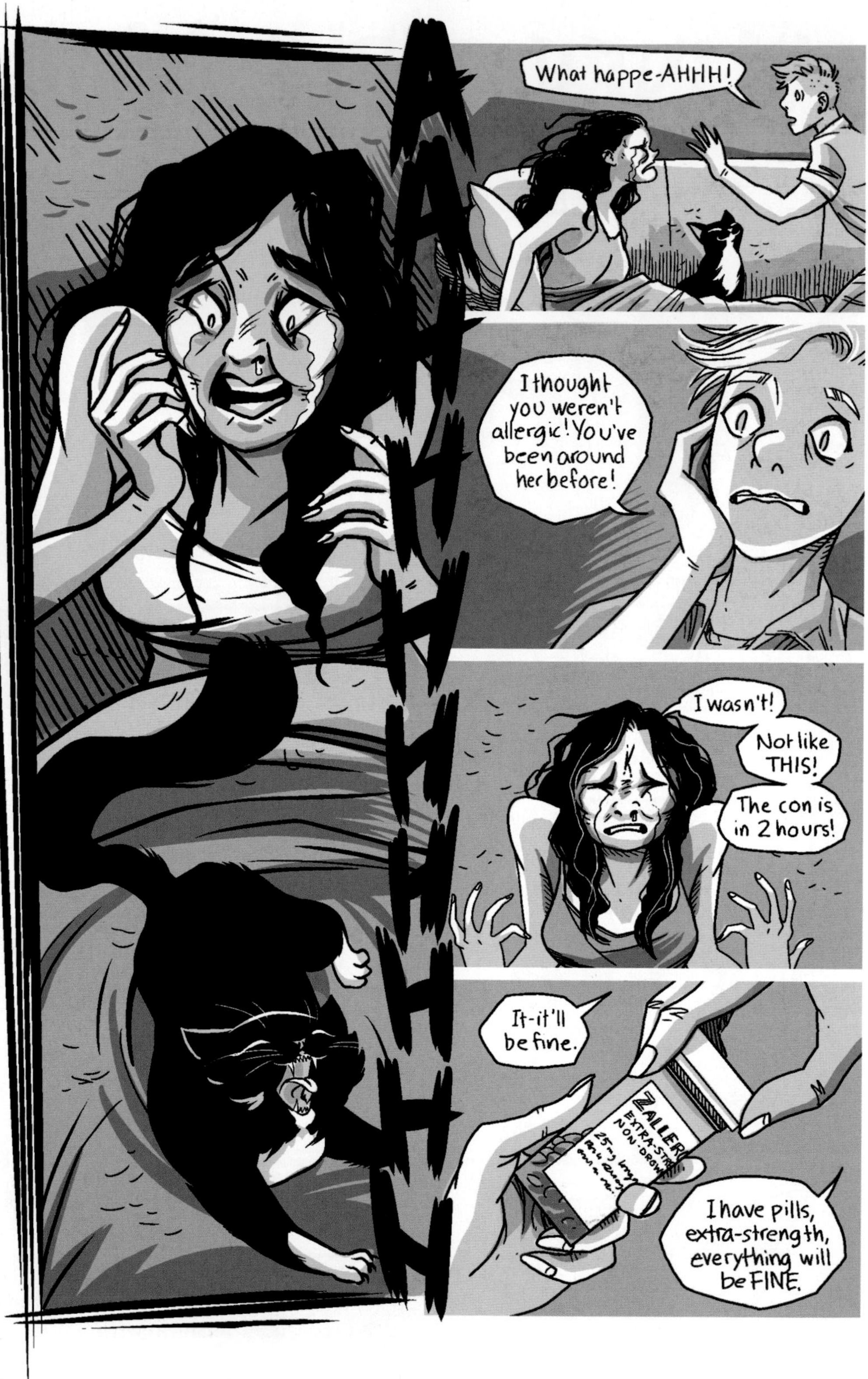
AAHHHHHHHH
What happe-AHHH!
I thought you weren't allergic! You've been around her before!
I wasn't!
Not like THIS!
The con is in 2 hours!
It-it'll be fine.
I have pills, extra-strength, everything will be FINE.

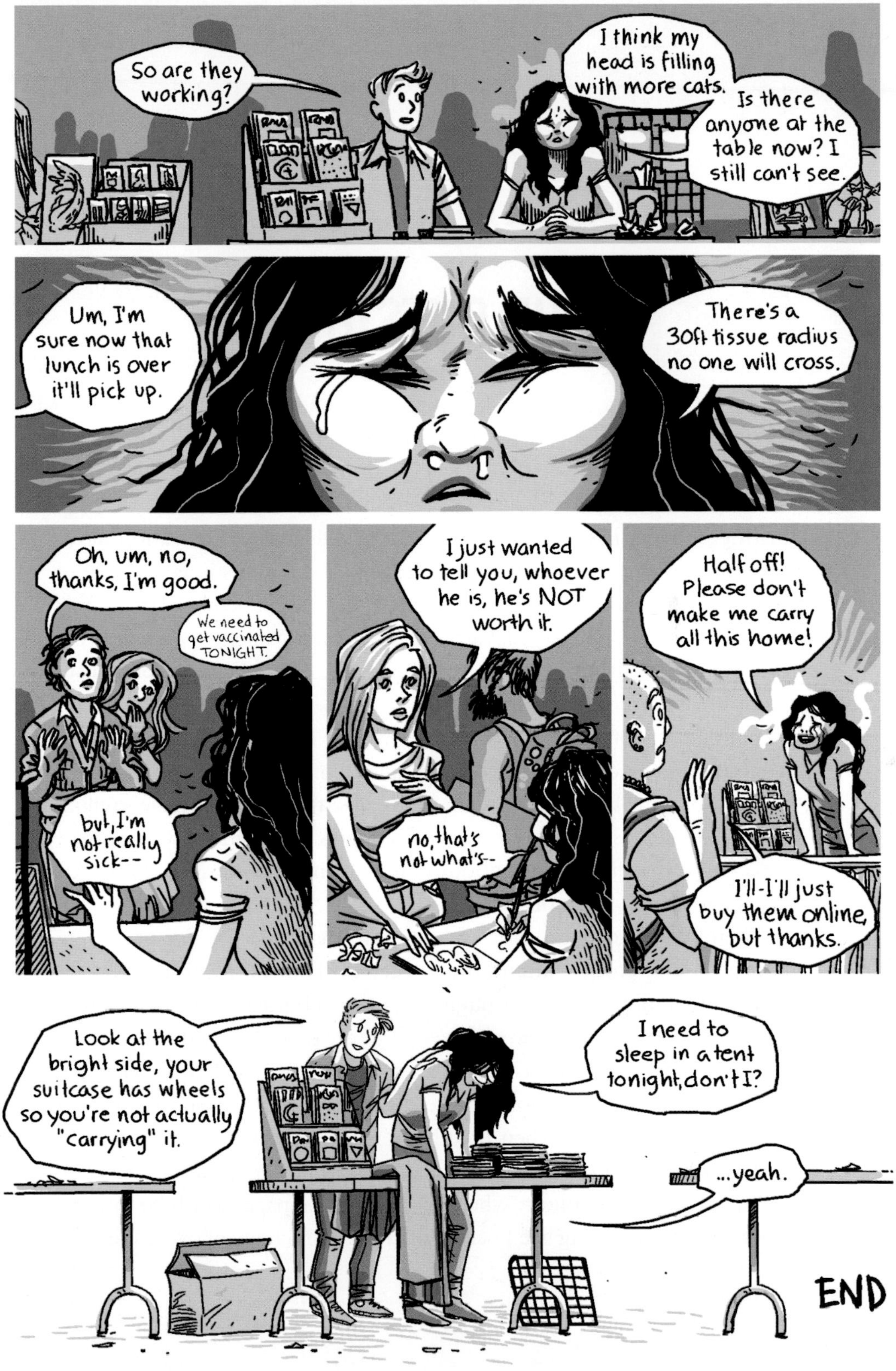
So are they working?
I think my head is filling with more cats.
Is there anyone at the table now? I still can't see.
Um, I'm sure now that lunch is over it'll pick up.
There's a 30ft tissue radius no one will cross.
Oh, um, no, thanks, I'm good.
We need to get vaccinated TONIGHT.
but, I'm not really sick--
I just wanted to tell you, whoever he is, he's NOT worth it.
no, that's not what's-
Half off! Please don't make me carry all this home!
I'll-I'll just buy them online, but thanks.
Look at the bright side, your suitcase has wheels so you're not actually "carrying" it.
I need to sleep in a tent tonight, don't I?
...yeah.
END

THE OUTSIDER

Bryan Hill

Writing, for me, has mostly been a path of solitude. Socialization never came into my mind when I first considered being a professional writer, but I had a specific understanding of what that life would be like. The writers I admired, Amy Hempel, Richard Wright, Frank Miller, *those folks*, were forces of nature. It seemed like everything they created was a report from the brink of extreme experience.

I found that comforting because my own life has exposed me to a lot of extremity. Writers didn't have to be pleasant, in my mind. Perhaps kind. Not pleasant. Not the kind of person you think of sitting behind a table, smiling and shaking hands, holding an army of Sharpies and chatting with people.

So I never really thought about conventions. Those were things for actors and artists, not writers.

When I first waded into writing comics, it was after a lifetime of reading them, of those stories finding me in very difficult times, times where I needed inspiration to move through my personal burdens. Stories of heroes overcoming adversity helped me overcome my own. It could have been a convenient delusion, but it was critically important that I could view my personal struggles in mythological terms. I read stories about heroes so I could become one, and when I felt like I gained the skill to write my own myths, I jumped into the snake-pit and tried to find my place.

I'm plagued with honesty whenever I'm on the page, so I'll be forward about never really feeling like I belonged in the community of comic creators.

I've never felt like it was a natural fit. In many ways, I'm too strange for the consensus culture, but I'm also not "nerdy" enough for the comic book subculture. My experience at conventions among other creators has been, and still is, one where I feel not quite welcome, not quite abandoned.

I'm tolerated, by the few I've known. Tolerated with civility.

I don't mind it. It is what it is, and I'm a private person by nature, so not being in the center of the clique is a dandy place for me. Conventions, for me, are incredibly awkward experiences. I tolerate them too. I appreciate how they allow fans and creators to interact and I see the strength and passion of the comics community there. It's illuminating, but I have yet to find my rhythm within the flow of the convention scene.

The reason I attend conventions is for the readers, not the other professionals. For no other reason than the way things are in this world, I am something of an anomaly. I'm a Black writer (I've never fully adopted the more gentile African American moniker) and I don't write things from what folks would call a "Black perspective," at least not all the time. Writing is a profession equated with intellect and Black men aren't often credited with intellect. We run fast. Jump high. Sing. Act.

We don't write books. At least not as an assumption.

I've come to realize from conversations with readers, from all cultures and races, that I represent a kind of possibility. The thing that makes me feel not quite in rhythm with the culture of comics is what a lot of readers respond to, being an outsider. I represent the possibility of contributing work to a culture that might not adopt them fully into its social circle, but will provide them a platform on the page. Some people are pure fans, but I find that the most dedicated fans of comics are also people who have their own stories to tell. I don't matter in comics, per se, but I have a little patch of land now and conventions are a place where I can tell people, in full honesty, that their visions of themselves *are* possible.

Conventions, for me, are also a responsibility. They're a place where I can give people the kind of positive experience I never had when I was on the other side of the table, standing in line, hoping that someone would give me a way into this world. I rarely socialize away from the floor. I never go to parties. I never go to the bar. I do the floor and then I explore the city or find solace in my hotel room with a half-decent salad and a bottle of light beer.

But conventions have changed me. Mainly they've made me more responsible and aware of the influence, intended and unintended, that creative work can have in the world.

I don't have a single, profound story. I have a collection of moments, a gestalt sense of experience from many brief memories. The POSTAL reader that tells me they've been diagnosed with Asperger's Syndrome and the portrayal of Mark in that series meant a lot to them. The kid who dreams of writing *Batman* and brightens up when I tell them, sincerely, that if I was able to do it, they can too. The young woman that comes up with a dog-eared and faded trade paperback of *ROMULUS* and tells me that the way I wrote Ashlar in that story helped them through a dark moment in their lives.

I don't think *I* am important, in fact I know I'm not, but any of us can have moments of importance, moments where we know we can make a real difference in someone's life. Perhaps because I still feel very much like an outsider, I'm able to speak to that feeling in others. Perhaps I'm holding onto that outsider feeling because it helps me define myself. It's a comfortable and familiar place for me, adversity is an old friend.

I'm still surprised when a company I'm working for gets me a pass and a hotel room. I'm grateful that now I have a floor where another creator can sleep if they need a roof for the weekend. Recently, I had my first real line and it's a surreal experience to see people waiting to meet me. I'm still that poor kid from Saint Louis who's spending lawn mowing money in his local comic book shop. I've been on panels with people I've wanted autographs from, and sometimes I still ask. Sometimes I don't. Whether I'm silent about it or not, the desire is always there.

I can't go to as many cons as I would like. Responsibilities get in the way, but I've made a promise to myself that whenever I do attend a convention, I would be there for the people who read my work, the people who are most important in the entire industry. Hollywood is a land of pretensions and silly hierarchies and comics is the one entertainment form where those things don't have to exist, where you don't have to be elevated above the people who enjoy your work. In comics, I can enjoy the creation of the work the same way people enjoy the consumption of it and we can all share that feeling on the same, solid ground.

I may never feel like I belong, but that's okay. I feel like I can make a positive difference and that's what comic conventions mean to me.

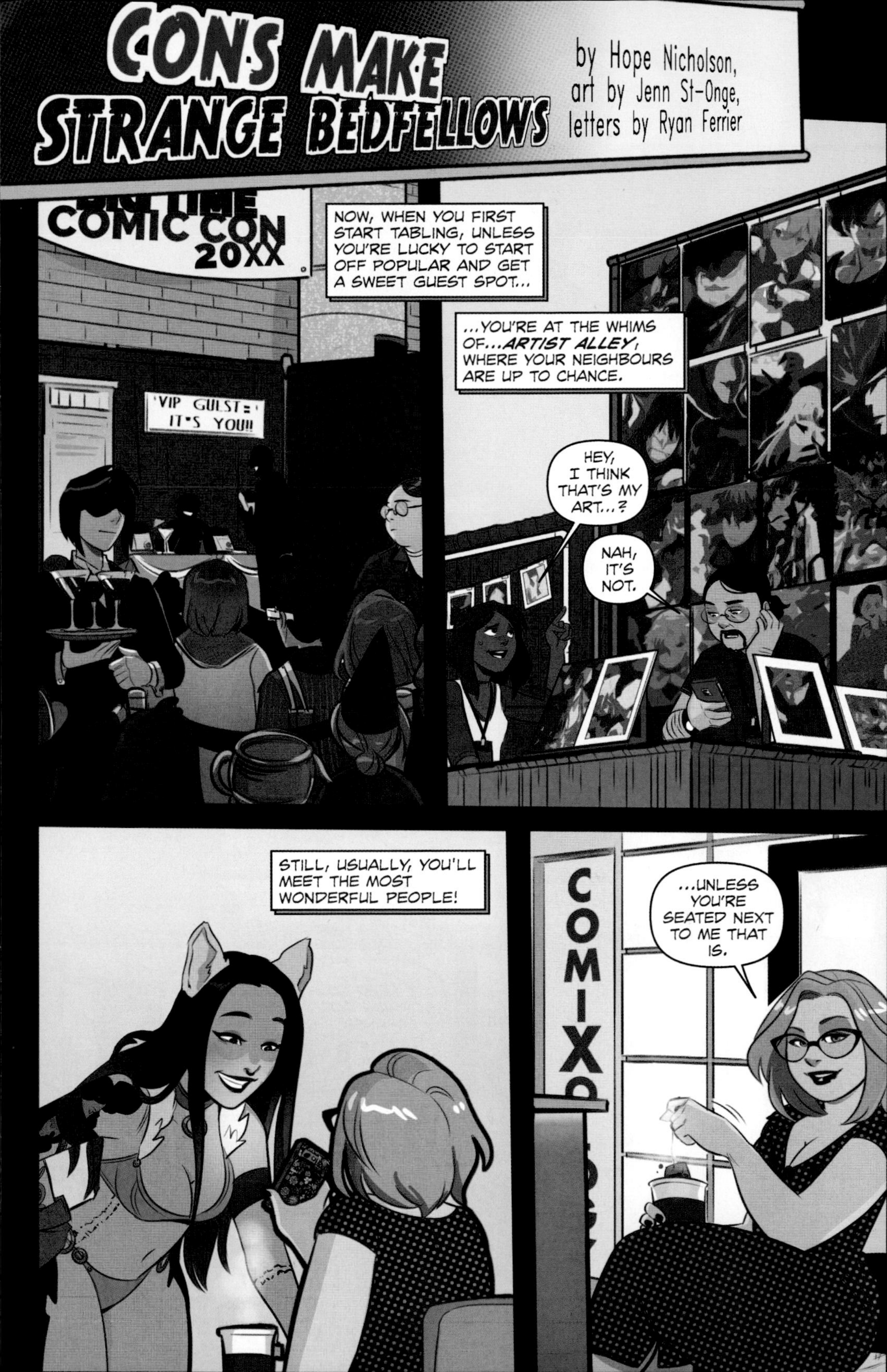
CONS MAKE STRANGE BEDFELLOWS
by Hope Nicholson, art by Jenn St-Onge, letters by Ryan Ferrier
COMIC CON 20XX
NOW, WHEN YOU FIRST START TABLING, UNLESS YOU'RE LUCKY TO START OFF POPULAR AND GET A SWEET GUEST SPOT...
'VIP GUEST' IT'S YOU!!
...YOU'RE AT THE WHIMS OF... ARTIST ALLEY, WHERE YOUR NEIGHBOURS ARE UP TO CHANCE.
HEY, I THINK THAT'S MY ART...?
NAH, IT'S NOT.
STILL, USUALLY, YOU'LL MEET THE MOST WONDERFUL PEOPLE!
...UNLESS YOU'RE SEATED NEXT TO ME THAT IS.

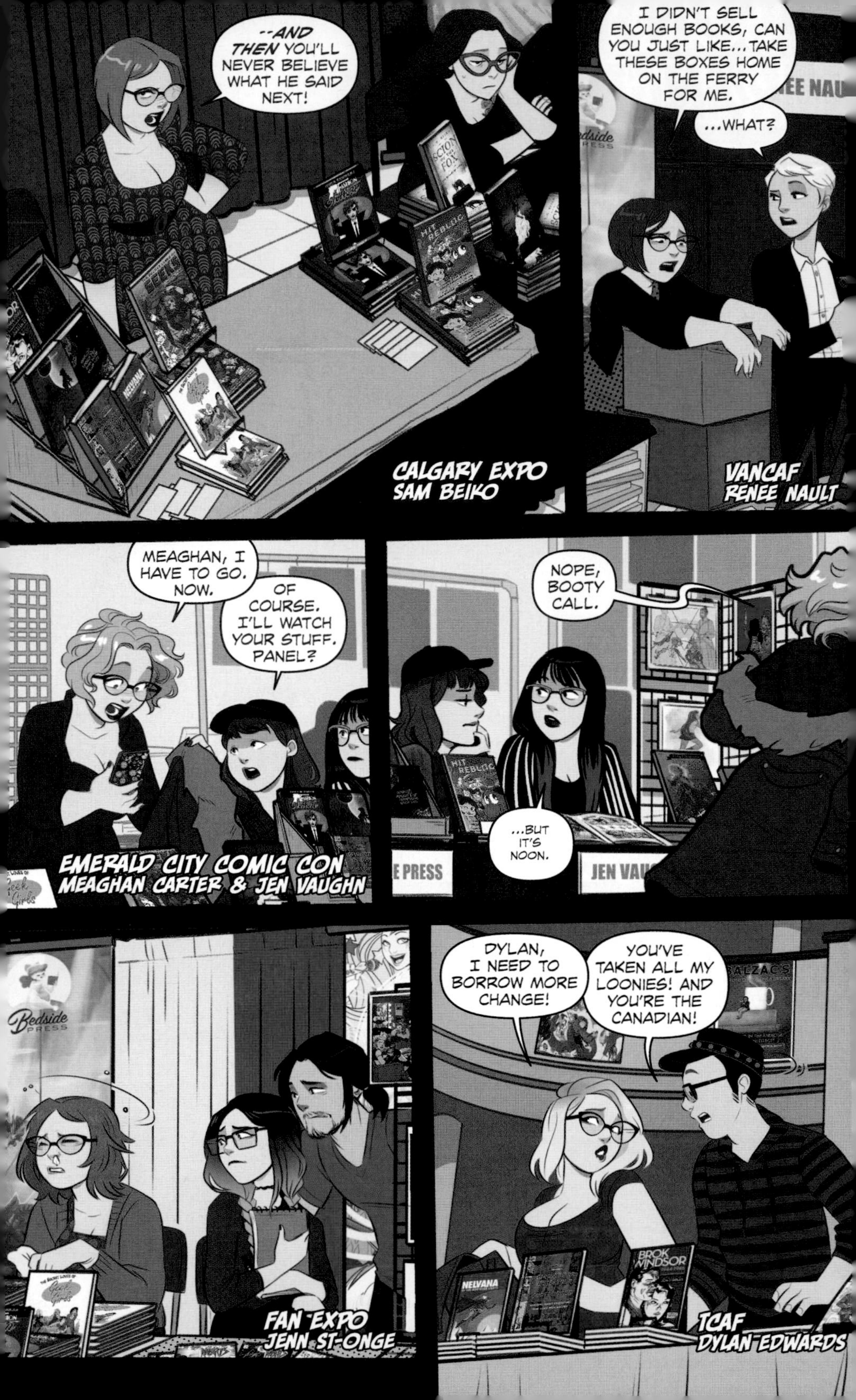
--AND THEN YOU'LL NEVER BELIEVE WHAT HE SAID NEXT!
CALGARY EXPO
SAM BEIKO
I DIDN'T SELL ENOUGH BOOKS, CAN YOU JUST LIKE...TAKE THESE BOXES HOME ON THE FERRY FOR ME.
...WHAT?
VANCAF
RENEE NAULT
MEAGHAN, I HAVE TO GO. NOW.
OF COURSE. I'LL WATCH YOUR STUFF. PANEL?
EMERALD CITY COMIC CON
MEAGHAN CARTER & JEN VAUGHN
NOPE, BOOTY CALL.
...BUT IT'S NOON.
DYLAN, I NEED TO BORROW MORE CHANGE!
YOU'VE TAKEN ALL MY LOONIES! AND YOU'RE THE CANADIAN!
FAN EXPO
JENN ST-ONGE
TCAF
DYLAN EDWARDS

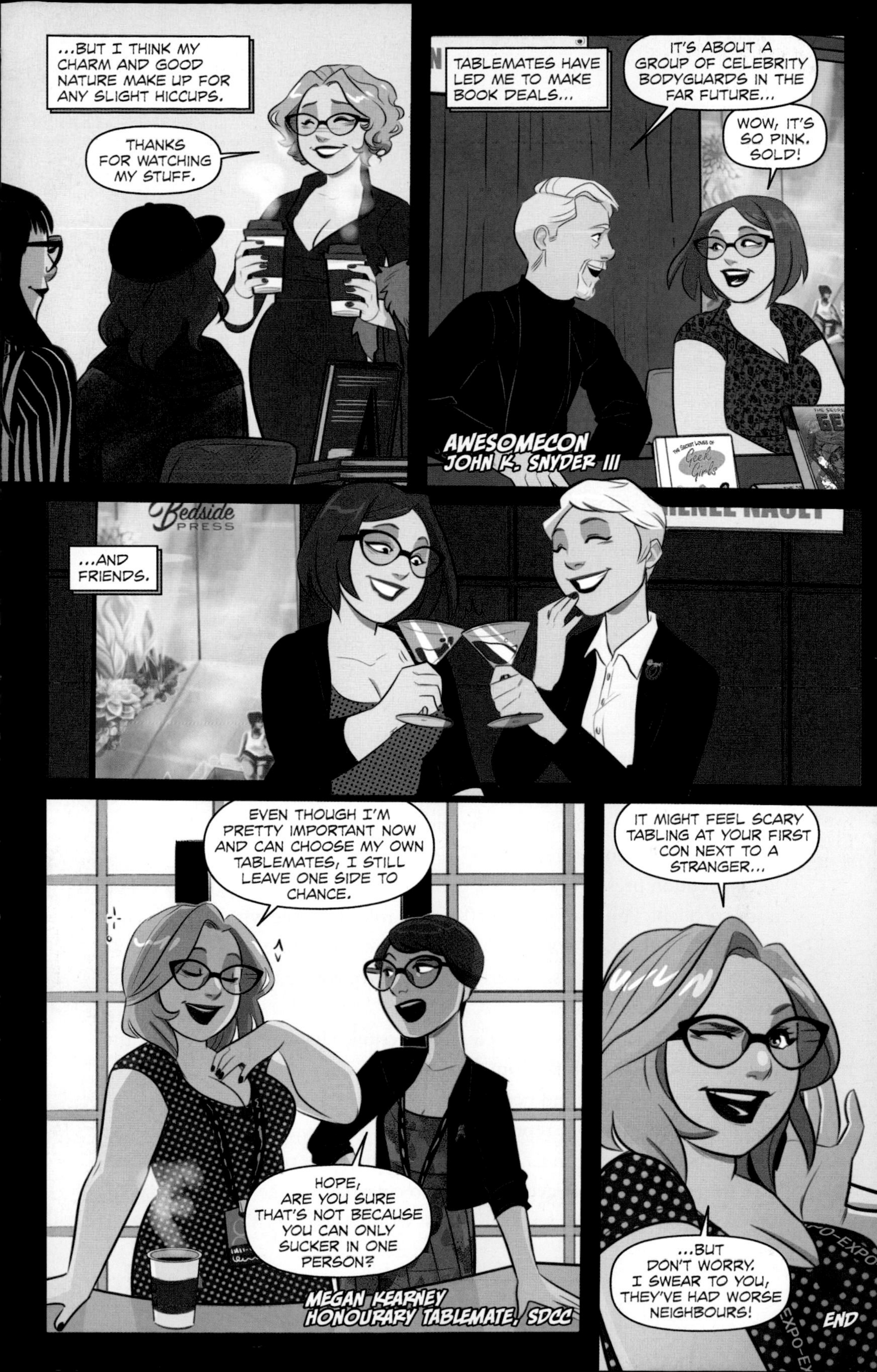
...BUT I THINK MY CHARM AND GOOD NATURE MAKE UP FOR ANY SLIGHT HICCUPS.
THANKS FOR WATCHING MY STUFF.
TABLEMATES HAVE LED ME TO MAKE BOOK DEALS...
IT'S ABOUT A GROUP OF CELEBRITY BODYGUARDS IN THE FAR FUTURE...
WOW, IT'S SO PINK. SOLD!
AWESOMECON
JOHN K. SNYDER III
...AND FRIENDS.
EVEN THOUGH I'M PRETTY IMPORTANT NOW AND CAN CHOOSE MY OWN TABLEMATES, I STILL LEAVE ONE SIDE TO CHANCE.
HOPE, ARE YOU SURE THAT'S NOT BECAUSE YOU CAN ONLY SUCKER IN ONE PERSON?
MEGAN KEARNEY
HONOURARY TABLEMATE, SDCC
IT MIGHT FEEL SCARY TABLING AT YOUR FIRST CON NEXT TO A STRANGER...
...BUT DON'T WORRY. I SWEAR TO YOU, THEY'VE HAD WORSE NEIGHBOURS!
END

STEP-BY-STEP GUIDE TO BECOMING A GEEK JOURNALIST

Karama Horne

Geek journalism is nestled somewhere in that otaku space between fan blogging and freelance writing. Made up of writers, producers, podcasters, bloggers, vloggers, comic book writers, and a celebrity or two, geek journalism has emerged as a lucrative subgenre. And nowhere is there more evidence of that than at places like San Diego Comic-Con and New York Comic Con, some of the biggest conventions in the country.

While most con goers are roaming the floor looking for a con-exclusive toy or game, waiting on line for a panel, or heading to artists alley to pick up a commission from their favorite comic book artist, there is another convention happening on the other floors and the surrounding buildings, and that is press coverage.

Convention press work is long, grueling, and contrary to popular belief, not sexy at all. Think about 10x10 rooms full of people who haven't slept (or sometimes bathed) for a few days at a time, all writing as fast as possible and cursing at the sluggish, overtaxed Wifi. No, you're not back in college, you're at a comic con.

And although we're finally seeing more comic characters that reflect the diversity of actual geek fandom, like Kamala Khan (*Ms. Marvel*), Lunella Lafayette (*Moon Girl*), and heck, Spock's own sister, who is a black woman, there is a lack of diverse representation in covering these same characters at conventions. I've been to so many cons where the press rooms are filled with straight white men, even assigned to cover shows like *Black Lightning*, *Supergirl*, or *Runaways*, which all boast women-led, LGBTQ, and diverse ethnicities as their main characters. And in the same year that Marvel's *Black Panther* has become the highest domestic grossing superhero film of all time, I'm often still the only person of color (sometimes even of any gender) when covering geekdom.

I've spoken to countless geek-journalist women of colour, who simply don't get invited to screenings or viewings like their white male counterparts do. It's a conversation I've repeatedly had at almost every convention. In researching why this disparity still exists, I have found, as suspected, that although racism is often at the root of bias, there are often two more other common reasons preventing folks like me from getting access, even from well-meaning publicists and marketers. The first is apathy, and the second is lack of experience.

Don't get me wrong, there are plenty of publicists out there, working hard to give access to women of color, but even the ones who do it right have told me that going out of their way to find us specifically to cover large events like comic book conventions is almost a job in and of itself. Some networks simply hire a local agency and let them "deal with the headache." Others that do reach out, don't always go about doing so the right way.

For example, I remember, one afternoon, after moderating a panel at a convention, being pulled aside by a white woman publicist who asked me nervously, in hushed tones, "Are there more of you?" With a raised eyebrow I asked, "More of what exactly? Moderators? Tall people? Humans? I'm really going to need you to be more specific." I was being cheeky, but really, I wanted her to articulate her meaning. She nervously laughed and asked me if I knew any more black geek-oriented women who wrote about pop culture or superhero shows on a regular basis.

One of the women that I ended up recommending soon contacted me in a panic, "I've never covered a comic book convention before! What do I do? How do I not mess this up?" I suddenly realized that although convention coverage is one of the easiest ways to break into geek journalism, there's no training available for a lot of young bloggers and writers to cover press at these events, which is especially important given that marginalized folks rarely get access to these opportunities, never mind a chance to learn on the job.

So, here's a little primer on how to access and cover conventions, as a geek journalist.

Getting Into the Con

Now, I know what you're thinking. How do I get a press pass to conventions? How do I find out where the interviews are? This is a numbers game, and it's often all about the outlet you write for, although your social media presence doesn't hurt either. The first thing you need to do is apply for a press pass. Every comic book convention has a press application. The stipulations all vary widely but smaller local conventions, especially newer ones, welcome the press. They often don't have a marketing budget and will probably send you a pass no matter how small you are just to get some free coverage. Keep in mind, though, that your press pass only covers admission to the convention, and getting yourself to the event is your responsibility, unless you have a company to cover your costs.

For popular conventions, what often works is applying through a popular website or outlet, preferably one that has a high unique visitor count within a month of your application. I've tested this theory myself and it does work, but it's still not an exact science.

A more surefire way to get a press pass is to write for an outlet that is already going to the con. This doesn't mean you have to try for i09 or Nerdist, (although that doesn't hurt either). I suggest looking at smaller sites that have a presence. The easiest way to figure out which those are is to look at coverage a week or two after a convention you've attended is over. Follow social media and YouTube channels to see who has articles and videos about a topic you know, or shows that you're looking to gain access to. Then, contact them through their site and ask if they are looking for writers to help cover a con. Just like retail stores who look for extra help around Christmas, outlets do the same thing around convention season. You might luck out and get a press pass that way.

Now, if you manage to contribute regularly to a site with previous press access to a convention near you, you may have a pretty good chance of getting in when convention season rolls around, especially if you live in a different city from that outlet's headquarters. C2E2 for instance, is in Chicago, IL. So, if you live in the Chicago area, and you know a New York-based outlet is looking for coverage, they may get you in, since it's always cheaper to send a local to cover a convention.

One of the biggest perks of getting a press badge to a convention is that it allows you to see the press emails sent through the convention organizer on behalf of various shows, events, actors, authors, and pop-ups. These e-mails provide access to talent and creators in several different ways. Here are some of the different setups you can find at a convention you might be covering:

The Roundtable

That's a panel where actors, producers and creators all sit at a literal round table with various media outlets present to ask questions. It's kind of like a mini controlled press conference. Usually these last anywhere from five to fifteen minutes at a time, with talent switching out after their allotted time is up. Recording devices are allowed here, but cameras are usually reserved for the press lines.

Press Lines

The press line at a convention is basically a mini red carpet with the convention logo in the background, where outlets have allotted spaces marked on the floor with the more popular ones getting first dibs at talking with talent. Actors, producers and directors are filed in one at a time and stop to talk to each outlet. This is where you'll find your camera crews and a host with a microphone talking with artists as they walk by. Press lines can get tricky. I have covered these with a cameraperson, sound engineer and a stick mic for myself. But I've also seen teams of one or two using a monopod, a mic, and a DSLR to record interviews, especially when there's not a lot of room.

Press Junkets

If you are lucky enough to be hired by an outlet to do a press junket, this is where you can really get the most publicity for your work. Press junkets are always two camera setups with a separate audio crew who will mic both you and the talent and check the audio levels the entire time. When you see interviews in a dark room, with the poster of the movie behind the artists and the interviewer sitting across from them, this is usually a standard press junket. These are usually recorded in a controlled environment like a room on a different level of the convention center or in a hotel nearby.

Different outlets will be set up in different rooms as talent is brought in for multiple interviews. These junkets are usually held right before film premieres, but have also taken place at conventions.

Man-on-the-street

These are your candid convention floor interviews in Artist Alley, with cosplayers and con-goers, which have largely been replaced by social media coverage and livestreaming.

Expectations

Once you're able to secure access, it's up to you to produce some content and get it into the hands of an outlet's editor as quickly as you can. This can be done by pitching editors directly, which I suggest you do before a convention starts, since you'll have your schedule laid out by then. If you've already been hired by an outlet, great, but keep in mind that these assignments usually involve quick turnarounds, especially if you're working on the newsfeed side. Many a press room and hallway at conventions are crowded with writers trying to get out leads and exclusives as fast as possible.

Finding Your Voice

Although some outlets are very open to their writers expressing their own opinion in reviews and highlights, if you are being paid to write general coverage, outlets are looking for a "neutral voice." Meaning that instead of saying "Along with most of Twitter, I think that the *Superman* reboot is ridiculous," you would say, "Twitter responded swiftly and negatively to the *Superman* reboot news, which trended for hours." More often than not, you are being paid to chronicle what you are covering instead of presenting a strong opinion about it. Sometimes, though, you will be asked to provide unique insight and opinions on shows, topics, actors and creators. It's a subtle art, finding that balance between standard reporting and op-ed writing. But if you can master it, and bolster your opinion with facts, you will absolutely gain followers and potential work from other outlets.

Building Your Own Brand

Even if you don't get into a convention with press credentials, there's still quite a bit you can do on your own. Simply buying a general ticket, but representing yourself as your own brand can get you some really great interviews, especially with people who don't often get a lot of press otherwise; indie comic book artists or cosplayers, for example, are great to approach. Your coverage also might gain the attention of an outlet this way. For example, personal website coverage of smaller cons, reviews of comics whose creators you met, and bites you post on Twitter, Facebook, and Instagram can get you noticed by other creators and outlets.

For a year or two I attended almost any convention that was in the New York, New Jersey, or Philadelphia area. I was simply taking notes, voice memos, and pictures with my iPhone. I didn't have any gear, since my budget went to travel and purchasing tickets. Although I did guest post on a few sites, I saved most of my coverage for myself and made sure my branded hashtag was on everything I posted. That body of work is what also got me out from behind a desk working with SYFY Wire, and on camera instead.

So if you've ever been to a convention livestage, or panel, or watched a live interview and thought "I could do that," the truth is, you can, and you should. Fandom needs more voices reporting from the front lines to give us fresh perspectives and ask new questions. Even if you don't have a website of your own, start posting on social media so the world can see who you are. Don't want to be on camera? That's fine; stick to roundtables and press rooms. But you too, can be a geek journalist, and the best place to start is at the next comic book convention.

MISTAKES WERE MADE

BY LUCY BELLWOOD

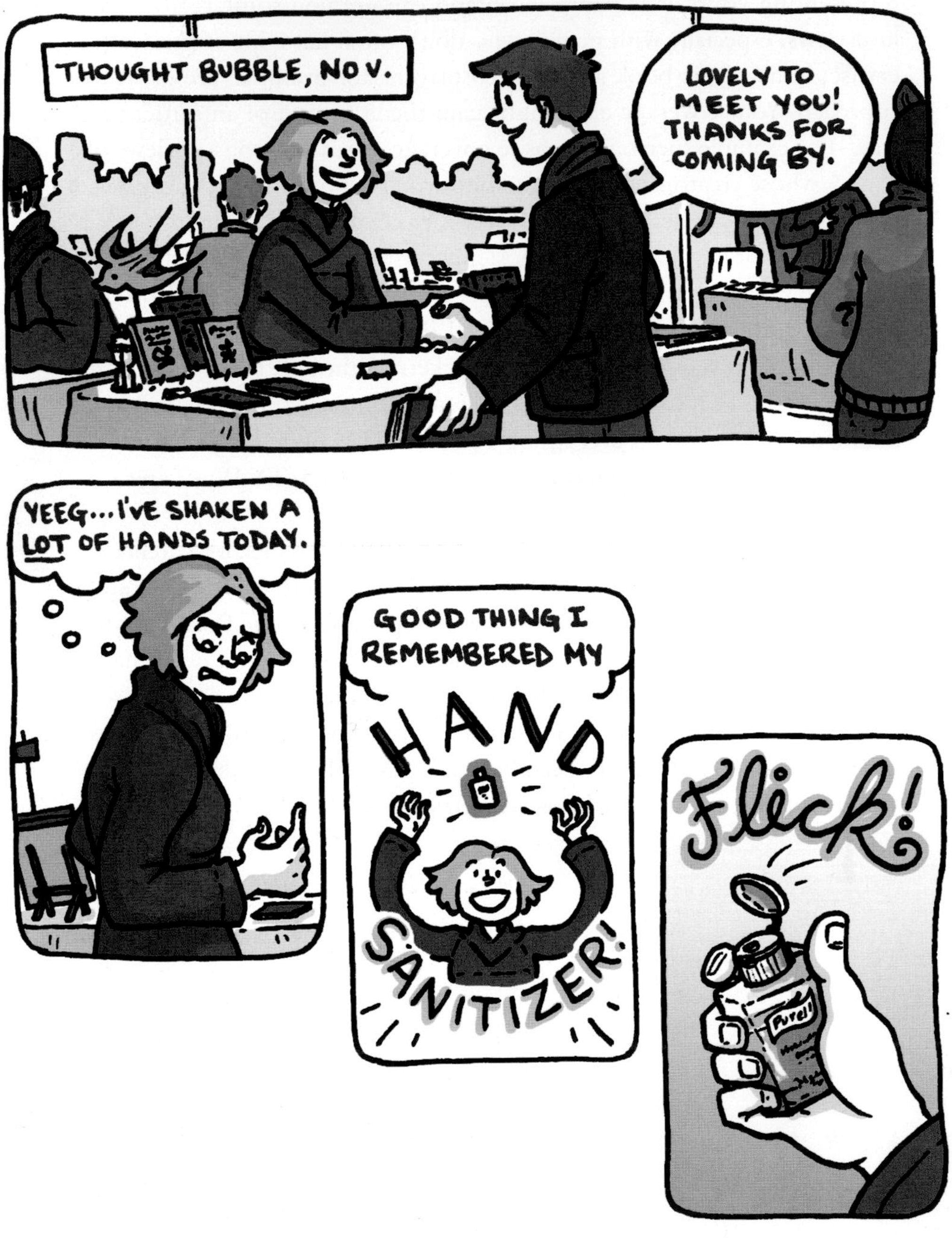
THOUGHT BUBBLE, NOV.
LOVELY TO MEET YOU! THANKS FOR COMING BY.
YEEG...I'VE SHAKEN A LOT OF HANDS TODAY.
GOOD THING I REMEMBERED MY
HAND
SANITIZER!
Flick!
Purell

DUMDEEDUMDUMDEEDADUMDU
SPLORT
6 MONTHS EARLIER...
RIGHT. TCAF. WHAT TO BRING? JACKET, TABLE, SOCKS, SIGNAGE, CH, PASSPORT, TOOTHPAST, BOOKS...
LUBE.

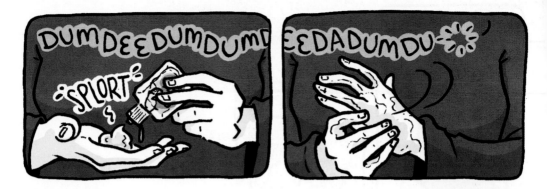

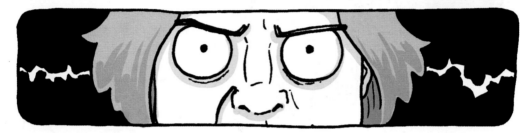

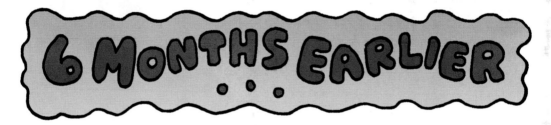

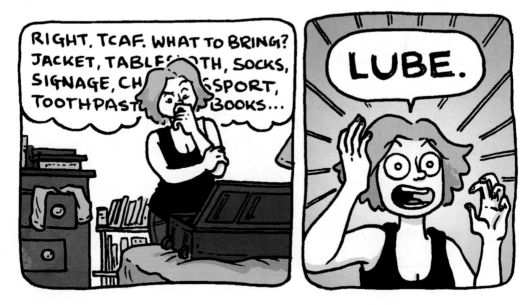

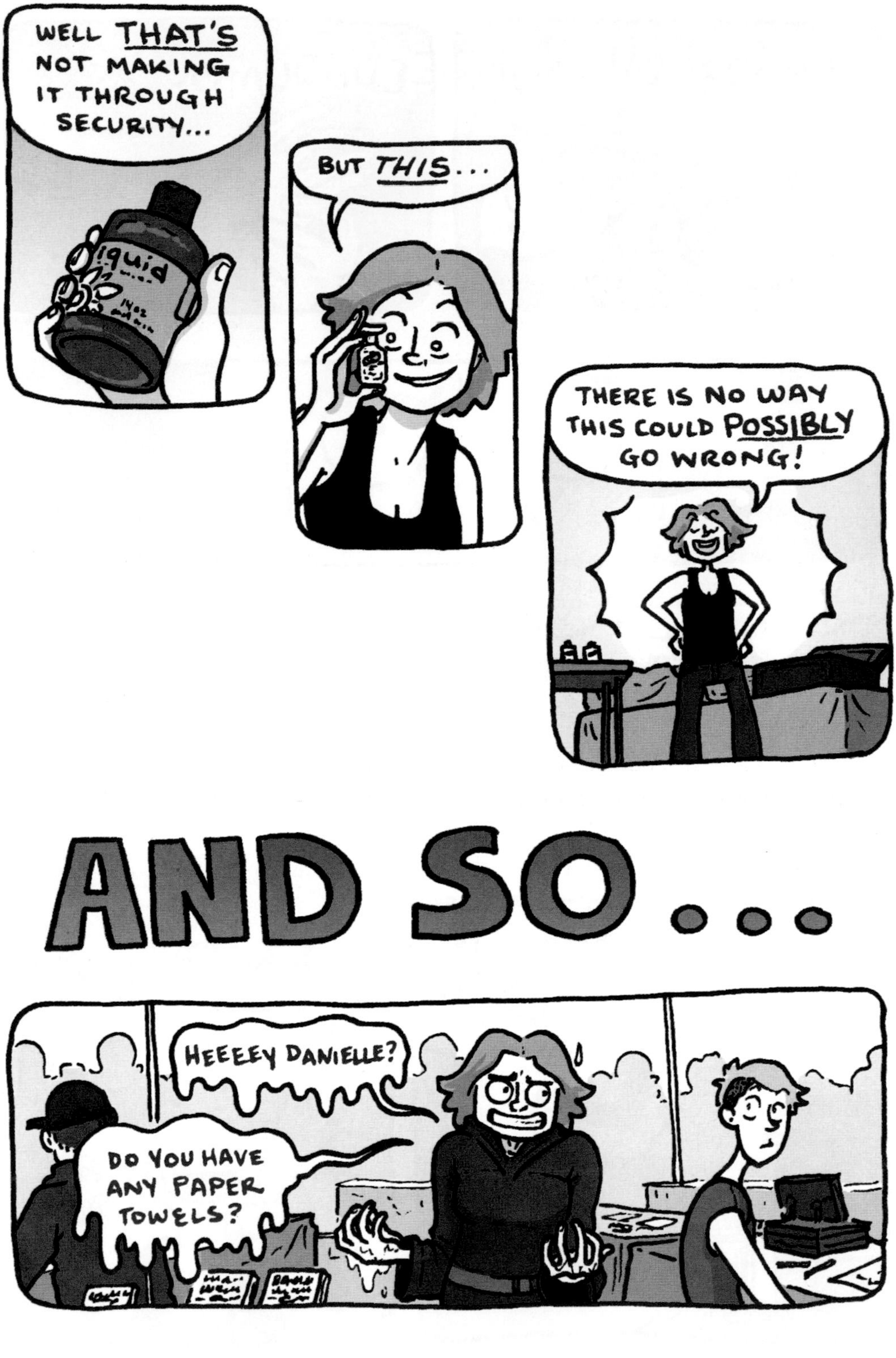
WELL THAT'S NOT MAKING IT THROUGH SECURITY...
liquid
BUT THIS...
THERE IS NO WAY THIS COULD POSSIBLY GO WRONG!
AND SO...
HEEEEY DANIELLE?
DO YOU HAVE ANY PAPER TOWELS?

CREE SUPERGIRL

📕

Sonya Ballantyne

I realized my jeans were too thick for the San Diego weather when I stepped out of the airport, heading to the hotel shuttle stop. Jeans seemed like a good idea when I'd left Winnipeg at 4 a.m., cold and exhausted.

I arrived at my hotel, the doors open to the humid sea air, and I wondered how anyone could prefer this to air conditioning. When I made it to the front desk, a bright-eyed, smiling clerk appeared before me without a second's delay. Being Canadian, I started with an apology.

"I'm super early, but I was wondering if I could check in or maybe drop off my luggage?" The clerk welcomed me warmly, offering me an assortment of key cards with *Riverdale* characters on them as he checked me in. I tried to remember which character my sister liked to guide my choice.

The clerk smiled and asked, "Here for Comic-Con?"

I nodded excitedly. "Yeah, I'm on a panel!"

When I found out I was going to Comic-Con, I told everyone I met, from the fruit stand lady I always saw on my way to work, to the random women sitting next to me on the plane. It wasn't that I couldn't believe how lucky I was, but that I deserved to be proud—I had to rely on my nerd cunning, and the support of various internet celebrities, just to make it to this point. I'd earned this.

My journey had begun just seven months before the con. I saw a Facebook post from Hope Nicholson, another fellow Winnipegger, asking for Canadian speakers for a SDCC panel. This immediately caught my attention, since I'd been to SDCC before and loved it. My professional nerd cred was thanks to my short films, where I told stories in genres that Indigenous people—Cree, specifically—are usually excluded from. Superhero stories. Sci-fi. You know, Indiginerd stuff. As a kid, I loved *Teenage Mutant Ninja Turtles*, comic books, and especially superheroes, but never saw stories featuring people like me and my family. So I made them myself. Along with that, I had more than a little speaking experience—I spoke, yeah you couldn't get me to shut up, actually, about positive media representation, at events like TedX and We Day in Winnipeg.

So, to get the chance to speak at the biggest comic convention in the world in front of tons of people? Of course I was down!

So, I tossed my hat into the ring, but Hope warned me, "The pitch probably won't be accepted."

Months and months later, I'd already forgotten about the panel. I was attending a conference on media as social justice, on Vancouver Island, where they had spotty cell service and completely meat-less catering.

I was on a break between sessions, wading in the seawater, so starved that I was eyeing up the wandering crabs to snatch and eat, when I got Hope's message: the panel had been accepted. My body about near burst with joy and I screamed so loud, I scared the crabs off, and set dogs barking across the island.

I called my parents to tell them the good news, which, like most things I do, they didn't understand, but were happy for me nonetheless. When I told my sister Kerri, though, she begged to come with. Otherwise, I kept my news on the down-low, it wasn't announced yet, so I couldn't say anything on social media. Still, I couldn't believe my good fortune, and walked around on a cloud. A friend mentioned it was likely I was going to be the first Swampy Cree woman to speak on a panel at Comic-Con. I felt like Superman when he spoke to the United Nations in *Superman 4*. But then, reality hit. With just a month to go before the con, how on earth was I going to pay for this last-minute trip?

Let's go back a bit. Like I said, I'm an Indiginerd, and I live in Winnipeg—the centre of Canada. I wasn't the only Cree person I knew, but the only Cree nerd? It wasn't until just a few years ago that I heard the term "Indiginerd" on the CBC (Canadian Broadcasting Corporation) and realized there were other people like me. Like, a lot of them.

Not only did I not know there were other Indiginerds, but I used to think that comic book conventions were either fictional or extinct. I only saw them on TV, on old sitcoms like *The Fresh Prince of Bel Air*, which at least had other nerds of colour on it. But there were rarely women nerds, and never any who looked like me.

Nerd culture seems like such a good fit for us Indiginerds, but before that show, I felt like I was the only one. Who knows the most about loss? Superheroes and Indigenous people. We *are* the first superheroes. We survived the loss of our Krypton, the loss of our families, and the loss of our culture. Nevertheless, we grow stronger: Indigenous Forever. A lot of science fiction, like *Star Trek*, comes from our stories.

I watched *Star Trek* as a kid every morning before school. Spock was my favourite character, and I adopted him as a Native person. He was kin, as I saw him going through the same struggles I was, trying to survive in one world, but belonging to another. The show gave me hope of a future where my being Indian wasn't going to matter, because if a half-Vulcan could be accepted by the crew, maybe we could be too. But even though I loved *Star Trek*, I felt like an outcast, because none of the other Native kids watched it.

When I finally discovered comic cons weren't imaginary, it was by finding out about my local convention in Winnipeg. The first year I went, I met one of my first heroes. Helen Slater. The original Supergirl.

My heart was in my throat as my sister and I approached her table, and saw her signing autographs with a line of people in front. She stood for a picture with a fan, and I was surprised that she was shorter than me. Maybe it was because I had always seen her through a child's eyes, but I thought she would be much taller. When I got to the front of the line, I told her that she was my hero, then she beamed at me and I saw the hero in her determined eyes, and her kind and reassuring smile.

I didn't see a lot of Indigenous people at this first con, it seemed to be just me and my sister, who I had converted into a nerd, just so I'd have someone to watch *Ninja Turtles* on the rez with me. Looking around at the mostly-white audience made me feel like I was still that awkward little Indian girl with no one else in the world like her.

Luckily, things change. More and more I saw other Indiginerds like me. Comics writers and artists like Jeffrey Veregge are getting Marvel gigs, actors like Cara Gee are getting gigs on major sci-fi shows, there's nerd podcasts like *Métis In Space,* and more and more, I see other Native kids in superhero costumes each year at my local con.

Eventually, it was time to upgrade, and years after this first con, me and my sister headed south—San Diego Comic-Con. The convention centre was bigger than the largest mall in Winnipeg, and I'd *never* seen so many people in one place before. Crossing the street with hundreds of people to get to offsite events was like being swept away in a riptide. My head whipped back and forth as I tried to take in everything at once: the costumes, the displays, the panels, the celebrities, and the general mayhem of this many nerds in one place.

The experience was perfect. I went to a *WWE* panel with my sister, sitting right behind The Miz at one point. I went to a *Hannibal* panel with my friend Angel, watching a blooper reel that had been unreleased before this point. It went on Tumblr a minute after but still, it felt so cool to be amongst the *first* to see something even if it only lasted a moment!

As I said, it was perfect—almost. Even though Winnipeg's con scene had changed, SDCC's audience didn't seem to have gotten the memo. Except for *Hannibal*, every other panel I went to was almost all men, and even in the huge crowd of fans I didn't see any other Indiginerds. I wasn't the only one to notice; during the *WWE* Q&A, Mick Foley asked the crowd, "I really appreciate you all, but could we get a woman to ask a question?" The all-male lineup at the mics had to grudgingly part to let one woman into the line. I didn't let being the only girl in the room affect my experience, but it just highlighted that again, this was my community, but also, it wasn't.

So here I was, five years later. Not just going to SDCC, but being asked to speak on a panel. A panel with other Canadian nerd celebrities—comic book creators Cecil Castellucci, Ian Boothby, and Pia Guerra. They, with Hope, were all going to SDCC anyway, so they had booked their flights and hotels months in advance. But flights from the middle of Canada to San Diego are a huge expense, and a last-minute hotel reservation during SDCC, if not impossible, costs at least a month's salary. There was no way I could do it. Canadian grants are great and all, but you need to apply for them months in advance, and with this late notice, it was a huge risk to gamble on getting one after paying for the trip out of pocket.

My friends suggested a GoFundMe campaign, but I was hesitant. All Indigenous people (and people of colour in general) know the sting of racist comments about "our need for handouts." But I didn't really have a choice, and I wasn't going to miss SDCC. I crossed my fingers and launched the campaign, hopeful I would get, at least, a few dollars to offset the cost.

In four days, the campaign reached its goal. The support was overwhelming, from the celebrities I looked forward to seeing at the con including comic writers, artists, actors, and celebrities, all were sending me tweets and funds and cheering me on. National news outlets like CBC and APTN (Aboriginal People's Television Network) started covering my mission to attend SDCC. But more importantly, other Indiginerds and people of colour were my biggest supporters, sharing the campaign far and wide, proud of me for going and representing my people.

The campaign wasn't without incident, though. I remember when a Yahoo story was put up, one of the first comments was "Why would anyone want to hear an Indian talk at comic con?" Another stated, "Tax payer gonna pay this injun's way." These comments weren't as disheartening as I feared, because everyone who supported the GoFundMe made it clear that they wanted to hear me speak. I felt powerful, like my voice was my superpower.

The goal was reached, I booked my hotel and flight, and a few weeks later, buoyed by everyone's support and love, I'd made it to SDCC.

I was excited, but also burdened with heavy responsibility. I was there to represent Indiginerds. I had to be cool. I had to look good. I had to make other Indigenous kids proud to see me up there. Luckily, I still felt like Superman, and no load was going to weigh me down for long. I might have been scared of looking like a fangirl in front of my heroes, but if it wasn't for doing things that scared me, I'd never have gone to my first con, I'd never have talked to Supergirl, and I definitely wouldn't be speaking at SDCC.

I went to the con an hour before the panel, killing time by wandering around the space. I saw something that stopped me dead in my tracks.

A familiar cloud of blonde hair.

A kind and patient smile.

A superhero who made up for her small size with her big heart.

Helen Slater.

Supergirl.

I was shaking just as much as when I first I met her. What were the odds, that she'd swoop into my life at my very first con, and again here before one of the most important moments in my life?

I blurted out that that this was a sign, and then we both laughed. If I had any nerves before, laughing with my favourite celebrity was weird enough that it shook me right out of them.

"I'm glad you're here," she told me. My hero.

I walked into the panel in a daze, on a high from this crazy trip. I took my seat and something landed in front of me suddenly.

"Holy shit."

A placard. With my name on it. At SDCC.

I looked into the crowded audience and saw that for once, it wasn't the same faces. There were a lot of women, and way more people of colour than the last time I was here. And here I was, sitting in front of them, not just as a fan, but a voice of power. Maybe, out there somewhere, was another little girl, at first con, getting to see someone who looked like her talk about the superheroes she was creating. Maybe, for someone, I'm their Cree Supergirl.

THERE YA GO. ONE SKETCH OF A HARDCORE NINJA COMMANDO!

TEEN! LOOK AT YOU! IT MUST BE SO INSPIRING TO DRAW THE COMIC CHARACTERS YOU READ ABOUT AS A KID.

YEAH, STEFANO, IT'S COOL. I'M LUCKY. I KNOW IT. IT'S JUST...

I DUNNO. THERE ARE A LOT OF RESTRICTIONS. I MEAN, I GET IT, IT'S A KIDS PROPERTY...

DON'T:
• SHOW BLOOD!
• MAKE POLITICAL STATEMENTS OR ANALOGIES TO REAL WORLD!
• SHOW GUNS POINTED AT PEOPL
• SHOW BUTTS!
• ...OF REAL WORLD
• ...GION
• A

BUT SOMETHING ABOUT BEING TOLD WHAT I CAN'T DO JUST MAKES ME WANT TO DO IT MORE, Y'KNOW?

YOU ALWAYS WANT WHAT YOU CAN'T HAVE.

AND I WANT A SKETCH.

ARE YOU GONNA DO ONE FOR ME OR NOT?

THE SECRET ORIGIN OF

HACK/ SLASH

A PARTIAL TRUTH

BY TIM SEELEY
COLORS BY CHRIS CHUCKRY
EDITS BY HOPE NICHOLSON

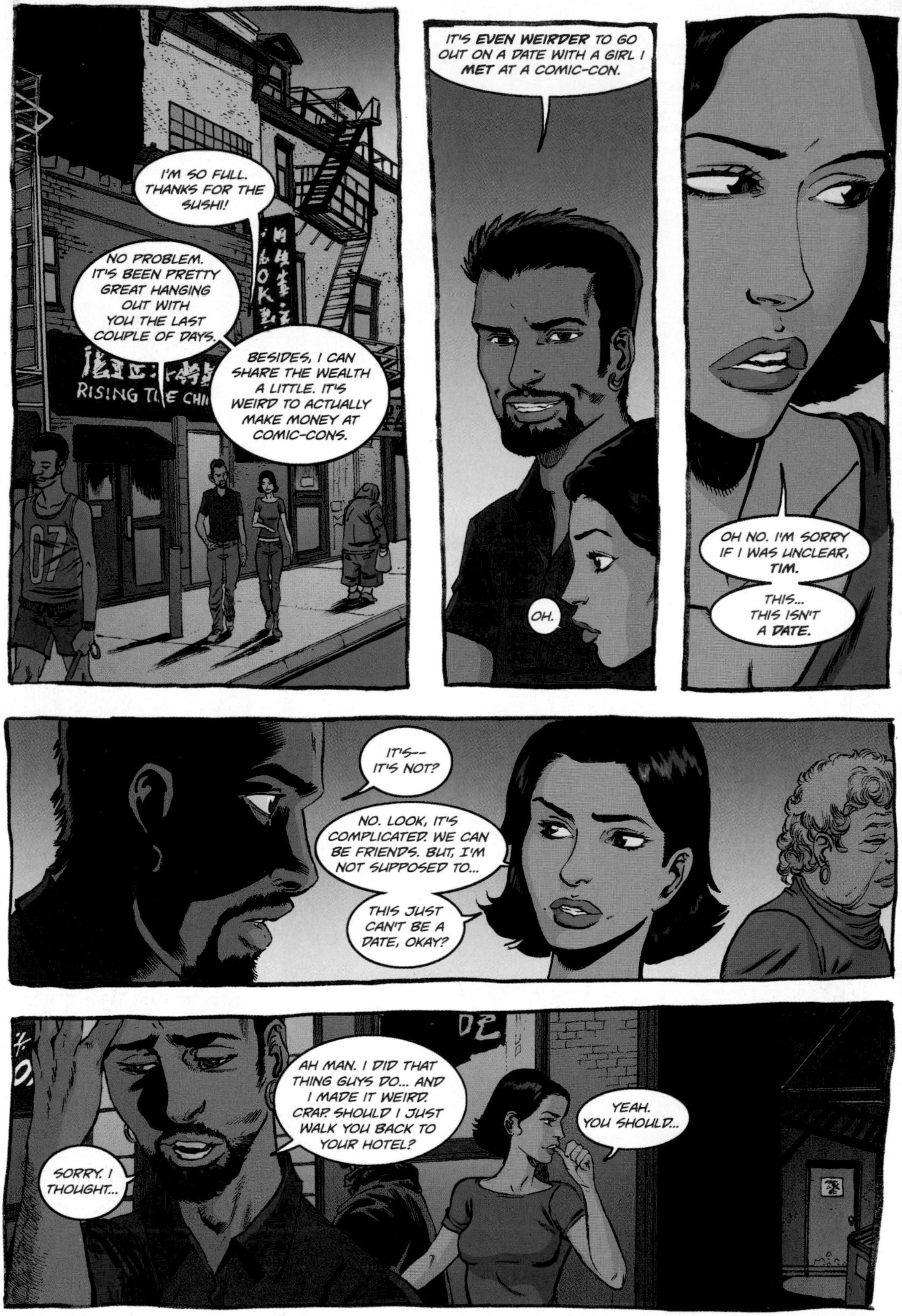
I'M SO FULL. THANKS FOR THE SUSHI!
NO PROBLEM. IT'S BEEN PRETTY GREAT HANGING OUT WITH YOU THE LAST COUPLE OF DAYS.
RISING TIDE CHI
BESIDES, I CAN SHARE THE WEALTH A LITTLE. IT'S WEIRD TO ACTUALLY MAKE MONEY AT COMIC-CONS.
IT'S EVEN WEIRDER TO GO OUT ON A DATE WITH A GIRL I MET AT A COMIC-CON.
OH.
OH NO. I'M SORRY IF I WAS UNCLEAR, TIM.
THIS... THIS ISN'T A DATE.
IT'S-- IT'S NOT?
NO. LOOK, IT'S COMPLICATED. WE CAN BE FRIENDS. BUT, I'M NOT SUPPOSED TO...
THIS JUST CAN'T BE A DATE, OKAY?
AH MAN. I DID THAT THING GUYS DO... AND I MADE IT WEIRD. CRAP. SHOULD I JUST WALK YOU BACK TO YOUR HOTEL?
YEAH. YOU SHOULD...
SORRY. I THOUGHT...

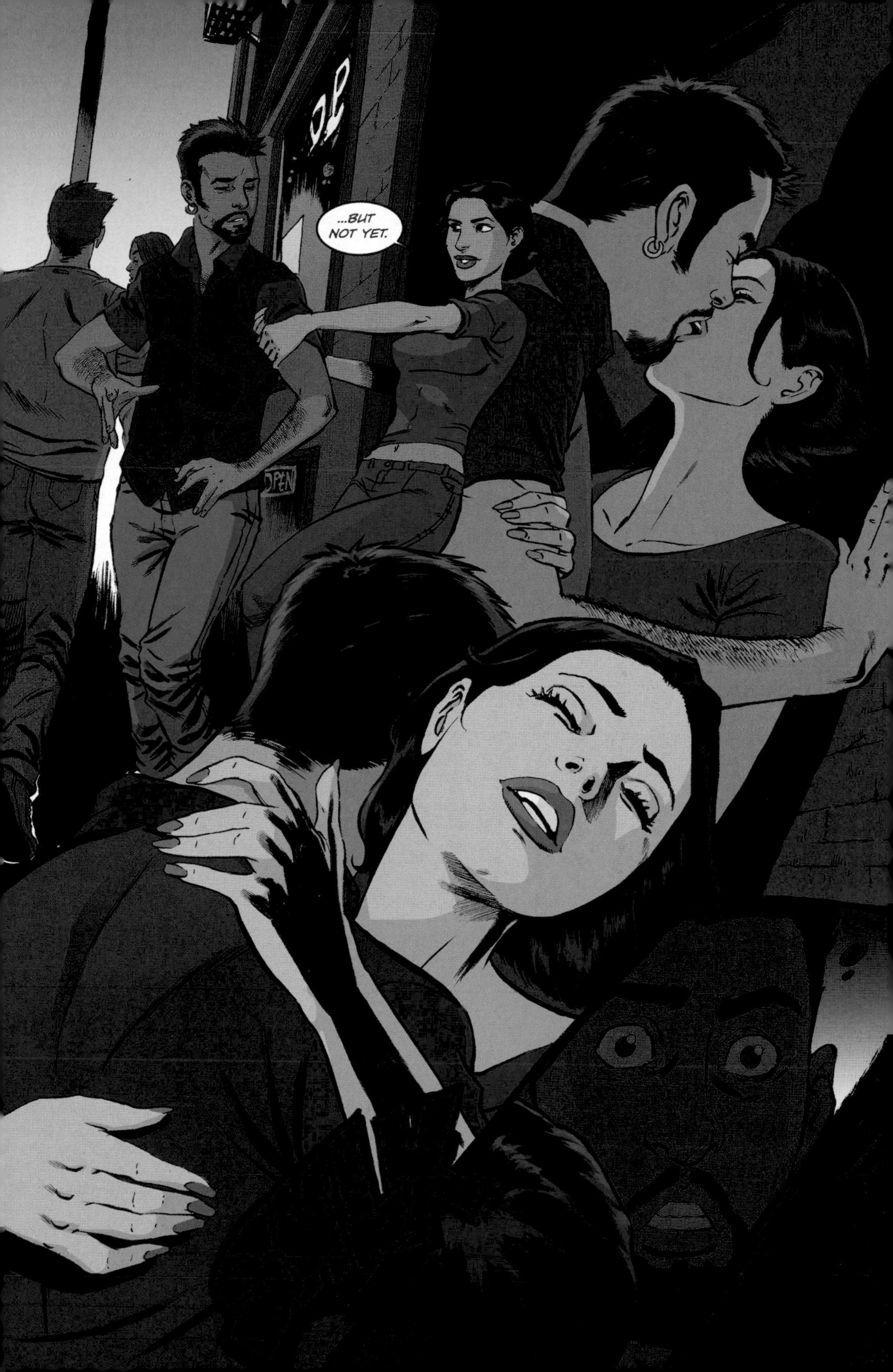
...BUT NOT YET.
OPEN

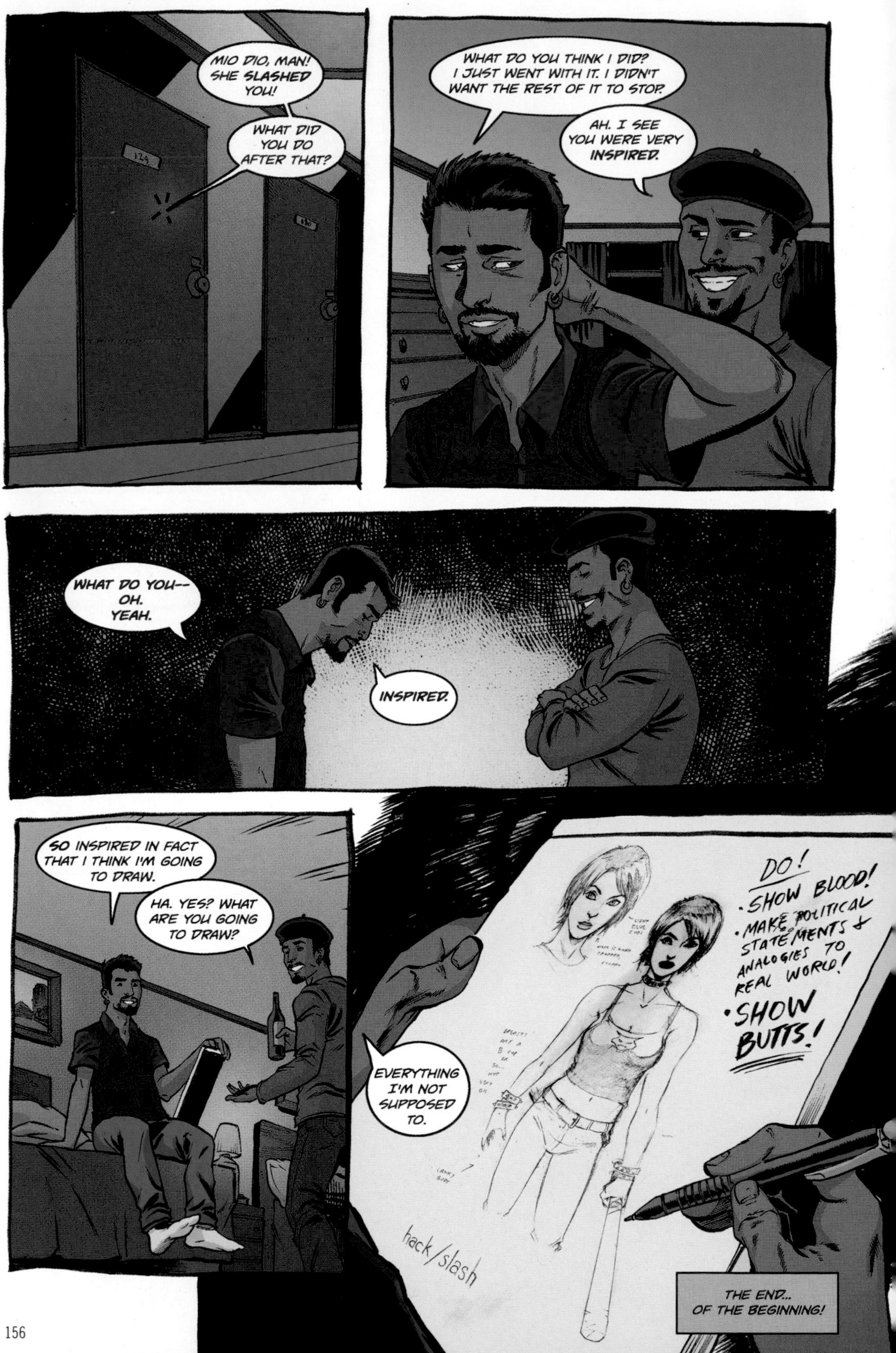
MIO DIO, MAN! SHE SLASHED YOU!
WHAT DID YOU DO AFTER THAT?
WHAT DO YOU THINK I DID? I JUST WENT WITH IT. I DIDN'T WANT THE REST OF IT TO STOP.
AH. I SEE YOU WERE VERY INSPIRED.
WHAT DO YOU-- OH. YEAH.
INSPIRED.
SO INSPIRED IN FACT THAT I THINK I'M GOING TO DRAW.
HA. YES? WHAT ARE YOU GOING TO DRAW?
EVERYTHING I'M NOT SUPPOSED TO.
DO!
·SHOW BLOOD!
·MAKE POLITICAL STATEMENTS & ANALOGIES TO REAL WORLD!
·SHOW BUTTS!
hack/slash
THE END... OF THE BEGINNING!

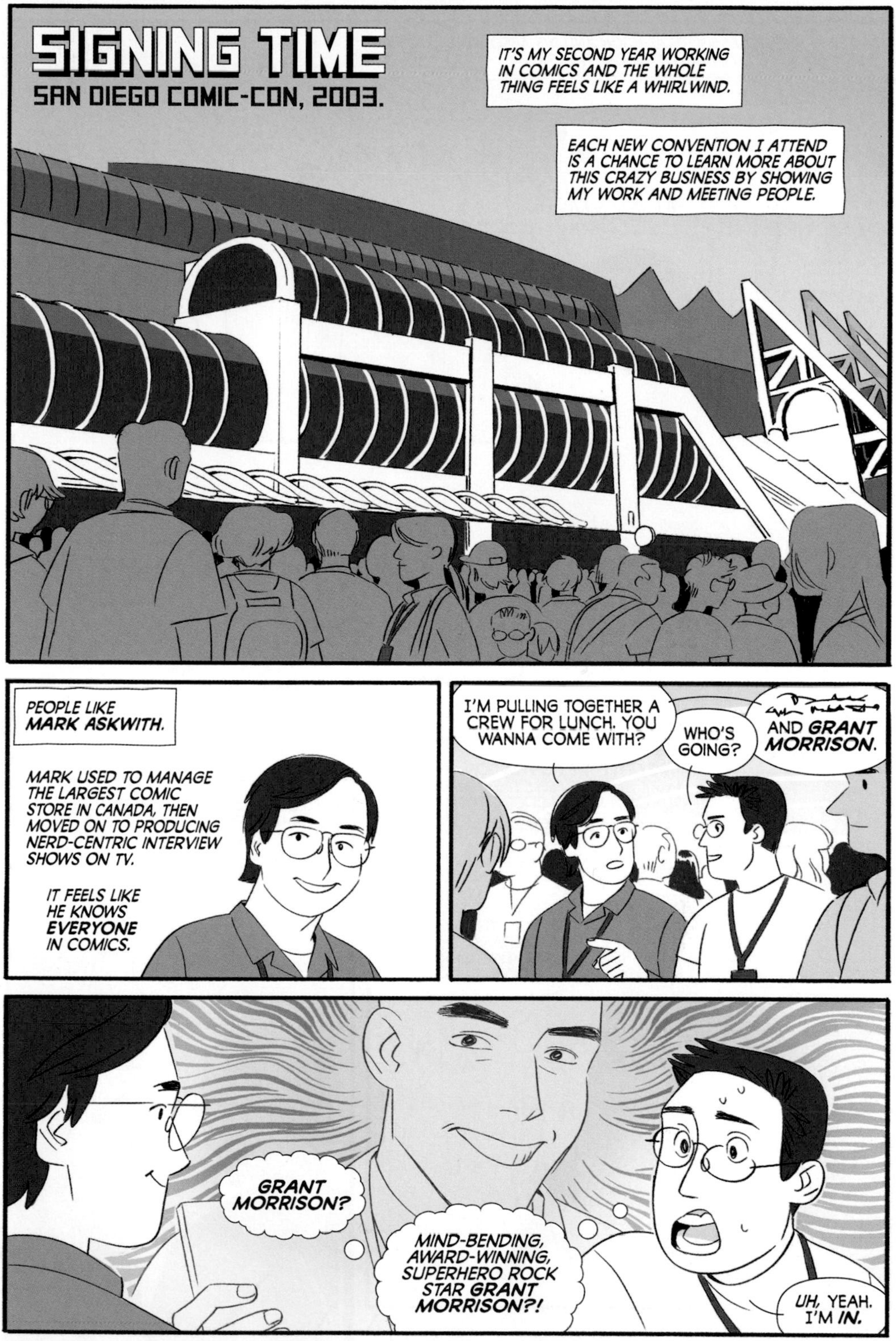
SIGNING TIME
SAN DIEGO COMIC-CON, 2003.
IT'S MY SECOND YEAR WORKING IN COMICS AND THE WHOLE THING FEELS LIKE A WHIRLWIND.
EACH NEW CONVENTION I ATTEND IS A CHANCE TO LEARN MORE ABOUT THIS CRAZY BUSINESS BY SHOWING MY WORK AND MEETING PEOPLE.
PEOPLE LIKE MARK ASKWITH.
MARK USED TO MANAGE THE LARGEST COMIC STORE IN CANADA, THEN MOVED ON TO PRODUCING NERD-CENTRIC INTERVIEW SHOWS ON TV.
IT FEELS LIKE HE KNOWS EVERYONE IN COMICS.
I'M PULLING TOGETHER A CREW FOR LUNCH. YOU WANNA COME WITH?
WHO'S GOING?
AND GRANT MORRISON.
GRANT MORRISON?
MIND-BENDING, AWARD-WINNING, SUPERHERO ROCK STAR GRANT MORRISON?!
UH, YEAH. I'M IN.

STORY JIM ZUB ART VIVIAN NG LETTERS MARSHALL DILLON

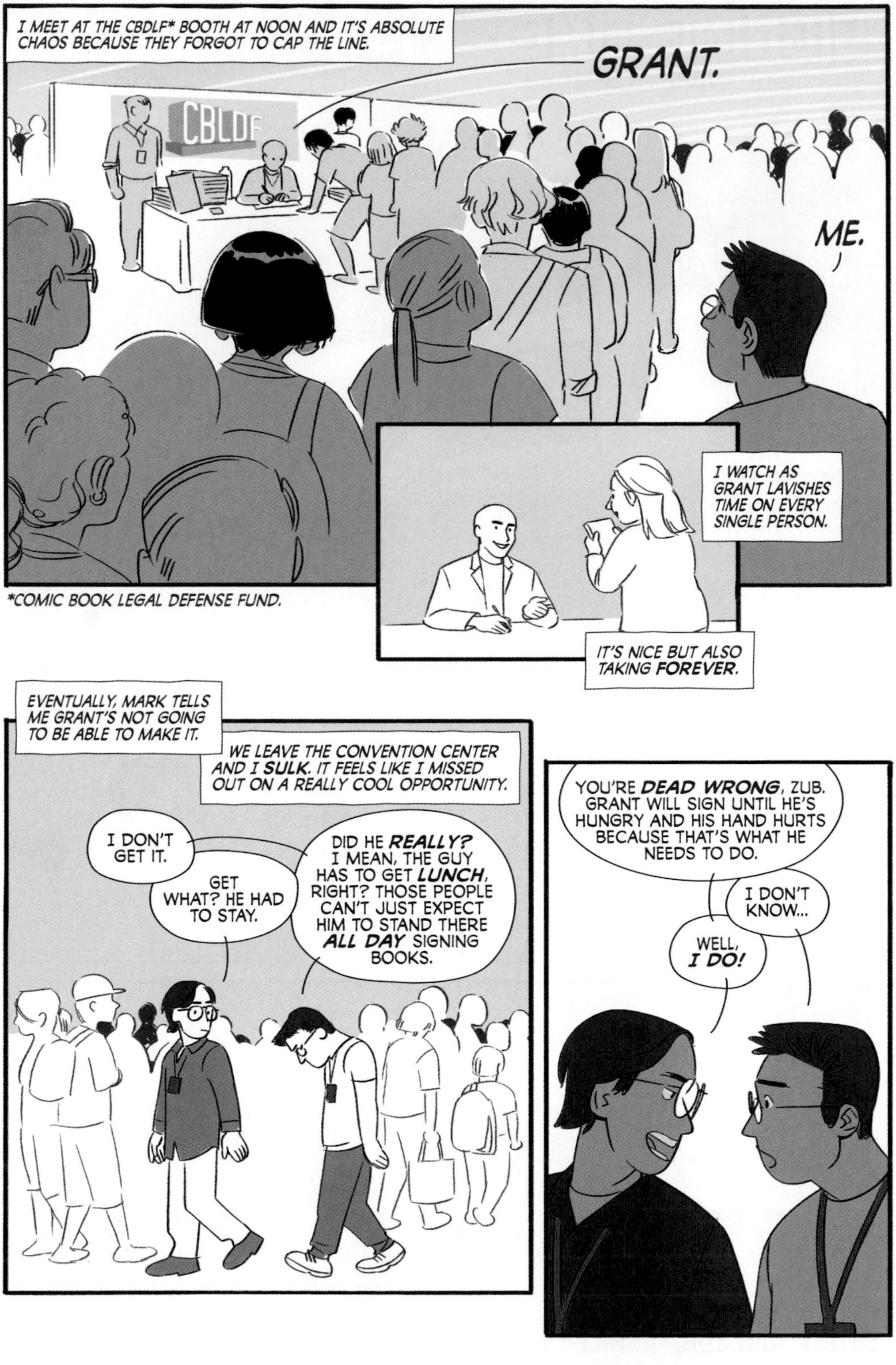
I MEET AT THE CBDLF* BOOTH AT NOON AND IT'S ABSOLUTE CHAOS BECAUSE THEY FORGOT TO CAP THE LINE.
GRANT.
CBLDF
ME.
*COMIC BOOK LEGAL DEFENSE FUND.
I WATCH AS GRANT LAVISHES TIME ON EVERY SINGLE PERSON.
IT'S NICE BUT ALSO TAKING **FOREVER**.
EVENTUALLY, MARK TELLS ME GRANT'S NOT GOING TO BE ABLE TO MAKE IT.
WE LEAVE THE CONVENTION CENTER AND I **SULK**. IT FEELS LIKE I MISSED OUT ON A REALLY COOL OPPORTUNITY.
I DON'T GET IT.
GET WHAT? HE HAD TO STAY.
DID HE ***REALLY?*** I MEAN, THE GUY HAS TO GET ***LUNCH***, RIGHT? THOSE PEOPLE CAN'T JUST EXPECT HIM TO STAND THERE ***ALL DAY*** SIGNING BOOKS.
YOU'RE ***DEAD WRONG***, ZUB. GRANT WILL SIGN UNTIL HE'S HUNGRY AND HIS HAND HURTS BECAUSE THAT'S WHAT HE NEEDS TO DO.
I DON'T KNOW...
WELL, ***I DO!***

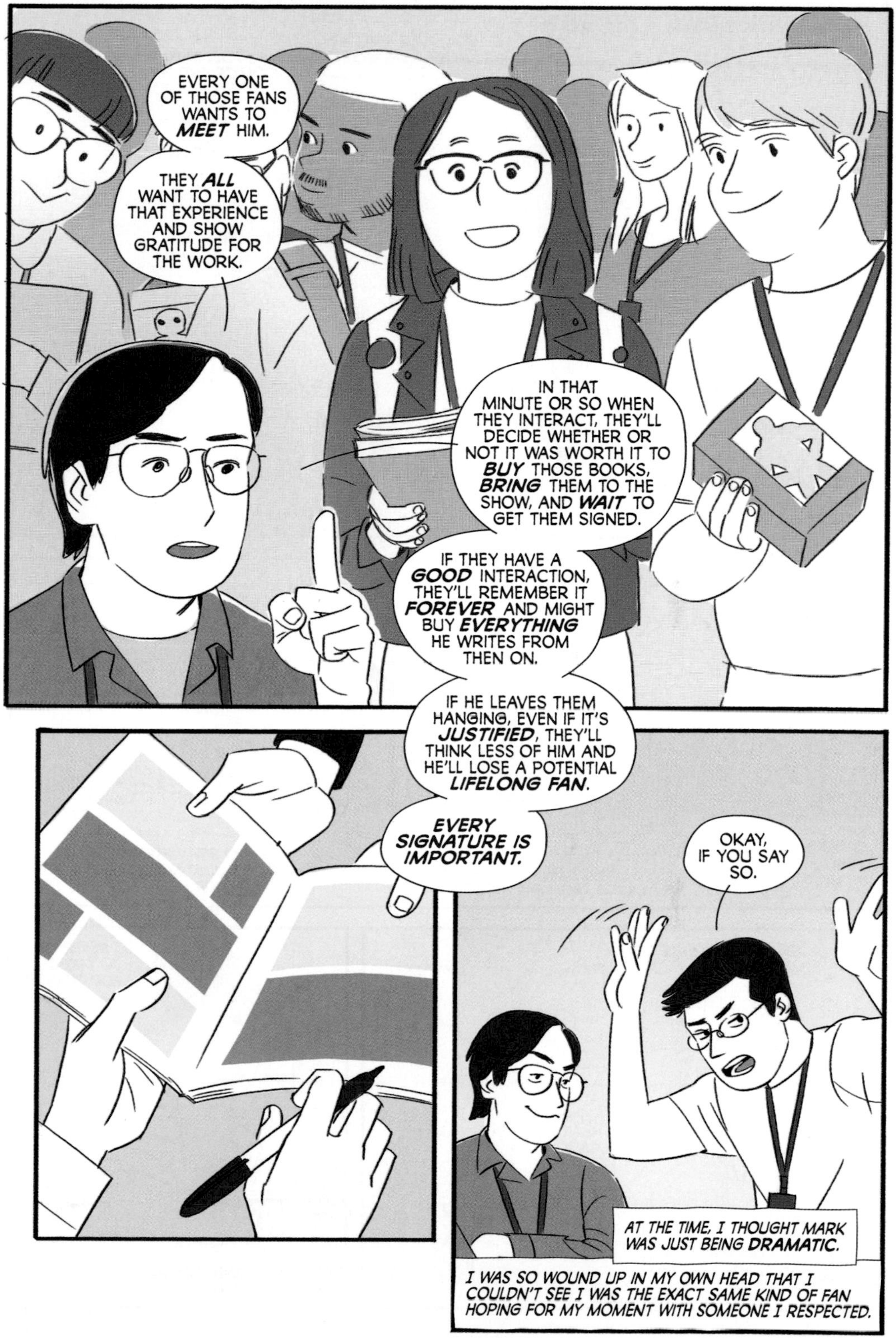
EVERY ONE OF THOSE FANS WANTS TO **MEET** HIM.
THEY **ALL** WANT TO HAVE THAT EXPERIENCE AND SHOW GRATITUDE FOR THE WORK.
IN THAT MINUTE OR SO WHEN THEY INTERACT, THEY'LL DECIDE WHETHER OR NOT IT WAS WORTH IT TO **BUY** THOSE BOOKS, **BRING** THEM TO THE SHOW, AND **WAIT** TO GET THEM SIGNED.
IF THEY HAVE A **GOOD** INTERACTION, THEY'LL REMEMBER IT **FOREVER** AND MIGHT BUY **EVERYTHING** HE WRITES FROM THEN ON.
IF HE LEAVES THEM HANGING, EVEN IF IT'S **JUSTIFIED**, THEY'LL THINK LESS OF HIM AND HE'LL LOSE A POTENTIAL **LIFELONG FAN**.
EVERY SIGNATURE IS IMPORTANT.
OKAY, IF YOU SAY SO.
AT THE TIME, I THOUGHT MARK WAS JUST BEING **DRAMATIC**.
I WAS SO WOUND UP IN MY OWN HEAD THAT I COULDN'T SEE I WAS THE EXACT SAME KIND OF FAN HOPING FOR MY MOMENT WITH SOMEONE I RESPECTED.

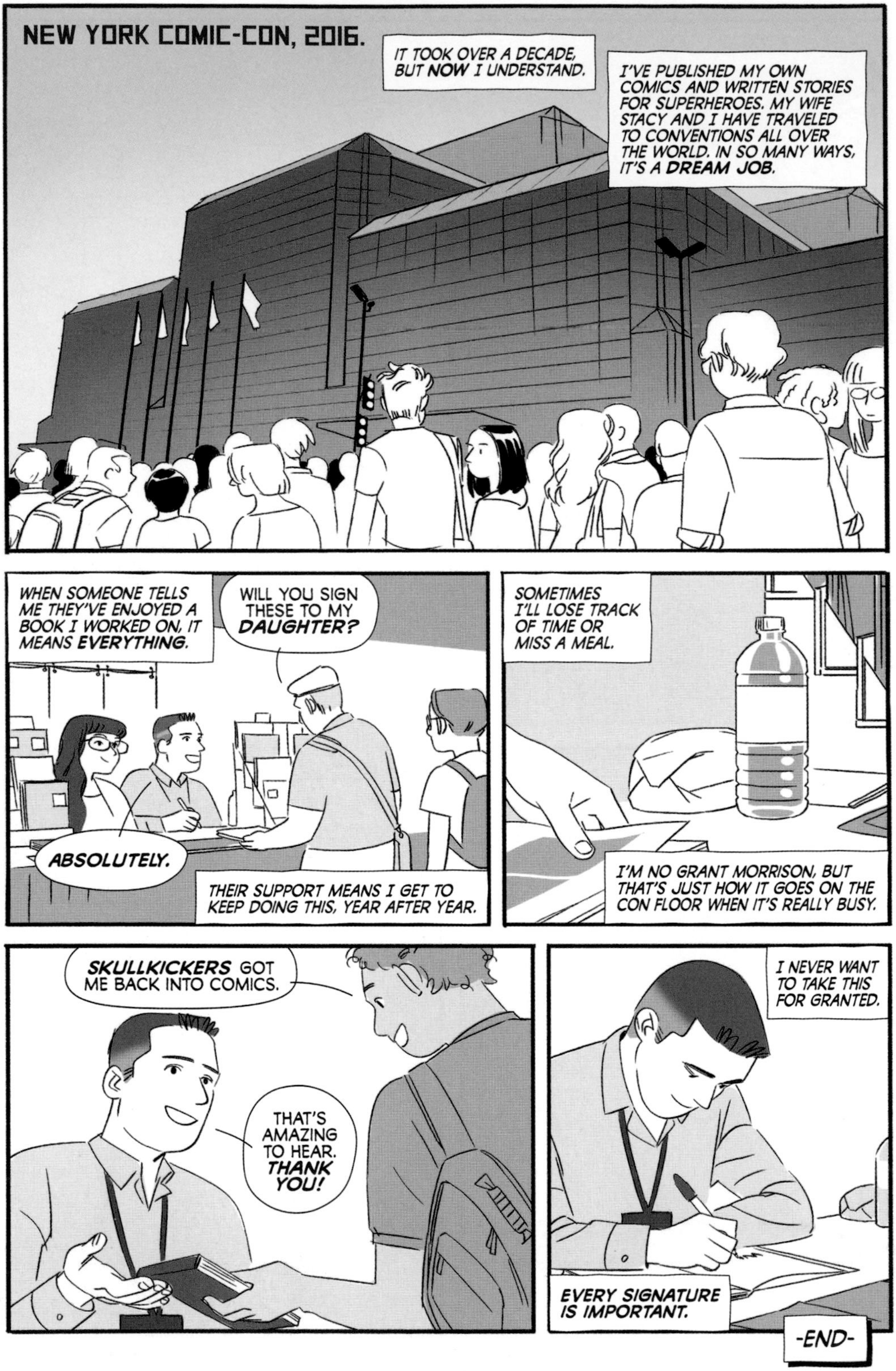
NEW YORK COMIC-CON, 2016.
IT TOOK OVER A DECADE, BUT NOW I UNDERSTAND.
I'VE PUBLISHED MY OWN COMICS AND WRITTEN STORIES FOR SUPERHEROES. MY WIFE STACY AND I HAVE TRAVELED TO CONVENTIONS ALL OVER THE WORLD. IN SO MANY WAYS, IT'S A DREAM JOB.
WHEN SOMEONE TELLS ME THEY'VE ENJOYED A BOOK I WORKED ON, IT MEANS EVERYTHING.
WILL YOU SIGN THESE TO MY DAUGHTER?
ABSOLUTELY.
THEIR SUPPORT MEANS I GET TO KEEP DOING THIS, YEAR AFTER YEAR.
SOMETIMES I'LL LOSE TRACK OF TIME OR MISS A MEAL.
I'M NO GRANT MORRISON, BUT THAT'S JUST HOW IT GOES ON THE CON FLOOR WHEN IT'S REALLY BUSY.
SKULLKICKERS GOT ME BACK INTO COMICS.
THAT'S AMAZING TO HEAR. THANK YOU!
I NEVER WANT TO TAKE THIS FOR GRANTED.
EVERY SIGNATURE IS IMPORTANT.
-END-

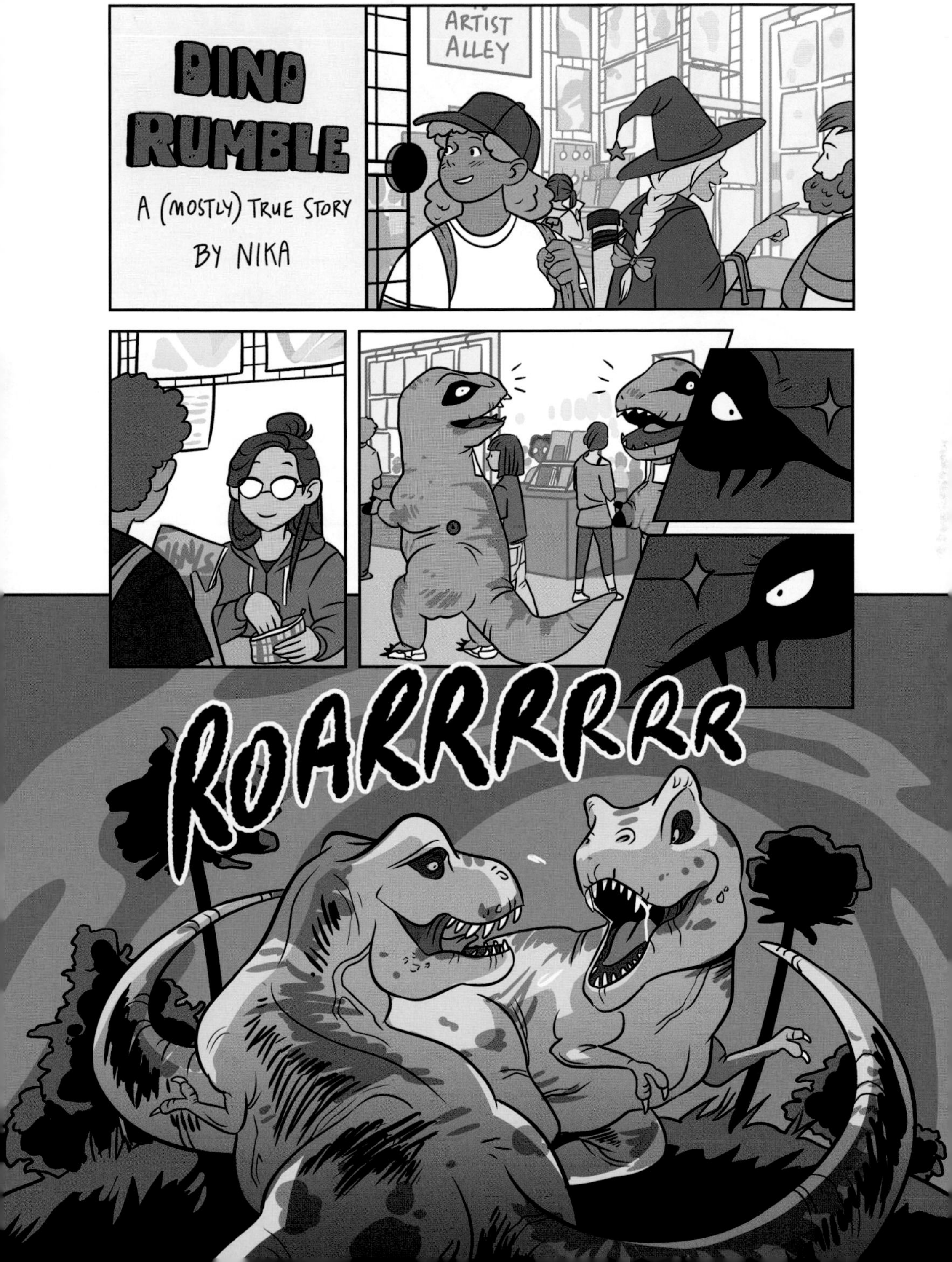
DINO RUMBLE
A (MOSTLY) TRUE STORY
BY NIKA
ARTIST ALLEY
ROARRRRRRR

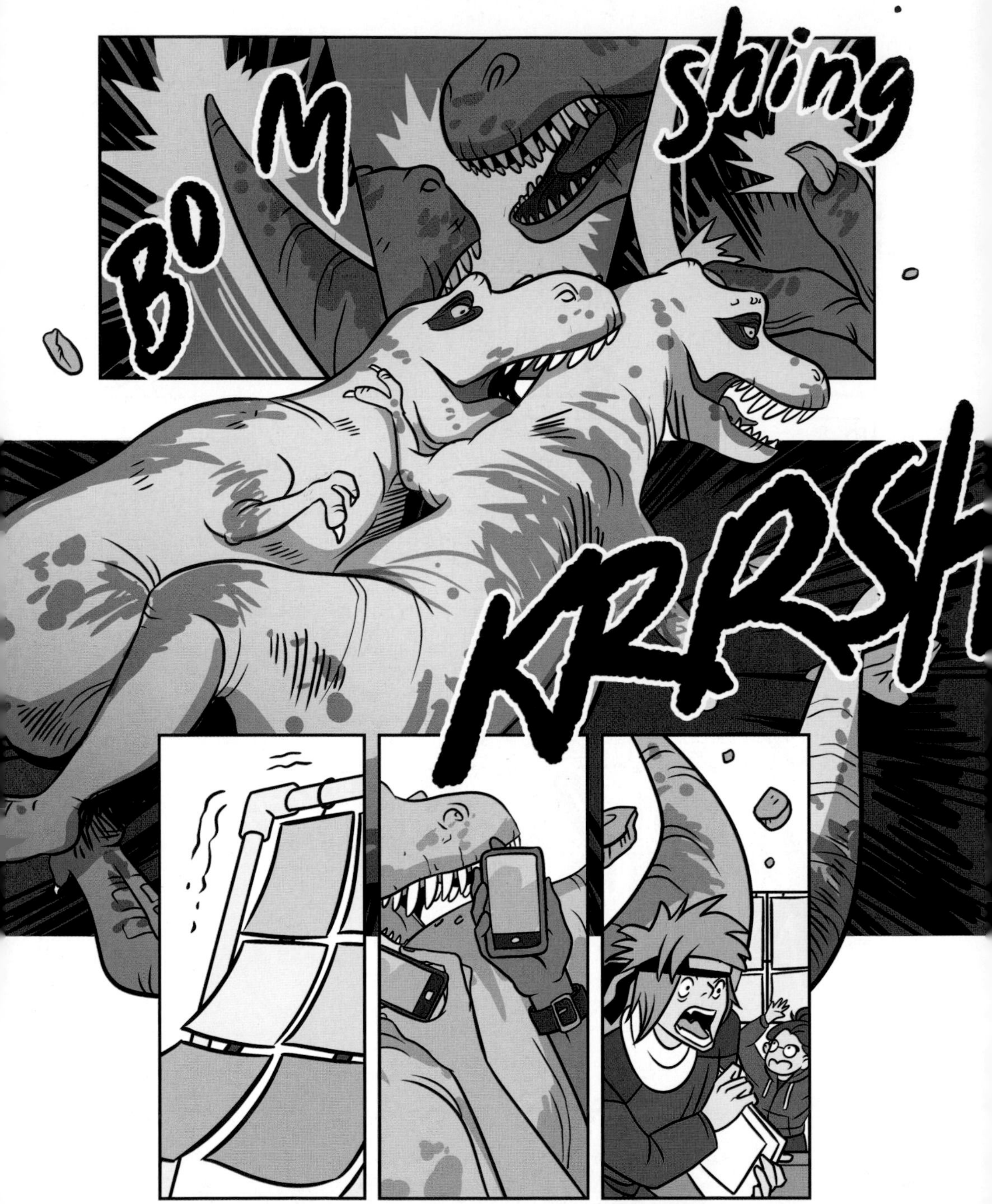
BOOM
shing
KRRSH

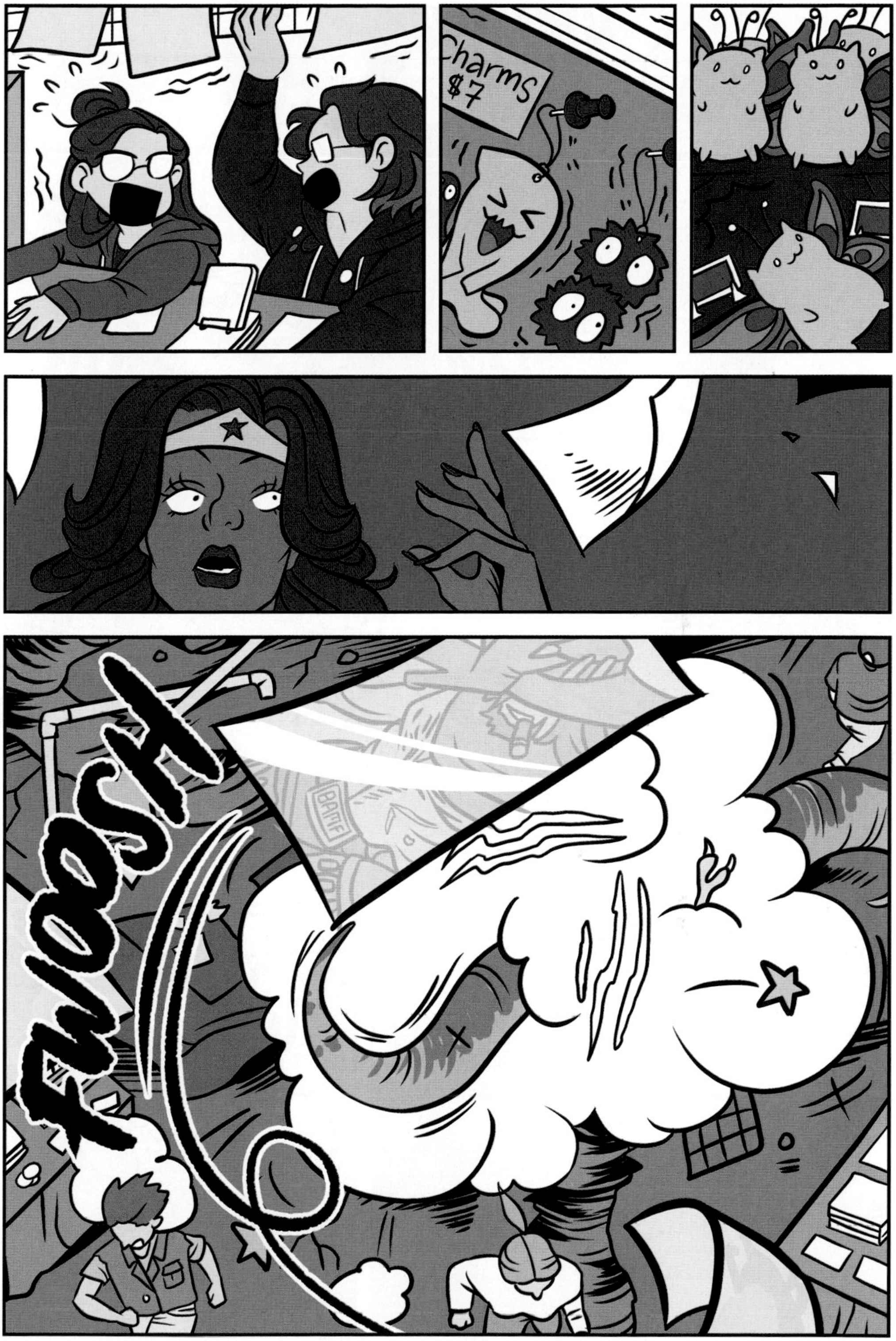
Charms
$7
BAMF
FWOOSH

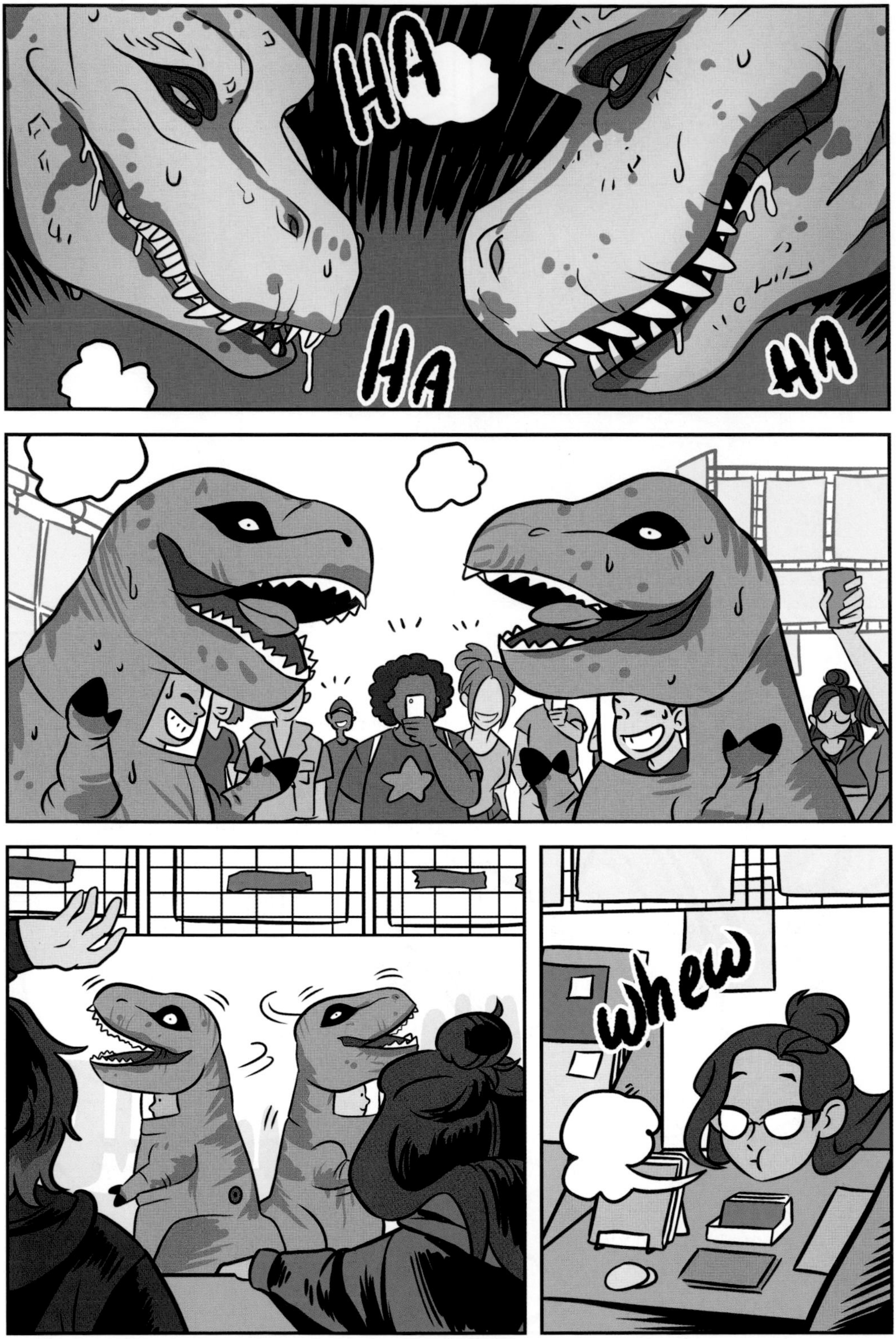
HA
HA
HA
whew

END.

BREAK EVEN

Tini Howard

Imagine you're me. The first time you go to a fan convention, you have no idea what you want to be when you grow up.

You're sixteen, around the age where it's no longer cute to suggest pie-in-the-sky daydreams when asked, "What would you like to do with your life?" One day it's cute when you answer with, "A marine biologist and a doctor and a talk show host and a writer," and the next day, it isn't. You have to choose one, and it's expected to be the *right* one, which always involves another ten years of being in school, which makes you wonder why you were supposed to answer so soon in the first place.

Anyway, you have no idea what you want to be when you grow up. And it's your senior year of high school. In an effort to drown out the rising anxiety in your chest, you spend a lot of time playing *Final Fantasy* games and reading vampire novels, which leads to logging on to the 2002 version of the Internet, looking for other people who play *Final Fantasy* games and read vampire novels, and from there, it's all over.

Your best friend, who is in the same AP Literature class as you, suggests that you two attend Katsucon, an event in the area for fellow anime and JRPG fans to get together. A convention. It's the first time you've ever heard of conventions outside of a Kevin Smith movie, but it seems *awesome*. A better selection of cool stuff than the weirdo basement "anime store" that's forty-five minutes away in traffic, and showings of recently-translated-movies and fan-made music videos on big screens (in 2002, streaming media was not yet a thing.) And there's *cosplay*.

Until now, cosplay has been a thing you and your best friend make fun of. You're not sure *why* you make fun of it. Probably because you're fascinated with it and haven't yet processed those feelings. Liking a character *so much* that you spend dozens of hours painstakingly recreating their costume to wear it around and *become* them? How . . . utterly strange and fascinating.

You're pretty sure it began as a joke. "What if we cosplayed, wouldn't that be weird?" You each have favorite characters from different Final Fantasy games. You've been told before that you look like Yuffie Kisaragi, the ninja character from Final Fantasy VII, so it would be *funny* if you dressed up as her. Sure, that's why.

For a joke, you scour the local Wal-Mart for a white turtleneck on clearance, a packet of green dye, styrofoam and silver fabric and sculpey clay. For a gag, you buy belts, shorts, fishnet stockings at a local thrift store to make into the pieces you need. For fun, you burn your fingers on dye baths and hot glue, staying up late into the night, even when classes start at 7:25 a.m., because you want to be Yuffie so badly.

You know, because it's *weird* or whatever.

You've been doing a lot of this on a broken foot. A stupid accident; you fell over on your way to the mailbox, running for the mail in the hopes of an acceptance letter to one of the colleges you actually care about. You didn't get in, but you did get an air cast that you have to wear sixteen hours a day. If you thought you didn't want to go to classes *before,* just *wait* until you have to hobble to each one on crutches. But even on crutches, you hop around the fabric store and the thrift store. You endlessly load your crutches into the back of your best friend's car and hop to the front seat, calculating how you can afford all of the bits and bobs you need to be an accurate Final Fantasy ninja (for a joke, of course) and also afford a peppermint mocha so you can stay awake to sew it.

The convention comes. You don't load your crutches into the back of your best friend's car this time—the air cast and crutches cramp your style. That's not what the character wears, so you don't wear it either. You'll tough it out and limp a little. It might be a joke, but it's even more pathetic if you look *bad*. The two of you are so amused by yourselves you pop out a handheld tape recorder—your cell phone just makes calls—and record yourselves. Making jokes, laughing. Singing made-up songs along to the Final Fantasy game soundtracks about how much the traffic into Washington D.C. sucks.

In ten years, when you are still cosplaying, you will still listen to that tape about how stupid this idea is, and how much you're only on your way to a con as a joke. Surely you, who sleeps in a Princess Leia t-shirt you ordered from the pages of *Star Wars Insider* magazine, who went to a friend's house so she could translate *Trigun* from her Chinese-subtitled tapes into English for you, who throws herself headlong into fanfiction every moment she isn't dragged from her disassociative play-places into the *real* world—surely you're not that big of a nerd.

You're only there, that Friday night, for a few hours. People like your costume, people take pictures. No one suspects that the metal stud on your armor is actually an old lip gloss tin, or that inside your sneaker, your broken foot is howling at you. You're Yuffie Kisaragi, Final Fantasy ninja. You are, for a moment, not yourself.

With that, you're off. Your heart immediately abandons the pretense of humor and the chains of your "cool" holding you in place rust and fall away. You find yourself floating, letting your "freak flag" fly, walking in circles and circles around the tables of nerds just like you. You look at file boxes full of manga and doujinshi, buy a vinyl decal of a favorite anime logo for the car you might get soon.

Over fifteen years later, you still remember what brought you to your knees at an artist's table. She was drawing Reno, a sloppy-suited, rangy miniboss from your favorite game, the one you're cosplaying from. He's your favorite character—he's cute, he's cool, he doesn't give a shit. You've written stories about him, what his life might have been like before he was a bad guy. The artist looks up from her work and is happy to see you—she likes your costume, too. You light up, and ask if you can watch her draw. You're too nervous to tell her about your story (over fifteen years later— you are glad that you did not tell her at length about your fanfiction.) But you sink slowly to your knees to watch, because your foot aches so badly, and because you're somewhat spiritually moved. You've never met another person, in the flesh, who loves this character like you do. And watching her pencil trace his cheekbones, (the same cheekbones you've imagined, despite the character only really existing in imperfect pixels), you lose yourself.

Until, of course, someone walking by steps on your broken foot. You feel it re-break, swallow your shout and lay your head down for a moment, grimacing. The artist asks if you're okay. You lie and say yes, and limp away. When you leave the convention for the night, you know you aren't coming back. You'll be laid up for *days* after being dumb enough to walk on your broken bone. But you already want more.

The silly weird convention trip that you did for a joke becomes a big part of your life. Upon seeing all of the costumes at the con, you instantly realize something—you need to level *up*. And the only way to level up, says a seasoned gamer like yourself—is to grind. You begin spending an absurd amount of your spare time and money on making costumes. Most of them never amount to anything, you hardly even get photos taken. But your whole *life* becomes the space between one convention and the next, what you'll wear when you're there. You break bones, break hearts, break your bank account at fabric stores, hardware stores, thrift stores, on your 1/8th cost of a two-person hotel room.

The anonymity that comes with embodying a character that isn't one's self is nothing new. The debauchery that comes after the masquerade is well-known enough that I won't retread it here. Imagine you're me— being someone else is what trains you to get to know people. I hated to go out and leave my LiveJournal behind, but this was like the same thing, the communities and friends, but in meatspace.

Imagine you're me—there comes a time when you begin to feel guilty. There's a pretty famous book that talks about putting aside childish things, and you've been spending a *lot* of money on costumes. In the time between graduating high school and gaining several levels in sewing, wig styling, and prop-work, you've become an adult. With a job you hate, but it's a good grown up job and it pays the bills. And when you go to conventions and look around you realize what you're seeing—a room full of adults who all had to choose what they wanted to be when they grew up, just like you, and they chose *this*.

The artists and writers you're gushing over, the vendors you're giving money to, they're all like you. You can get a table, sit on the other side, wearing no costume but your own best sales-pitching self, and sell your stories. Maybe one day, you'll walk out of a con with more money than you came in with. Theoretically. And even if you don't make a dime, just the prospect of being on the other side of the table is thrilling.

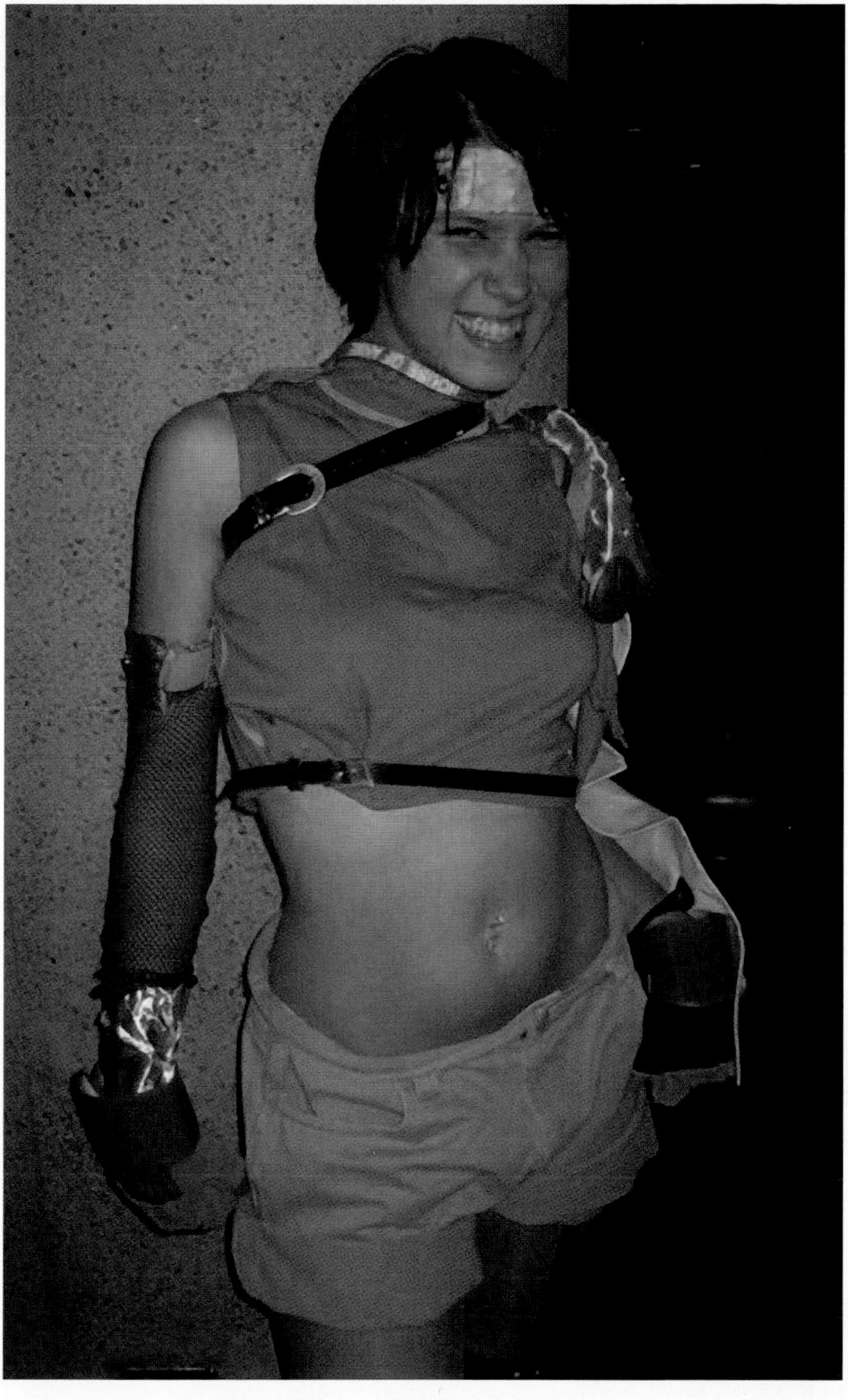

You start small. You start scheduling less costumes and more stylish-professional outfits, start booking your convention time less around late-night parties and more around early-morning breakfast meetups. You feel your former favorite hobby become *work* and the change is strangely welcoming. You bring less costumes, then just one costume, and then none. You pack an outfit for meetings with editors, an outfit for a book release event, and plenty of comfy clothes to wear while you're skipping parties, up late hitting deadlines in your room. The girl who once took her broken foot out of a cast for a costume now spends $100 on good sneakers to wear for fourteen hour shifts on the con floor.

"Do you miss it?" People ask you this all the time. "Do you miss having *fun* at conventions?" You don't know how to say that it's something other than fun. Conventions used to be a cupcake at the mall, and now they're bread and meat, a fundamental part of your life and career. Sitting in your hotel room writing the adventures of characters you used to cosplay is something that *barely existed* in the era before you. You're part of a generation of professionals that came up afraid for anyone to find out we wrote fanfiction and now it's something people come up to your table to ask you about. Your table, where you sit—they come to *you*.

There was a time when you too hid your past—your cosplay and your fanfiction. Now people cheer when you bring it up, because they're sitting in the audience at your panel, and they're just like you.

You think of yourself at sixteen, sitting in a panel room with a throbbing broken foot and questioning if all of this is a waste of time, comic books and costumes.

You know someone's going to ask her what she wants to be when she grows up.

You hope you can save her some time, time you spent trying to fit yourself into a mold of "adulthood" that was never going to work out.

And you would make sure to tell her—your costume looks *great*.

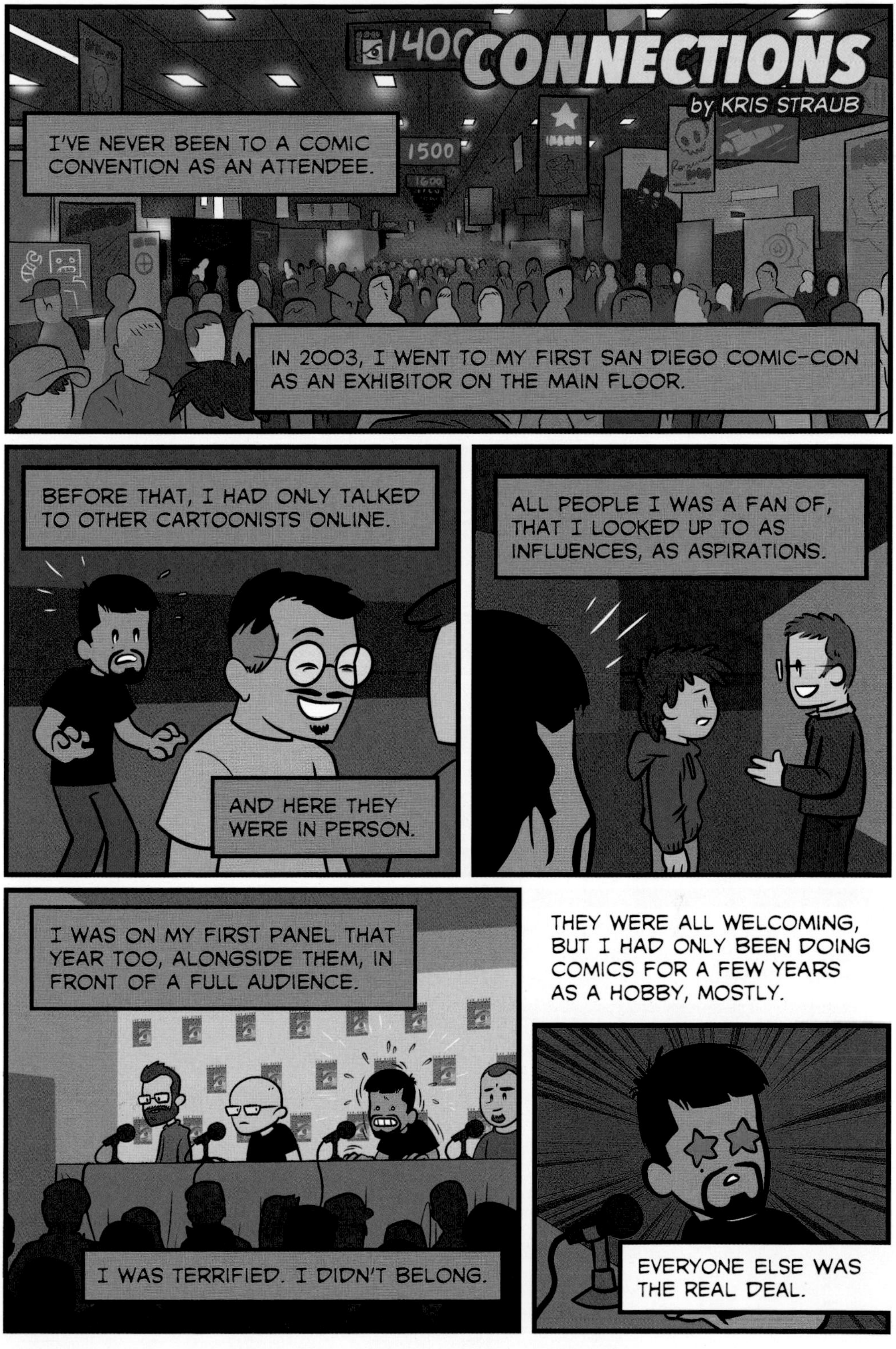
CONNECTIONS
by KRIS STRAUB
I'VE NEVER BEEN TO A COMIC CONVENTION AS AN ATTENDEE.
IN 2003, I WENT TO MY FIRST SAN DIEGO COMIC-CON AS AN EXHIBITOR ON THE MAIN FLOOR.
BEFORE THAT, I HAD ONLY TALKED TO OTHER CARTOONISTS ONLINE.
AND HERE THEY WERE IN PERSON.
ALL PEOPLE I WAS A FAN OF, THAT I LOOKED UP TO AS INFLUENCES, AS ASPIRATIONS.
I WAS ON MY FIRST PANEL THAT YEAR TOO, ALONGSIDE THEM, IN FRONT OF A FULL AUDIENCE.
I WAS TERRIFIED. I DIDN'T BELONG.
THEY WERE ALL WELCOMING, BUT I HAD ONLY BEEN DOING COMICS FOR A FEW YEARS AS A HOBBY, MOSTLY.
EVERYONE ELSE WAS THE REAL DEAL.

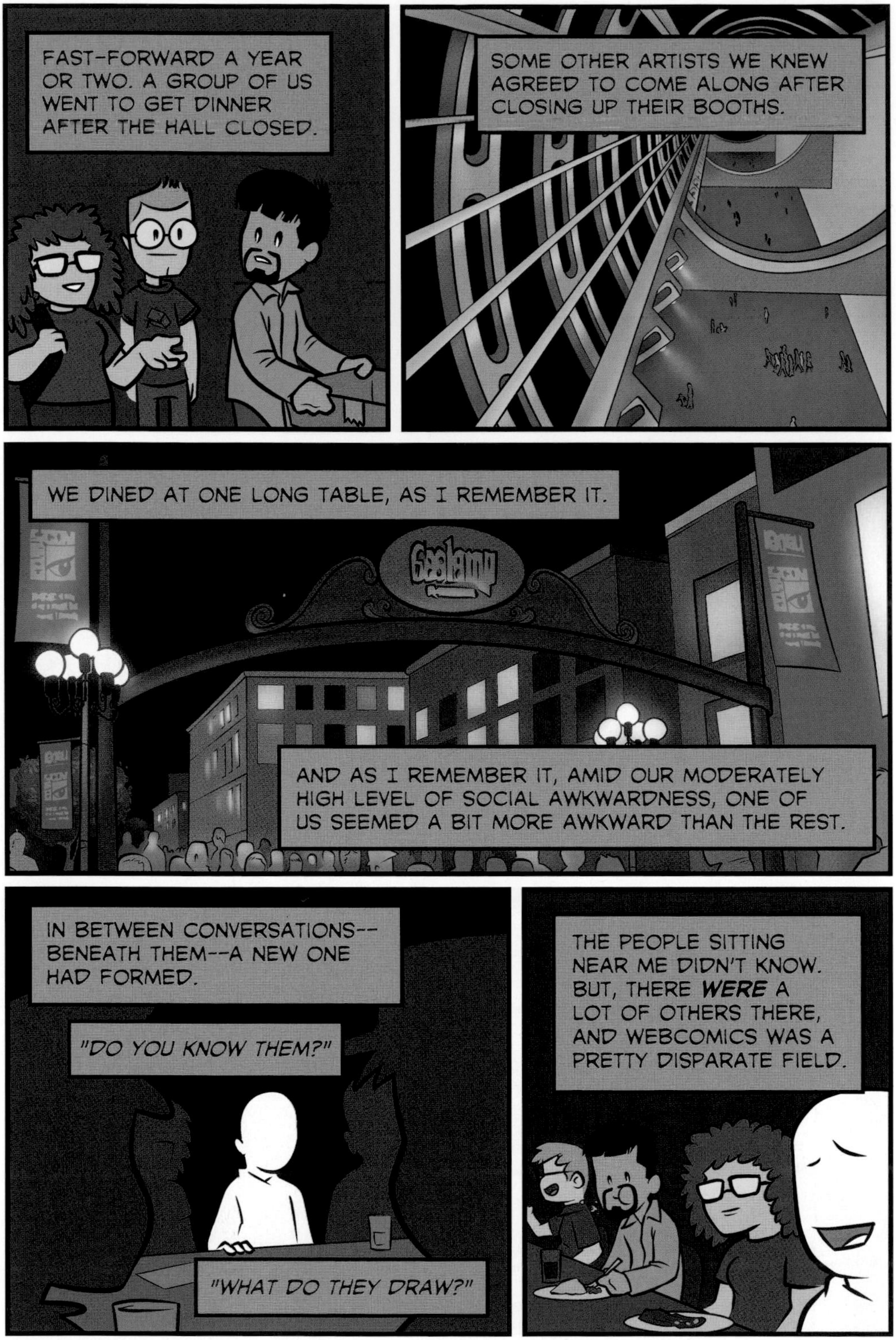
FAST-FORWARD A YEAR OR TWO. A GROUP OF US WENT TO GET DINNER AFTER THE HALL CLOSED.
SOME OTHER ARTISTS WE KNEW AGREED TO COME ALONG AFTER CLOSING UP THEIR BOOTHS.
WE DINED AT ONE LONG TABLE, AS I REMEMBER IT.
AND AS I REMEMBER IT, AMID OUR MODERATELY HIGH LEVEL OF SOCIAL AWKWARDNESS, ONE OF US SEEMED A BIT MORE AWKWARD THAN THE REST.
IN BETWEEN CONVERSATIONS-- BENEATH THEM--A NEW ONE HAD FORMED.
"DO YOU KNOW THEM?"
"WHAT DO THEY DRAW?"
THE PEOPLE SITTING NEAR ME DIDN'T KNOW. BUT, THERE *WERE* A LOT OF OTHERS THERE, AND WEBCOMICS WAS A PRETTY DISPARATE FIELD.

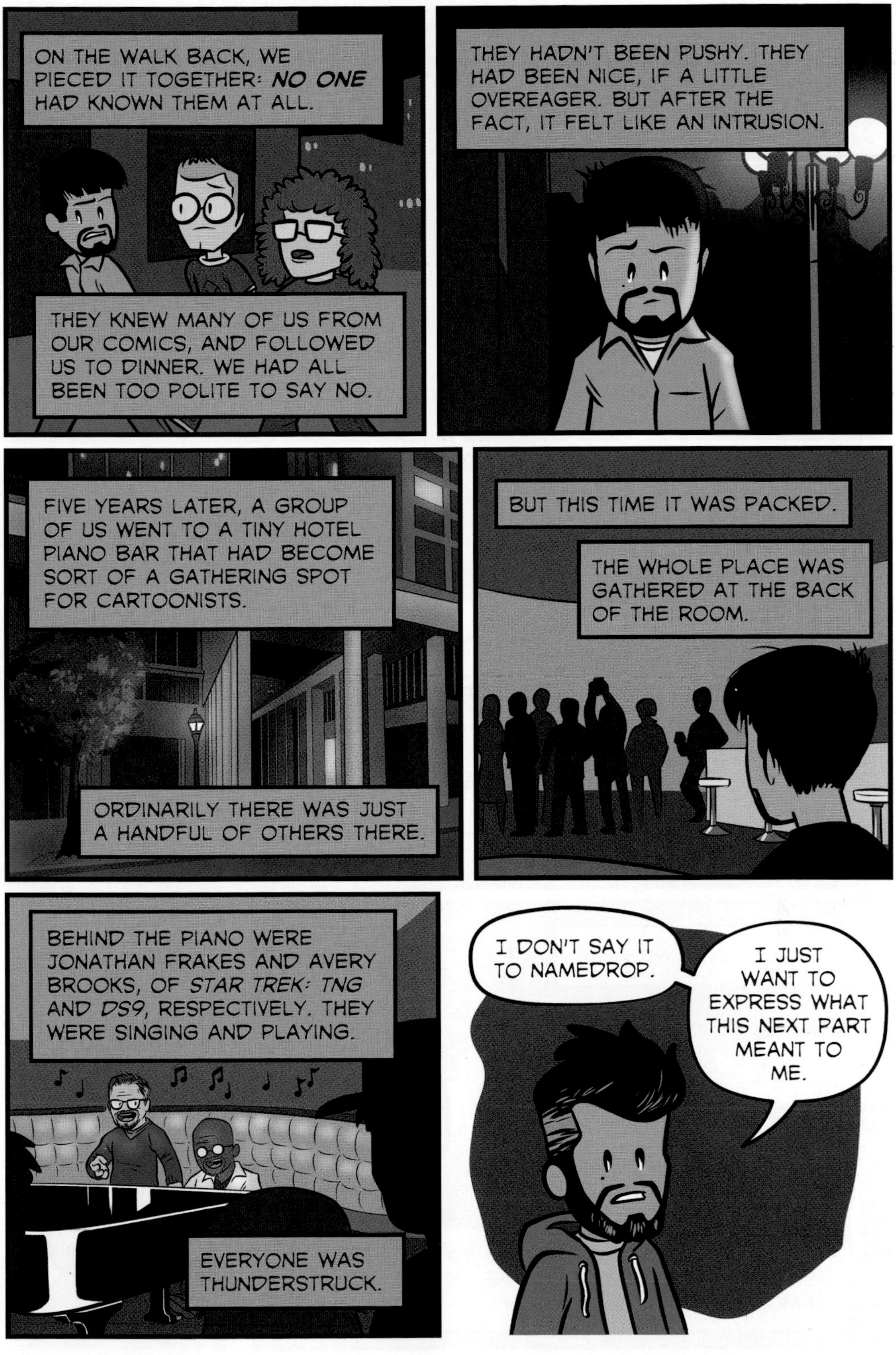
ON THE WALK BACK, WE PIECED IT TOGETHER: NO ONE HAD KNOWN THEM AT ALL.
THEY KNEW MANY OF US FROM OUR COMICS, AND FOLLOWED US TO DINNER. WE HAD ALL BEEN TOO POLITE TO SAY NO.
THEY HADN'T BEEN PUSHY. THEY HAD BEEN NICE, IF A LITTLE OVEREAGER. BUT AFTER THE FACT, IT FELT LIKE AN INTRUSION.
FIVE YEARS LATER, A GROUP OF US WENT TO A TINY HOTEL PIANO BAR THAT HAD BECOME SORT OF A GATHERING SPOT FOR CARTOONISTS.
ORDINARILY THERE WAS JUST A HANDFUL OF OTHERS THERE.
BUT THIS TIME IT WAS PACKED.
THE WHOLE PLACE WAS GATHERED AT THE BACK OF THE ROOM.
BEHIND THE PIANO WERE JONATHAN FRAKES AND AVERY BROOKS, OF STAR TREK: TNG AND DS9, RESPECTIVELY. THEY WERE SINGING AND PLAYING.
EVERYONE WAS THUNDERSTRUCK.
I DON'T SAY IT TO NAMEDROP.
I JUST WANT TO EXPRESS WHAT THIS NEXT PART MEANT TO ME.

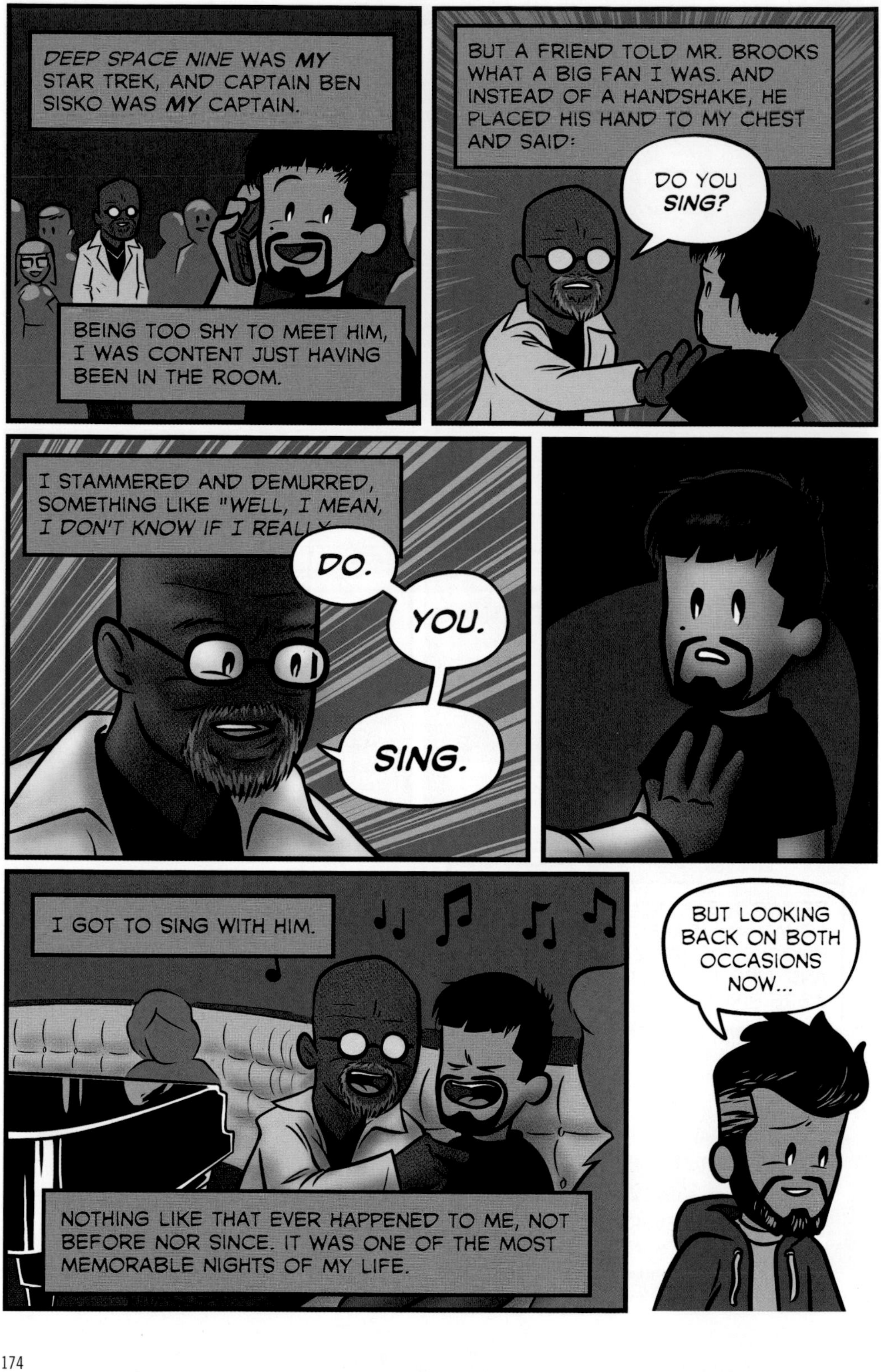
DEEP SPACE NINE WAS MY STAR TREK, AND CAPTAIN BEN SISKO WAS MY CAPTAIN.
BEING TOO SHY TO MEET HIM, I WAS CONTENT JUST HAVING BEEN IN THE ROOM.
BUT A FRIEND TOLD MR. BROOKS WHAT A BIG FAN I WAS. AND INSTEAD OF A HANDSHAKE, HE PLACED HIS HAND TO MY CHEST AND SAID:
DO YOU SING?
I STAMMERED AND DEMURRED, SOMETHING LIKE "WELL, I MEAN, I DON'T KNOW IF I REALLY...
DO.
YOU.
SING.
I GOT TO SING WITH HIM.
NOTHING LIKE THAT EVER HAPPENED TO ME, NOT BEFORE NOR SINCE. IT WAS ONE OF THE MOST MEMORABLE NIGHTS OF MY LIFE.
BUT LOOKING BACK ON BOTH OCCASIONS NOW...

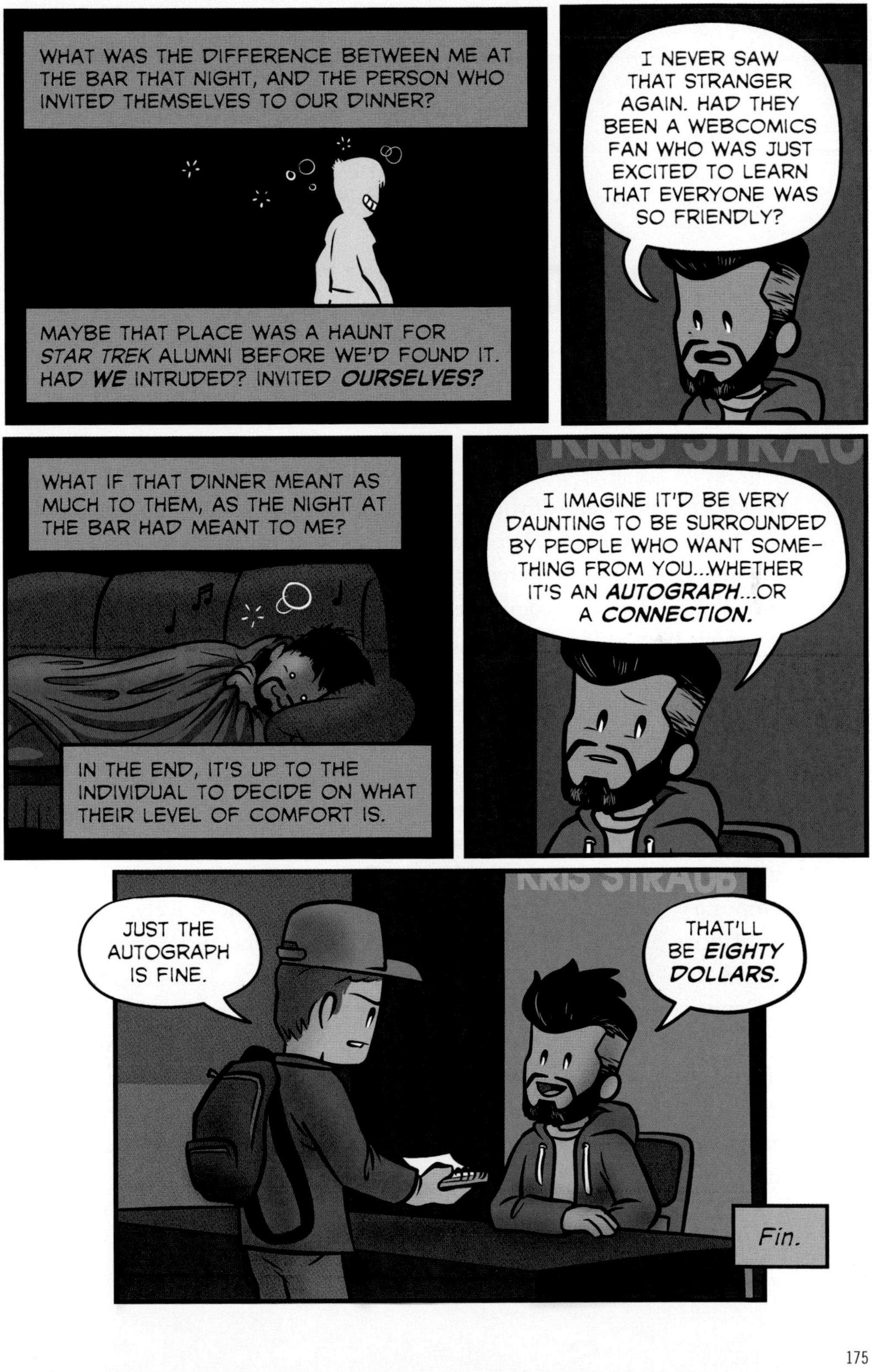
WHAT WAS THE DIFFERENCE BETWEEN ME AT THE BAR THAT NIGHT, AND THE PERSON WHO INVITED THEMSELVES TO OUR DINNER?
MAYBE THAT PLACE WAS A HAUNT FOR STAR TREK ALUMNI BEFORE WE'D FOUND IT. HAD WE INTRUDED? INVITED OURSELVES?
I NEVER SAW THAT STRANGER AGAIN. HAD THEY BEEN A WEBCOMICS FAN WHO WAS JUST EXCITED TO LEARN THAT EVERYONE WAS SO FRIENDLY?
WHAT IF THAT DINNER MEANT AS MUCH TO THEM, AS THE NIGHT AT THE BAR HAD MEANT TO ME?
IN THE END, IT'S UP TO THE INDIVIDUAL TO DECIDE ON WHAT THEIR LEVEL OF COMFORT IS.
I IMAGINE IT'D BE VERY DAUNTING TO BE SURROUNDED BY PEOPLE WHO WANT SOMETHING FROM YOU...WHETHER IT'S AN AUTOGRAPH...OR A CONNECTION.
KRIS STRAUB
JUST THE AUTOGRAPH IS FINE.
THAT'LL BE EIGHTY DOLLARS.
Fin.

THE CALIFORNIA GUYS

Bud Plant

Hello! I'm Bud Plant—if you are an old-timer, or maybe even not so old, you might recognize me. I've been doing catalogs of comics-related material since 1970 and I exhibited at every San Diego Comic-Con from 1970 until 2017. I was also a comics distributor from 1982–88, and opened and ran comic book stores in 1968, 1969–70, and 1972–88.

I discovered comics first through a subscription my family had to *Walt Disney's Comics & Stories* in the late 1950s, soon after I discovered the joy of buying my own ten-cent books, including *Fantastic Four* #1!

I started collecting regularly in 1964, a year later I was introduced to my comic buddies across town, then to comics fandom, and I never stopped falling in love with comics. It's a different world today—there were less than a dozen monthly Marvel titles in 1964—and I don't read many contemporary comics. But I still greatly enjoy graphic novels, French translations, and am deep into learning about the early artists, writers and publishers of comics through comic histories.

Comic conventions have always been an integral part of my life. I currently attend five or six per year. If you add in antiquarian book shows, where I also buy and sell comics, I exhibit at nearly one every month. Up until 2018, I never had a time in my life where I attended as a fan without setting up to sell. I love turning fellow fans and collectors on to "the good stuff," so I always find an excuse to set up at a show.

But that doesn't mean I haven't spent countless hours going through dealers' and fellow collectors' comics to find missing issues for my own collection!

That's how it all began and it's still the fuel I run on.

From the early days of just a handful of used comic dealers in the late sixties and maybe a hundred fans buying stock, to now giant conventions with overwhelming media displays and hundreds of thousands of fans packed into cons all weekend, conventions have changed and grown considerably. But while San Diego Comic-Con might be too exhausting (or impossible) to attend, that doesn't mean that there aren't small local cons even now, where you can still get that personal experience of looking for treasures, shoulder to shoulder with buddies or newly met collectors. And talk about favorite comic stories, artists, and covers with other fans.

A surprising number of these "other fans" who date back to my teen-aged years became my closest friends, business partners, and travelling companions. When I first met Phil Seuling in 1970, he dubbed us "The California Guys." Buddies at other shows did the same. In the early seventies, we were a little hardcore group of collectors, wheeling and dealing at every show that we could. We were so devoted to comics we spent weeks together on the road. Living on the cheap, sleeping in rest areas, enduring breakdowns, flat tires, even wrecking one van and buying a new one in Texas one year. All to get to meet our heroes—and buy a whole lot of old comics.

My very first show was BerkeleyCon, the World Science Fiction Convention (also known as WorldCon or BayCon), in August 1968. I was sixteen, and already the owner, with five other comic fans, of the Seven Sons Comic Shop in San Jose, California. Some call it the first comic shop, though like everything in comics, this is very debatable. At the least, we were the first free-standing comic store on the west coast. Bert Blum's Cherokee Books in LA pre-dated us, but it was an adjunct to a larger book store. We opened up just one month before Gary Arlington started his San Francisco Comic Book Company—but he gets full credit for running that shop through thick and thin much longer than we did.

A few months after we opened up, four of us headed north to BerkeleyCon, ostensibly to pick up stock for the store, but really, to add to our own personal collections. My buddies and I took our sleeping bags and actually got away with sleeping overnight on the grounds of the Clairmont Hotel. Not so different from the people camping out in front of SDCC still today, save that we were doing it to save money, and not to get a good spot for a movie sneak-peek. A very young Harlan Ellison was one of the guests, and the four of us from San Jose (a sixty-mile drive away) shared *one* table. Most of our time at the convention was spent looking for goodies for our own personal collections—two dealers from New Orleans, who quickly became convention buddies, kindly watched our neglected table while we roamed the dealer's room.

In 1969, we went a bit further, going to Houston Con, then OAF-Con, our first *real* comic convention. We all drove together and were generally pretty ditzy—spilling drinks in the car, flying stiff taco shells like frisbees out the car window, experiencing the interior roof melt and separate so that it ended up on our heads. We once passed a cop when we were going ninety mph, in Arizona or New Mexico (he was hidden in front of the car we were passing)–but luckily he didn't bother to stop us.

At the show we met many, many dealers and collectors, the heart of comics fandom in the area—people I still know today. The annual OAF-Con in Oklahoma (Oklahoma Alliance of Fandom, started in the late sixties) brings these guys all back together each year. We all became honorary members even though we all lived in California.

We bought out one fellow's tables at the end of the show, stuffed several thousand comics into the car's trunk and back seat—piled loose between two of us (boxes to protect them? Nahh!), and drove home to open our second store, Comic World, the same month.

But those trips were just preamble for the real thing . . . Phil Seuling's New York Comic Art Convention, preceded by a return trip to OAF-Con. This was 1970 and New York was our comics mecca. San Diego had only had just one tiny show the same year—which we also trekked to—but back then, New York was *the* place to go. Oklahoma City was part of a triumvirate of Houston, Dallas and OK-city shows, also outstripping the then-teenie little San Diego Comic-Con.

Here's that story, from memory but also from my informal diaries in which I kept of all my comic book activities c.1964–72. Quotes are direct from there.

Friday, June 12, 1970
Packed up and left about 11:30 for conventions

We left our store, Comic World, in the hands of three comic buddies. This was our second store. Six of us had opened Seven Sons in 1968, but five of us had sold out our shares to one of the partners in the same year.

Coming on the trip were Michelle (then Mike) Nolan, Larry Strawther, John Barrett, and myself. I had just graduated from high school. Well, sort of.

We had to leave for the east before the last days of the school year, but fortunately after finals. I made up a story that my folks were taking me on vacation. The school bought it. So I missed the graduation ceremony, and those precious last days with friends, which I do feel melancholy about now. But I'd do it all again. Comics were our life. John had graduated the year before, and Michelle was already well into college, and Larry, too, I expect. So it was summer vacation time for all of us.

Michelle had driven back east the previous year on a long road trip with Larry, so she knew the ropes already. She'd been to New York Con, met Phil Seuling, who was already a bit of a legend among comic collectors, and stayed at his family's apartment, working for him at the show. I think she also drove by Cape Canaveral for the moon launch as part of the trip.

It was the four of us in a short baby blue Dodge Tradesman van, with boxes of old comics, and underground comics that I'd bought for the trip—about a thousand just purchased a week earlier, titles like *Skull Comics* #1, R. Crumb's *Motor City* #2, *Hydrogen Bomb* #1, *Slow Death Funnies*, *Zap* #5, and *Insect Fear*. We brought whatever we thought might sell, to turn into more comics for our collections.

My dad and I installed rear windows in the utility van and put in a cool little stereo system, with a cassette player and speakers on each side of the car, mounted into plywood panels that came with the van. My sister or my mom added curtains for the side and rear windows that we could draw closed at night, if we were sleeping inside or wanted to hide the boxes.

I'd bought the van just for this trip. John Barrett's dad had loaned us his Ford LTD for the Houston trip last year in 1969. That wasn't going to happen again. I don't think the car was ever the same. That's another story there.

I borrowed the money from my folks, $1,800 for my first car . . . well, in my case, van. We immediately had a tire disintegrate just thirty miles south of San Jose, in Gilroy. Turned out the van was sporting retread tires, nicely spray painted on the sides to look like new. The load was immediately too much for them.

I think we managed to lose all four of them by the end of the trip, broken under the weight of all our comic collections. We were off to a questionable start, but nothing was going to stop us!

Saturday, June 13
Pulled into LA (Los Angeles)—bought nine originals by Joe Kubert and Russ Heath

Most likely these were DC war pages—and probably intended for sale at the shows, since I don't have them anymore. Back then we were more into old comics than original comic pages. I also scored the new book "*The Pulp Heroes, Arkham Collector* #6 . . . " and assorted new paperbacks with cover art by Jeff Jones (later Jeffrey Catherine Jones) and Frank Frazetta.

We would have made the rounds of the three sources of old comics in Hollywood: Collector's Book Store, Cherokee Book Store, and Bond Street Books (see *Comic Shop* by Dan Gearino, 2017, for more details on these first stores), looking for cheap comics to take to the shows to resell. But I think we were saving our money, what little we had, for the show itself.

The next few days were fairly unremarkable; we travelled up to Oklahoma City, staying in rest areas at night, and cooked up hot cereal on a little camp stove we brought along. We survived mostly on fast-food burgers and gas station junk food.

Thursday, June 18
Undergrounds sold well.

We finally made it to Oklahoma City, and set up our table there for the first day of the convention. Another friend from San Jose, Jim Vadeboncoeur, Jr., had flown in for the con. Jim was big time, he had a real job and everything, so he had no patience for the long van route. Along with Jim came a co-editor of ours from *Promethean*, Al Davoren. Jan Strnad, who'd already collaborated with artist Richard Corben on several comics and would go on to a successful comics career, joined us as well.

Jim and I, along with Al Davoren, had co-edited—and hand-folded, collated, and stapled—two issues of our own fanzine, *Promethean Enterprises*, which mixed drawings and sketches by regular comics artists like Al Williamson and Frank Frazetta with underground work by Rick Griffin, who did the first two covers, Robert Crumb, who did the cover of issue #3 and had work inside most issues, and many others. The second issue had just been put together in early June, so I also had that and #1 for sale at the show.

A note about fanzines: before modern times when fans can break into print easily with print-on-demand, not to mention blogs and social media, the only way we could communicate was by letter and fanzine. Fans as famous as Roy Thomas got their start doing amateur strips and history-of-comic articles in short-run amateur publications, often printed with inexpensive ditto machines, an ugly but very cheap medium. Zines were an outgrowth of science fiction fandom, who'd been producing them since the thirties. As editors got a bit more funding and print runs went up, these went to photo-offset, our modern method of printing, and even into full color. These were the publications I loved, and that I began to buy for resale to other fans through the mail and at shows.

Selling these fanzines along with underground comics was quickly to become my new, fledgling mail order business that began in the fall following these shows, and continues today as *Bud's Art Books.*

John Barrett and I bought two original Reed Crandall paintings. Mine (which I still own) featured John Carter, Dejah Thoris, Tars Tarkas, and other Martian green men being attacked by the Black Pirates. It was an unfinished painting Reed had supposedly intended to give to his friend Al Williamson, who had encouraged him to paint it (see Roger Hill's biography of Crandall, which mentions it). It was never finished, and somehow Jerry Weist ended up with it. Jerry had published it in his fanzine *Squa Tront*, where I'd first seen it. But never like this.

I had fallen hard for Reed Crandall's work early in my collecting. To me, he was every bit as good as Frazetta, Wood, and the other giants we all collected. So not only was I seeing his original artwork for the first time, here was a chance to own something very special.

Suddenly John and I went from strictly comics fans to collecting original art. John bought a finished John Carter/Green Martian piece for himself. Jerry, who sold me the painting, went on to open The Million Year Picnic in Boston, with Chuck Wooley—one of the premier early comic stores. He also curated the first comic book auctions from Sotheby's in the nineties, and wrote books about EC and Ray Bradbury . . . but here we were still just a bunch of young comic fans doing our thing.

More acquisitions included the legendary Frazetta solo-comic book, *Thunda* #1, a Bernie Wrightson original, two Roy Krenkel originals (I think I still have mine, a lovely time-travel pen and ink), and a Crandall sketch which I sold in New York. And the list goes on, comics with Reed Crandall, ECs, Atlas comics, even *Uncle Scrooge* and *Mickey Mouse* magazines from 1936.

Friday, June 19
picked up Donald Duck Four Color #*159, 1947,*
"The Ghost in the Grotto," The Fine Line of Al Williamson

The Fine Line was compiled and published by Jim Vadeboncoeur, so I assume he introduced it here at the show.

Saw Buster Crabbe

This line in my journal is as understated as you can get since he was the guest of the show! Buster Crabbe was the handsome star of the thirties *Flash Gordon* film and numerous other features. The show was called "Multi-Con" for a reason, since its themes embraced comics *and* old movies and serials, beloved by the older fans there (and just being introduced to us youngsters, since we hadn't grown up on Saturday matinees in the forties and early fifties, as they had).

Sunday June 21
Dealer's room went all night

While movies were playing, the dealers' room remained open all through Saturday night and Sunday morning, and we evidently stayed up all night. We moved between watching movies—remember, most of these would have probably never made it to TV, being genre westerns, sci-fi, and serials—and hanging out together in the dealers' room.

Left hotel in evening . . . sacked out for 14–18 hours.

What this meant was we drove a little way out of Oklahoma City, found a rest area, and slept well into the next day. Clearly we were all burnt out from the all-nighter plus all the show goings-on. I don't think I'd ever slept so long before.

John and I made a grand total together of $450 at the show, which if you adjust for inflation would be around $3,000 today. That was *big* money for us, and now we were set for New York. Since John and I were already partners in Comic World (and had also been partners in Seven Sons), we worked in partnership at the shows this year, sharing acquisitions and then splitting up the loot, depending on which books we liked the most. Often we'd draw cards to see who would get first pick, then go from there. That's just what we used to do in the store, even with our many partners, when comics would come in that were destined for our collections.

We were now on our way to New York City for the next big event, which was to begin on July 3.

In New York, we would do a whopping $750—mostly selling comics bought from the OK show, and picked up a few acquisitions too. But somehow, by the end we still ended up $500 in debt to Phil Seuling, as you'll see below.

But first, we had a week to make it to New York City, and lord knows exactly what we did in that week. We dropped Michelle off in the south somewhere, so that she could take a bus through Arkansas, one of the very few states she'd never been in before, and meet us back north. We ended up coming into Washington, DC on a rainy, miserable day, probably June 30 or July 1. We did a quick tour of the Washington Monument and the Lincoln Memorial, and decided to head out for New York. We were supposed to meet Michelle at Phil Seuling's apartment a day or so later, but we jumped the gun and arrived late in the evening.

Being bold and naïve, we parked the car in Luna Park, just off Coney Island, and trekked up to the thirteenth floor to Phil's apartment. No cell phones in those days, so no calling in advance for us. It was about 10:30, but we could hear a radio or TV through the door, so we went ahead and knocked.

This big hulking guy comes to the door in his briefs—well, it was summertime in muggy New York—takes a look at us, and declares, "You must be the California guys." And the three of us proceed to spread out our bedrolls in his kitchen.

The next morning we met Phil's wife Carol and his two kids, Gwen and Heather, who were probably about eight and ten years old. Phil proudly announced he'd laid in lots of breakfast cereal for Michelle—who proceeded to roll in a few hours later.

If this seems a bit strange, we were probably some of the very, very few fans crossing the country to do the show, so we were welcomed with open arms. And Phil was like that. A high school teacher, he was the most out-going and generous man I'd ever met, the life of every party, enthusiastic, passionate. He'd recruit his students as help at the show . . . just as he recruited all of us to do security detail in the dealer's room, and transport stuff from his apartment there in Brooklyn to the Statler Hilton Hotel in Manhattan . . . and back again. Like many New Yorkers, Phil had never owned a car. You took the subway or cabs or car service, which we would soon learn all about.

Friday, July 3
Convention opened

Helped Phil with con for room and board/table next to Dorry [Phil's table help] and Dale Manesis

Dale was a slightly older guy, in his thirties like Phil, a dealer from Milwaukee, where he had a store devoted all sorts of paper and toy nostalgia. He was a notorious drinker who would leave a table filled with empty bottles after each show. And a great character who quickly became another long-time friend. We visited him later at his show and his home, where his basement was filled with wonderful items in his collection.

We were in a spot of honor being next to Phil's table. On our other side were Jack Diamond and Roger Nelson from New Orleans, who watched our table at our first-time show, BerkeleyCon. We eventually visited them on our way through New Orleans for a wild night of adventure. I spent the day buying and selling comics, scoring more forties and fifties comics with Frazetta, Wood, and Williamson.

Saturday, July 4
Steranko Portfolio, Cheech Wizard, The Machines, Bode poster

Jim Steranko, already a good friend of Phil's (he drew originals for Heather and Gwen's bedroom at the apartment) introduced his new portfolio at the show. He berated me for mispronouncing his name Ster-on-ko, but we also became friends pretty quickly. He was as much a huckster there at the show as he was an artist/celebrity, pushing his own publications as well as art and pin-up books. From then on he and I bought publications from each other, swapped tips about new products to handle and about catalog layout (he was light-years ahead of me).

Vaughn Bode was there with his *Cheech Wizard and The Machines* booklet and a poster. As much as I could, I would buy multiple copies of all these new publications at wholesale and bring them home to sell in the store and in my mail order business. That's how immediate so much of distribution was in those days—find it at a show, buy a bunch of copies, start a relationship with the publisher.

Sunday, July 5
Bought and had signed Frazetta original, Krenkel sketches, Jones sculpture

There was an auction, undoubtedly overseen by Seuling. I bought a Frazetta drawing and had it signed by Frank, a wonderful page from *Heroic Comics*. Phil was selling Roy Krenkel sketches, a few on each 8.5x11 page on regular white paper, for $10 each. I bought several. And Jeff Jones unveiled his amazing statue, the nude cave girl, of which he only made fifty or so copies. Phil went on to buy several and sell them through his own small mail order business. Every one was broken in the mail, most at the knees. Jeff added a metal rod for the second edition. Fortunately, mine has never been stressed and remains just as I bought it, flaws and all.

Monday, July 6
With Barry to Abe Paskow's, missed baseball game with Fritz, Torres & Morrow

I don't remember if we spent Sunday at the hotel or went back to Phil's apartment on Sunday night. But that day was my greatest "fish that got away" story. Barry Bauman, another young collector from Oakland, California was at the show and knew an old timer named Abe Paskow, who sold original art. Paskow even had legendary stuff like *Little Nemo* Sunday by Winsor McCay. So we headed over to his place where I found myself a lovely V.T. Hamlin *Alley Oop* daily, and a piece by Will Eisner.

Meanwhile, my partner John played baseball with Phil, Frazetta, Angelo Torres, and Gray Morrow, undoubtedly with other volunteers from the con.

Oh, my, goodness.

All that I can say about missing the chance to play baseball with these legends is that I had been held back in "farm league" for three years of Little League baseball. I was absolutely appalled at the idea of making a fool of myself playing baseball with my heroes, even though I had been invited. I'm sure my joy at spending an afternoon with such company might have overcome my embarrassment, but I'll never know.

Tuesday, July 7
*Left Phil's place—goodbye to Carol, Gwen & Heather,
Sal, Dorry, Eric, etc.*

Sal was probably Sal Quartuccio, still a publisher today as SQP—he produced Phil's con booklets for these first years.

Wednesday, July 8
Through Ohio, Indiana. Axel broke

The next few days were spent making the same trip in reverse. We burned up a rear axle in Brimfield, Illinois. We got to spend a night there while the gas station manager made a special trip back into the big city and got us a new axle, while we goofed around cleaning up his station for his assistant, in return for free cokes and playing a yard dart game in the side lawn. We slept in our sleeping bags in the back yard of his attached house.

Friday, July 10
dropped off Lucas, Mike and Larry.

We covered a lot of ground on our last day. We had picked up another buddy from Oakland, Lucas Dang, at the New York show. I'd almost forgotten this. He had flown to New York for the show, so he hitched a ride back home with us. He and his brother Ted Dang collected and bought and sold comics—I still find occasional books with their address stamped on the first page.

And then, the California Boys were home. We came back home stone-cold broke, borrowing money from one another for hot chocolate over the Sierras. Phil Seuling had sent us on our way owing him $500—for yet another batch of Joe Kubert and Russ Heath original art pages and other stuff. I think the pages ran us $4 each. We proceeded to flip them in *Comic World* at a whopping price of $10 each. I still delight in how this great guy from New York gave a couple teenagers credit of $500 and sent us on our way.

That was the beginning of an amazing relationship. Phil and I went on to co-publish and co-distribute books and fanzines, swap fanzines, underground comics and other books, and set up at shows together. He came out beginning the next year to San Diego Comic Cons, and I went back east for the next twelve years of Phil's own shows in New York, until he gave them up due to his health.

The experience of travelling together bonds people like nothing else. Some of us are still friends to this day, others went on to do other things, but I still have incredible memories from this whirlwind trip.

Where are they now:

Michelle Nolan has probably attended more comic conventions than nearly any other fan, still driving to several each year. She's a professional journalist, but also has written for *Comic Book Marketplace, The Comics' Buyer's Guide,* and other comic spots. She's written two books for McFarland including *Love on the Racks,* about the romance comics of the fifties, and received an Inkpot Award in 2014.

Larry Strawther was never a big comics fan and dropped out of our circle. He went on to write for Merv Griffin and several other popular television shows.

John Barrett, **Bob Beerbohm** and I started Comics & Comix, which became the first comic store chain. We had seven stores by 1988 when we sold out, and they continued to 2004, when then-owner Ross Rojack was arrested for security fraud. In 1987, **Barrett** founded the Wonderful World of Comics Convention (later known as WonderCon). He died in 2002.

Phil Seuling (1934–84) is commonly considered the founder of the Direct Market, the system of distribution that led to the exponential growth of comic book stores. He ran the NY Comic Art Convention from 1969–

1980s, as well as the monthly Second Sunday show in NYC.

And I, **Bud Plant**, am still as enthusiastic as ever about collecting comics, learning about artists, and sharing my discoveries with friends and customers. It often surprises me when someone is in turn surprised that I still am actively collecting. Why not? There's just so much out there to learn about, to enjoy. I love finding more and more obscure Golden Age comics. My interests also have expanded into the history of illustration, so I have built quite a collection of illustrated books, circa 1850–1950, vintage magazines with special artists, pulps, and ephemera. And, yes, original art to keep my Reed Crandall company.

I think it has been an advantage for me to be a lifetime dealer in all this, and it's given me the time, the access, and the means to keep pushing my interests out into new fields. But I've never left comics behind and still love all those books from my youth and the hallowed years before I was born. And there's still nothing like hunting for treasures at comic and book shows . . . you really never, ever, know what is going to turn up. But great stuff always does.

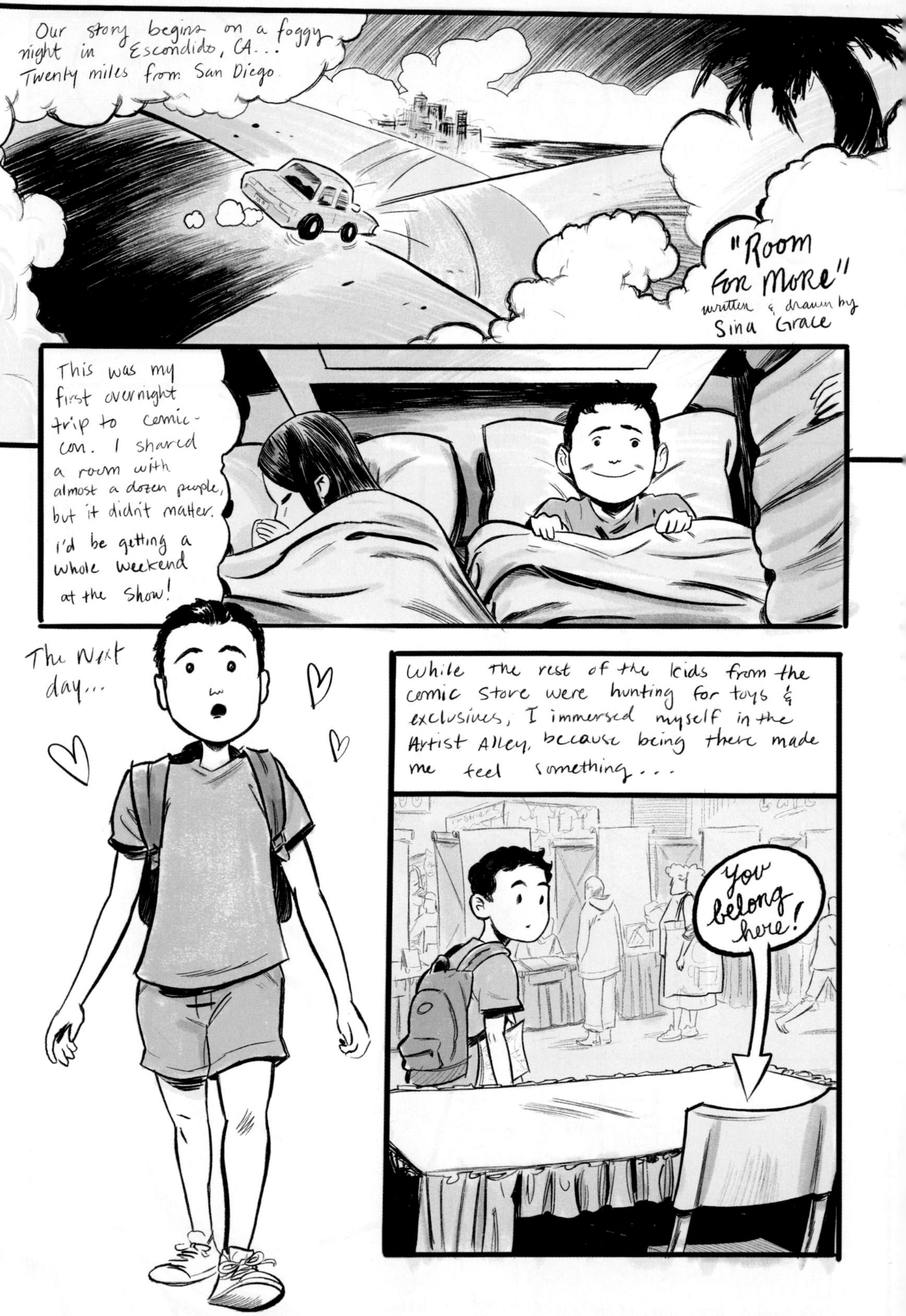

Our story begins on a foggy night in Escondido, CA... Twenty miles from San Diego.
"Room for More"
written & drawn by Sina Grace
This was my first overnight trip to comic-con. I shared a room with almost a dozen people, but it didn't matter. I'd be getting a whole weekend at the Show!
The Next day...
While the rest of the kids from the comic store were hunting for toys & exclusives, I immersed myself in the Artist Alley, because being there made me feel something...
You belong here!

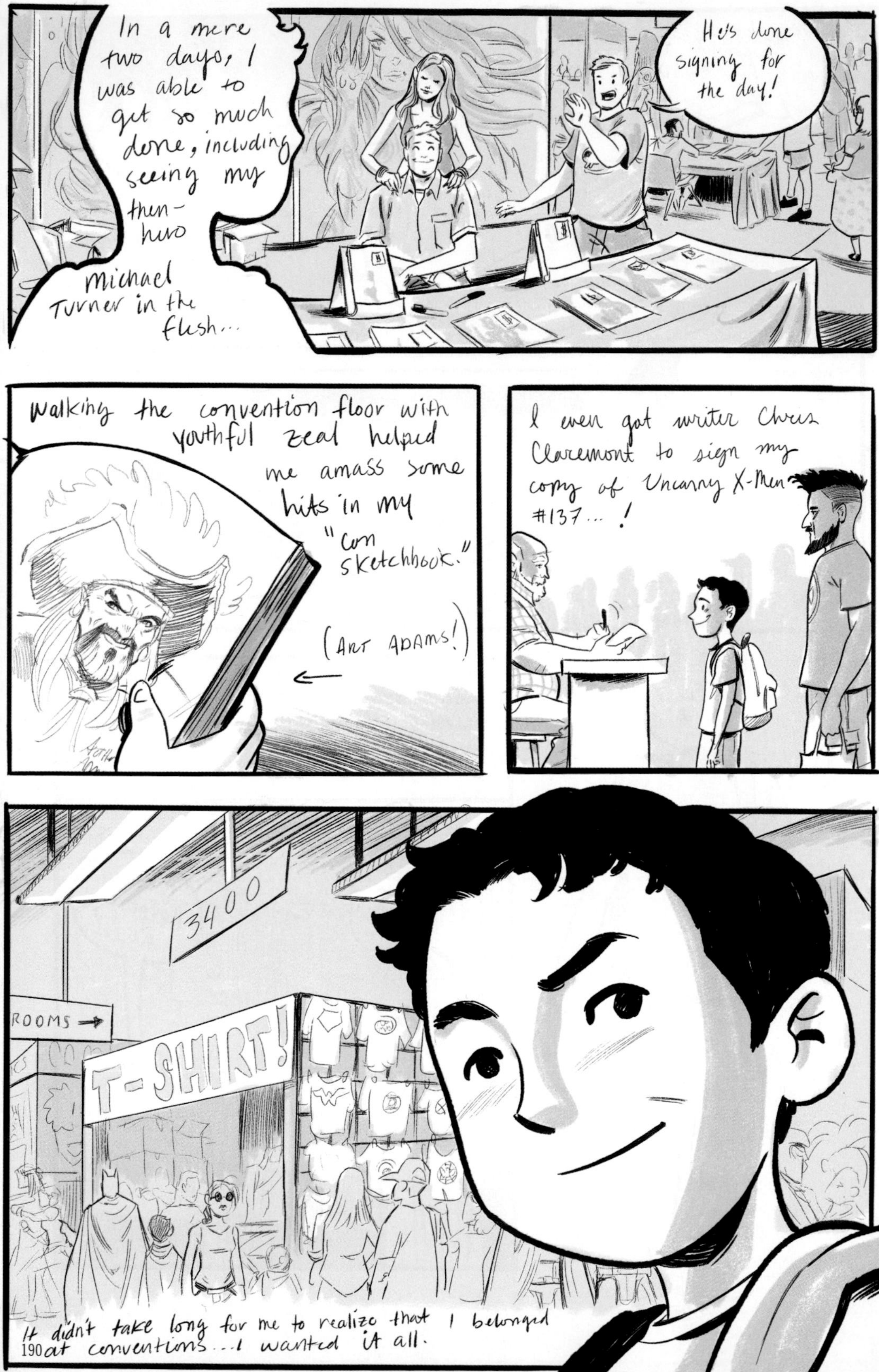
In a mere two days, I was able to get so much done, including seeing my then-hero Michael Turner in the flesh...
He's done signing for the day!
Walking the convention floor with youthful zeal helped me amass some hits in my "con sketchbook."
(ART ADAMS!)
I even got writer Chris Claremont to sign my copy of Uncanny X-Men #137... !
3400
ROOMS
T-SHIRT!
It didn't take long for me to realize that I belonged at conventions... I wanted it all.

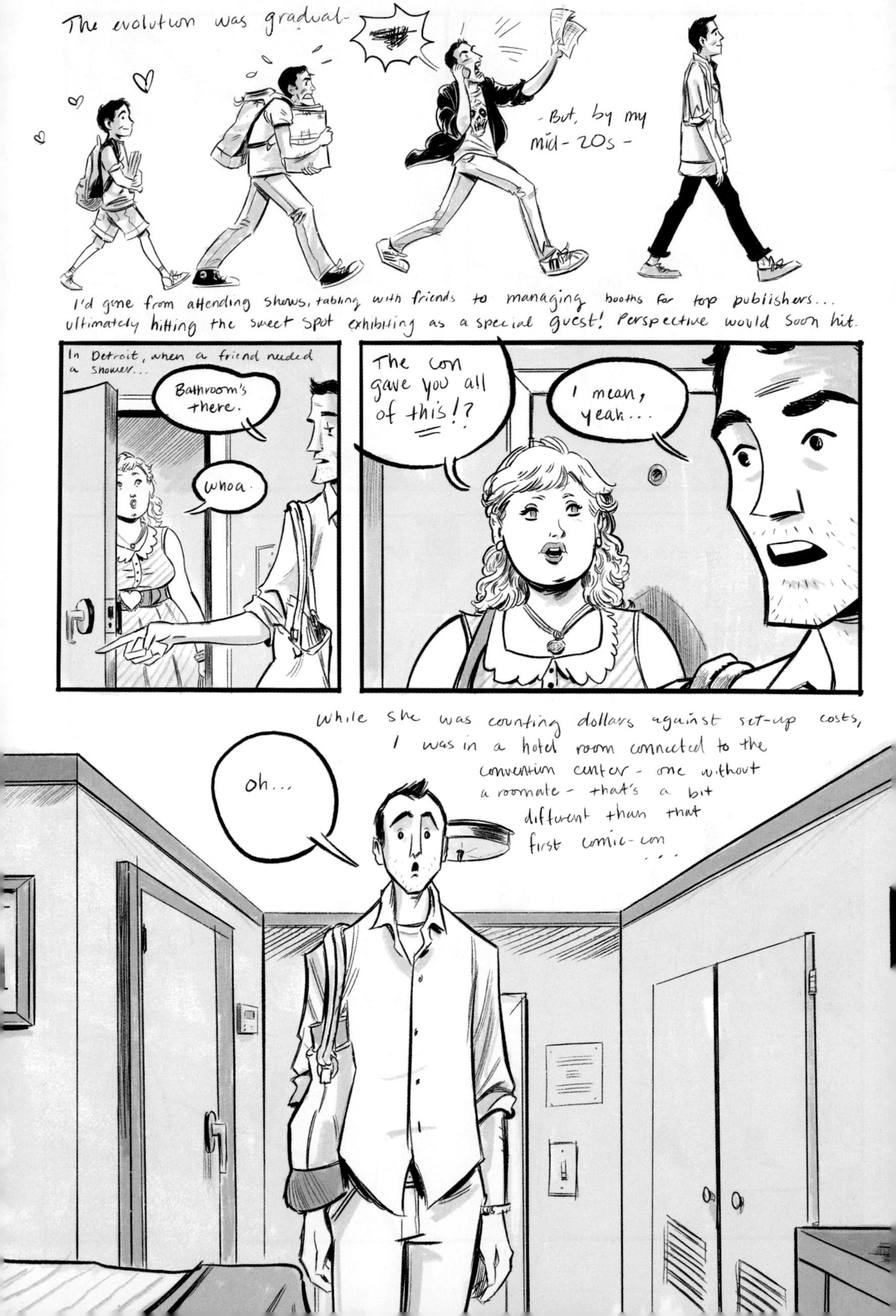
The evolution was gradual-
-But, by my mid-20s-
I'd gone from attending shows, tabling with friends to managing booths for top publishers... ultimately hitting the sweet spot exhibiting as a special guest! Perspective would soon hit.
In Detroit, when a friend needed a shower...
Bathroom's there.
whoa.
The con gave you all of this!?
I mean, yeah...
While she was counting dollars against set-up costs, I was in a hotel room connected to the convention center- one without a roommate- that's a bit different than that first comic-con ...
oh...

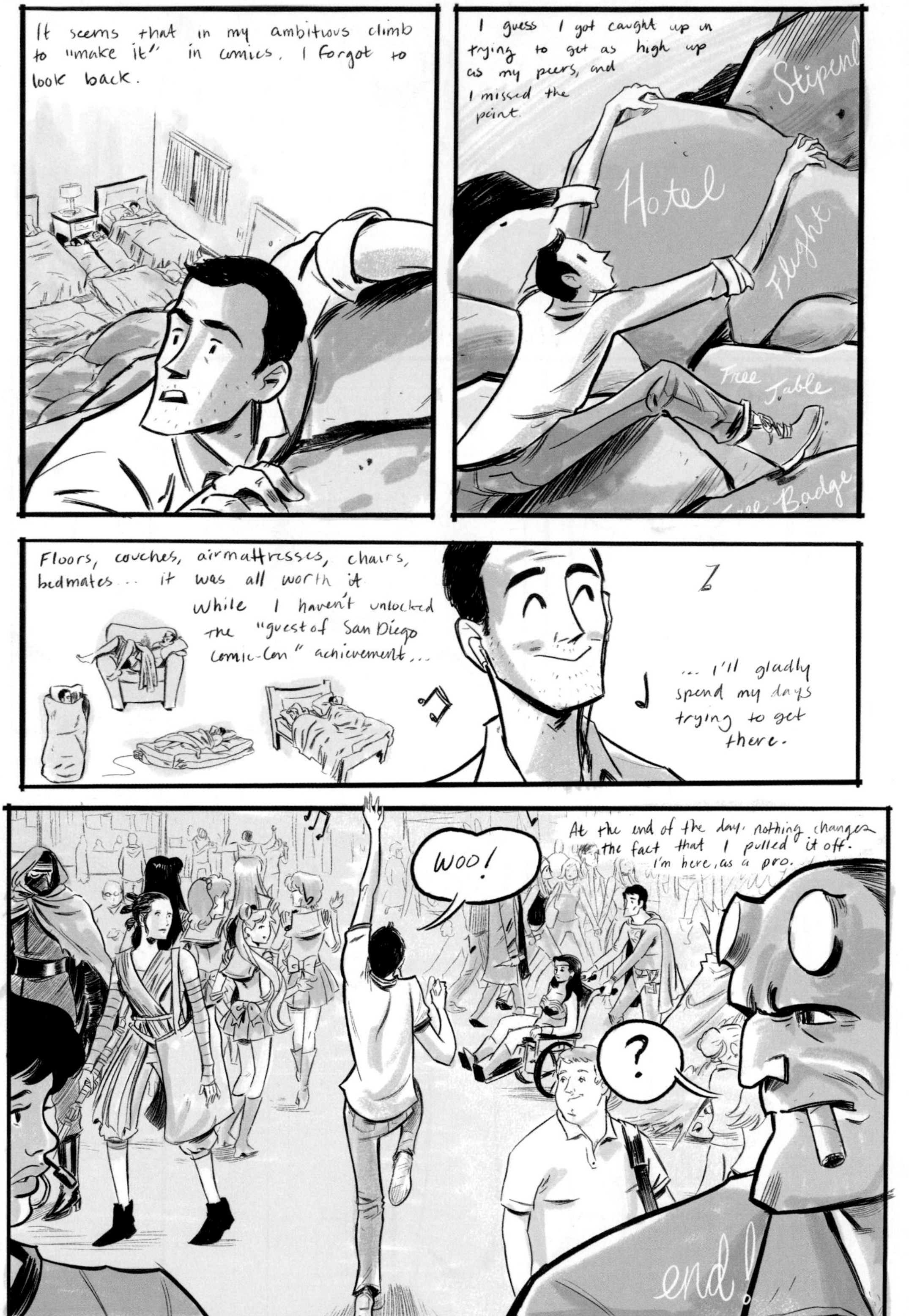
It seems that in my ambitious climb to "make it" in comics, I forgot to look back.
I guess I got caught up in trying to get as high up as my peers, and
I missed the point.
Stipend
Hotel
Flight
Free Table
Free Badge
Floors, couches, airmattresses, chairs, bedmates... it was all worth it.
While I haven't unlocked the "guest of San Diego Comic-Con" achievement...
Z
...I'll gladly spend my days trying to get there.
At the end of the day, nothing changes the fact that I pulled it off. I'm here, as a pro.
WOO!
?
end!

CREATOR BIOS

Nyala Ali is a freelance comics journalist and editor based in Winnipeg, Manitoba. She has taught comics to undergrads and is a book reviewer for the Winnipeg Free Press.

Chris Arrant (@chrisarrant) is the editor of Newsarama.com, and author of *Modern Masters: Cliff Chiang*. He has written for *Life*, *USA Today*, and *Publishers Weekly*, and is a judge in the 2019 Will Eisner Comic Book Industry Awards.

Sonya Ballantyne is a filmmaker and writer originally from Misipawistik Cree Nation in Northern Manitoba. Her work focuses on Indigenous women and girls in non-traditional film genres such as horror, sci-fi, and fantasy. Her first film *Crash Site* has played in festivals internationally and she hopes to direct a *Superman* film in the future.

Lucy Bellwood (@lubellwoo) is the creator of *100 Demon Dialogues*. She lives (nominally) in Portland, Oregon, but spends most of her time going on adventures.

Marlene Bonnelly (@marlene) spends far too much time on the Internet. Surprisingly, that's worked out to her advantage. Catch her on Twitter, or in the office at Tumblr HQ.

Bonnie Burton (@bonniegrrl) is a Los Angeles-based author who writes books and comics about sea monsters, Wookiees, mean girls, crafts, magical things, robots, and aliens. Her latest book is *Crafting with Feminism*.

Louie Chin is an illustrator living in NYC. He has worked with a variety of publications and companies including the *New York Times* and Nike. He has a new children's book out called *Don't Ask a Dinosaur*.

Amy Chu (@amychu) is a comics writer for DC, Marvel and many other publishers. Amy loves travel, coffee, whiskey, and Lego (not necessarily in that order).

Chris Chuckry is a veteran colourist who has worked for DC, Marvel, Image, Dark Horse, and many other comic book publishers in North America and Europe. A founder of the seminal comic book color studio, Digital Chameleon Ltd., Chris lives in Canada with his wife and two sons.

Tania del Rio @taniadelrio is a Los Angeles–based comic artist, writer, and author of the *Warren the 13th* middle grade trilogy. When she's not busy creating stories, she's probably taking photos of her dogs.

Dylan Edwards is an award-winning creator of queer and trans comics. His current project is *Valley of the Silk Sky*, a queer YA science fiction webcomic.

Scott A. Ford is an award-winning comic creator, illustrator, and designer from Winnipeg, Manitoba. His most recent graphic novel, *Ark Land* (ChiZine Publications), is a full-length sci-fi/fantasy adventure, full of robots, alien creatures, and strange places. scottafordart.com.

Kieron Gillen is a writer based in London. He is the co-creator of *the Wicked + the Divine* comic series. He likes to disco, rock 'n' roll, hip-hop, and not let the music stop.

Sina Grace is a writer and artist living in Los Angeles, CA. While he is best known for his slice-of-life memoir at Image, and writing *Iceman* at Marvel, his biggest accomplishment to date is having a cat and dog who get along.

Barbara Guttman (@MarteaniArt) is a Minneapolis-based author and illustrator of creepy stories about strange creatures and the mutability of identity in the face of darkness.

Bryan Edward Hill is a writer-filmmaker (*Batman and the Outsiders*) who lives and works in Los Angeles.

Morgan Hoffman was a former host on InnerSpace for over five years, covering everything from red carpets to comic conventions. Currently the digital reporter for ET Canada.

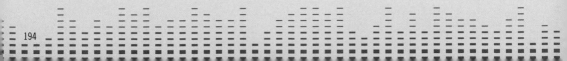

Karama Horne is a contributing editor, producer, and talent host for SYFY Wire and the founder and creator of the theblerdgurl brand. She hosts her own podcast as well as co-hosts the Who Won the Week Podcast for SYFY as well. When she's not trying to get sleep she's listening to k-pop and writing about indie comics and anime.

Tini Howard (@tinihoward) writes comics and lives in North Carolina.

Zak Kinsella is a cartoonist from Denver who's known for his sci-fi comic series *Outré Veil*.

Leonard Kirk is an artist in Canada who has been working in comics far longer than he would care to admit and, currently, draws a number of *Star Wars* projects for Marvel. He would say more but he's only operating on three hours sleep and skipped breakfast.

Adrienne Kress (@adriennekress) is a Toronto-based author, actor, playwright, screenwriter, director, cinephile, and fan of lists. Her latest project is The Explorers series for Penguin Random House.

Andy Kuhn is the artist and co-creator of the comic series *Firebreather*, with writer Phil Hester. In 2010 *Firebreather* was adapted into an Emmy Award–winning animated film for Cartoon Network. He is currently working on a new series with writer James Robinson for Image Comics. Andy lives and works in New Mexico.

Jackson Lanzing is a writer for page and screen who primarily operates as one half of Lanzing.Kelly (*Joyride*). He lives in Los Angeles with his wife Alex and their cat, who has been crawling all over the keyboard while he tries to write this, so sorry for any typos.

Melonami is a cat-adoring Brooklyn-based illustrator, comic artist, and animator. As such, all her time goes to her cat.

Randy Milholland has drawn the online comic *Something*Positive* (somethingpositive.net) since 2001. When not drawing the adventures of pudding cats or painting unfortunate Halloweens for Trick-or-Treaters, he lives in

Savannah, Georgia with an academic librarian, a baby, three cats, and a crested gecko who needs to learn his place. He probably owes Hope a drink.

B. Clay Moore (@bclaymoore) has written for virtually every major publisher in comics at one time or another. He is perhaps best known for his creator-owned work, including *Hawaiian Dick* (Image Comics).

Laura Neubert is an artist and storyteller from the Southwestern US. She enjoys exploring new storytelling venues, talking with new people, and harassing her cat.

Vivian Ng (@vviinng) is a comics artist, background painter, and plant parent working in Toronto. They are also secretly eight plants in a trench coat and would die without regular sunlight.

Hope Nicholson (@hopelnicholson) is a comics publisher and freelance comics curator based in Winnipeg, Manitoba. She made this book to bring people together for the very long winter months when there're no cons at all.

Nika (@onelemonylime) is a DC-based writer and artist whose current webcomic *Signals* is serialized on Tapas.io and Patreon.

Anthony Oliveira @meakoopa is a writer, PhD, film programmer, and pop-culture critic. You can keep up with his work on twitter, or on his podcast, *The Devil's Party*, as he reads through Milton's *Paradise Lost* and its demonic twists and turns.

Greg Pak (@gregpak) is a comic book writer and filmmaker best known for *Planet Hulk*. gregpak.com

It's been fifty years since **Bud Plant** and his high school buddies opened their first comic store in San Jose, Calif. For all that time, Bud has sold—and avidly collected—comics and related material. It began with fifty-copy runs of a one-page list on a Hectograph, up through the full-color glossy *Incredible Catalog*, still published regularly. He's online at budsartbooks.com

Erik Radvon (@radvon) is a writer and journalist based in Massachusetts, where he lives with his wife Jessika and a seemingly immortal guinea pig. His latest comic is *Crisis Vector*, a time-traveling adventure story inspired by Jack Kirby and Japanese roleplaying games.

Sara Richard (@sararichard) is an Eisner-nominated artist based in spooky Salem, MA. Sara has worked on covers for many titles including *My Little Pony*, and illustrated the book *The Ghost, The Owl*. She is a sharer of ghost stories, cleaner of gravestones, a karaoke aficionado, and obsessed with owls.

Trina Robbins has been drawing and writing comics since 1966. In 1970, she produced the very first all-woman comic book, *It Ain't Me, Babe*. In 1972 she was one of the founding mothers of *Wimmin's Comix*, the longest-lasting women's anthology comic book. (1972–1992). In her histories, she has been responsible for rediscovering previously forgotten early women cartoonists like Nell Brinkley, Tarpe Mills, and Lily Renee. In 2013 Trina was inducted into the Will Eisner Comic Book Hall of Fame.

Julia Scheele (@juliascheele) is a freelance illustrator and comics artist based in Glasgow, and the illustrator of *Queer: A Graphic History*, written by Dr. Meg-John Barker and published through Icon Books.

Diana Schutz has been working in comics since 1978, as an editor, an educator, and most recently a literary translator.

Tim Seeley is one of those "slash" people . . . a writer-slash-artist. He has drawn a number of different comic book series. His writing work includes *NY Times*–bestselling *Hack/Slash*. He resides in Chicago, Illinois and works at Four Star Studios where he is never far from his eighties action figure collection.

Jenn St-Onge (aka "Princess Jem") is the tatted Canadian cat mommy/comic artist behind Dynamite's *Nancy Drew*. She loves coffee, Bioshock, and anything spoopy; she is definitely not several cats stacked in a trench coat (probably).

Kris Straub is a cartoonist, writer, and performer behind the comics

Chainsawsuit, *Broodhollow*, and *Starslip*. Kris also appears weekly on the D&D stream Acquisitions Inc: The "C" Team and co-hosts the Australian gaming podcast 28 Plays Later with Paul Verhoeven.

Tia Vasiliou (@portraitofmmex) is a senior digital editor and comics content specialist at comiXology. You can find her monthly comics recommendations at The Mary Sue.

Jim Zub is a teacher and comic writer living in Toronto, Canada. He writes for Marvel, Image, IDW, Dark Horse, and anyone else who lets him run wild with swords & sorcery goodness.

MORE TITLES YOU MIGHT ENJOY

ALENA
Kim W. Andersson
Since arriving at a snobbish boarding school, Alena's been harassed every day by the lacrosse team. But Alena's best friend Josephine is not going to accept that anymore. If Alena does not fight back, then she will take matters into her own hands. There's just one problem . . . Josephine has been dead for a year.

$17.99 | ISBN 978-1-50670-215-5

ASTRID: CULT OF THE VOLCANIC MOON
Kim W. Andersson
Formerly the Galactic Coalition's top recruit, the now-disgraced Astrid is offered a special mission from her old commander. She'll prove herself worthy of another chance at becoming a Galactic Peacekeeper . . . if she can survive.

$19.99 | ISBN 978-1-61655-690-7

BANDETTE
Paul Tobin, Colleen Coover
A costumed teen burglar by the *nome d'arte* of Bandette and her group of street urchins find equal fun in both skirting and aiding the law, in this enchanting, Eisner-nominated series!

$14.99 each
Volume 1: Presto! | ISBN 978-1-61655-279-4
Volume 2: Stealers, Keepers! | ISBN 978-1-61655-668-6
Volume 3: The House of the Green Mask | ISBN 978-1-50670-219-3

BOUNTY
Kurtis Wiebe, Mindy Lee
The Gadflies were the most wanted criminals in the galaxy. Now, with a bounty to match their reputation, the Gadflies are forced to abandon banditry for a career as bounty hunters . . . 'cause if you can't beat 'em, join 'em—then rob 'em blind!

$14.99 | ISBN 978-1-50670-044-1

HEART IN A BOX
Kelly Thompson, Meredith McClaren
In a moment of post-heartbreak weakness, Emma wishes her heart away and a mysterious stranger obliges. But emptiness is even worse than grief, and Emma sets out to collect the pieces of her heart and face the cost of recapturing it.

$14.99 | ISBN 978-1-61655-694-5

HENCHGIRL
Kristen Gudsnuk
Mary Posa hates her job. She works long hours for little pay, no insurance, and worst of all, no respect. Her coworkers are jerks, and her boss doesn't appreciate her. He's also a supervillain. Cursed with a conscience, Mary would give anything to be something other than a henchgirl.

$17.99 | ISBN 978-1-50670-144-8

DARKHORSE.COM AVAILABLE AT YOUR LOCAL COMICS SHOP OR BOOKSTORE • TO FIND A COMICS SHOP IN YOUR AREA, VISIT COMICSHOPLOCATOR.COM
For more information or to order direct: • On the web: DarkHorse.com • Email: mailorder@darkhorse.com • Phone: 1-800-862-0052 Mon.–Fri. 9 AM to 5 PM Pacific Time.
Alena™, Astrid™ © Kim W. Andersson, by agreement with Grand Agency. Bandette™ © Paul Tobin and Colleen Coover. Bounty™ © Kurtis Wiebe and Mindy Lee. Heart in a Box™ © 1979 Semi-Finalist, Inc., and Meredith McClaren. Henchgirl™ © Kristen Gudsnuk. Dark Horse Books® and the Dark Horse logo are registered trademarks of Dark Horse Comics, Inc. All rights reserved. (BL 6041 P1)

MORE TITLES YOU MIGHT ENJOY

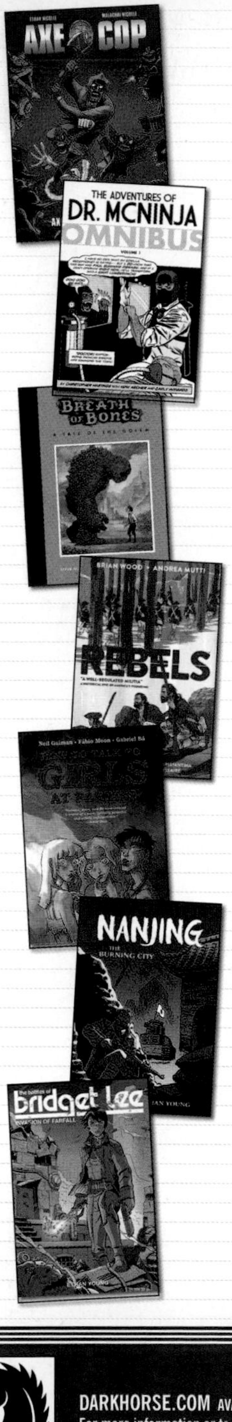

AXE COP
THE ADVENTURES OF
DR. MCNINJA
OMNIBUS
BREATH OF BONES
BRIAN WOOD • ANDREA MUTTI
REBELS
NANJING
bridget Lee

AXE COP

Malachai Nicolle, Ethan Nicolle

Bad guys, beware! Evil aliens, run for your lives! Axe Cop is here, and he's going to chop your head off! We live in a strange world, and our strange problems call for strange heroes. That's why Axe Cop is holding tryouts to build the greatest team of heroes ever assembled.

Volume 1 ISBN 978-1-59582-681-7 $14.99
Volume 2 ISBN 978-1-59582-825-5 $14.99
Volume 3 ISBN 978-1-59582-911-5 $14.99
Volume 4 ISBN 978-1-61655-057-8 $12.99
Volume 5 ISBN 978-1-61655-245-9 $14.99
Volume 6 ISBN 978-1-61655-424-8 $12.99

THE ADVENTURES OF DR. MCNINJA OMNIBUS

Christopher Hastings

He's a doctor! He's a ninja! And now, his earliest exploits are collected in one mighty omnibus volume! Featuring stories from the very beginnings of the Dr. McNinja web comic, this book offers a hefty dose of science, action, and outrageous comedy.

$24.99 | ISBN 978-1-61655-112-4

BREATH OF BONES: A TALE OF THE GOLEM

Steve Niles, Matt Santoro, Dave Wachter

A British plane crashes in a Jewish village, sparking a Nazi invasion. Using clay and mud from the river, the villagers bring to life a giant monster to battle for their freedom and future.

$14.99 | ISBN 978-1-61655-344-9

REBELS

Brian Wood, Andrea Mutti, Matthew Woodson, Ariela Kristantina, Tristan Jones

This is 1775. With the War for Independence playing out across the colonies, Seth and Mercy Abbott find their new marriage tested at every turn as the demands of the frontlines and the home front collide.

Volume 1: A Well-Regulated Militia
$24.99 | ISBN 978-1-61655-908-3

HOW TO TALK TO GIRLS AT PARTIES

Neil Gaiman, Gabriel Bá, Fábio Moon

Two teenage boys are in for a tremendous shock when they crash a party where the girls are far more than they appear!

$17.99 | ISBN 978-1-61655-955-7

NANJING: THE BURNING CITY

Ethan Young

After the bombs fell, the Imperial Japanese Army seized the Chinese capital of Nanjing. Two abandoned Chinese soldiers try to escape the city and what they'll encounter will haunt them. But in the face of horror, they'll learn that resistance and bravery cannot be destroyed.

$24.99 | ISBN 978-1-61655-752-2

THE BATTLES OF BRIDGET LEE: INVASION OF FARFALL

Ethan Young

There is no longer a generation that remembers a time before the Marauders invaded Earth. Bridget Lee, an ex–combat medic now residing at the outpost Farfall, may be the world's last hope. But Bridget will need to overcome her own fears before she can save her people.

$10.99 | ISBN 978-1-50670-012-0